ROBERT HARRIS

Robert Harris is the author of eleven bestselling novels: *The Cicero Trilogy – Imperium, Lustrum* and *Dictator – Fatherland, Enigma, Archangel, Pompeii, The Ghost, The Fear Index, An Officer and a Spy*, which won four prizes including the Walter Scott Prize for Historical Fiction, and *Conclave*. His most recent novel, *Munich*, was published in September 2017. Several of his books have been filmed, including *The Ghost*, which was directed by Roman Polanski. His work has been translated into thirty-seven languages and he is a Fellow of the Royal Society of Literature.

MIKE POULTON

Mike Poulton's work for the RSC includes *Wolf Hall* and *Bring Up the Bodies* (Stratford/West End/Broadway); *Anjin, The English Samurai* (RSC, Horipro at Sadler's Wells, Tokyo and Osaka), *Morte d'Arthur, The Canterbury Tales, St Erkenwald*.

His other work includes *Kenny Morgan* (Arcola); *The York Mystery Plays* (York Minster); *A Tale of Two Cities* (Royal & Derngate, Northampton/tour); *Fortune's Fool* (Old Vic); *Uncle Vanya, Judgment Day* (Print Room); *Luise Miller* (Donmar); *The Bacchae* (Royal Exchange); *Dance of Death* (Red Bull, New York); *Mary Stuart, The Cherry Orchard* (Clwyd Theatr Cymru); *Il Sindaco, Wallenstein, The Father, The Cherry Orchard, Uncle Vanya, Fortune's Fool* (Chichester); *Don Carlos* (Sheffield Crucible/West End); *Don Carlos* (Aarhus, Göteborg); *The Lady from the Sea, Three Sisters* (Birmingham Rep); *Ion, The Seagull, Three Sisters, Uncle Vanya, Dance of Death* (Colchester); *Ghosts* (Plymouth); *Uncle Vanya* (Broadway); *Fortune's Fool* (Broadway).

IMPERIUM

The Cicero Plays

Adapted for the stage by
Mike Poulton
From the novels by
Robert Harris

With an introduction by Mike Poulton

NICK HERN BOOKS
London
www.nickhernbooks.co.uk

ABOUT THE ROYAL SHAKESPEARE COMPANY

The Shakespeare Memorial Theatre opened in Stratford-upon-Avon in 1879. Since then the plays of Shakespeare have been performed here, alongside the work of his contemporaries and of living modern playwrights. In 1960, the Royal Shakespeare Company was formed, gaining its Royal Charter in 1961. The founding principles of the Company were threefold: the Company would embrace the freedom and power of Shakespeare's work, train and develop young actors and directors and, crucially, experiment in new ways of making theatre. The RSC quickly became known for exhilarating performances of Shakespeare alongside new masterpieces such as *The Homecoming* and *Old Times* by Harold Pinter. It was a combination that thrilled audiences and this close and exacting relationship between writers from different eras has become the fuel that powers the creativity of the RSC.

In 1974, The Other Place opened in a tin hut on Waterside under the visionary leadership and artistic directorship of Buzz Goodbody. Determined to explore Shakespeare's plays in intimate proximity to her audience and to make small-scale, radical new work, Buzz revitalised the Company's interrogation between the contemporary and classical repertoire. Reopened in 2016 under the artistic directorship of Erica Whyman, The Other Place is once again the home for experimentation and the development of exciting new ideas.

In our 55 years of producing new plays, we have collaborated with some of the most exciting writers of their generation. These have included: Edward Albee, Howard Barker, Alice Birch, Richard Bean, Edward Bond, Howard Brenton, Marina Carr, Caryl Churchill, Martin Crimp, David Edgar, Helen Edmundson, James Fenton, Georgia Fitch, Fraser Grace, David Greig, Tanika Gupta, Ella Hickson, Dennis Kelly, Anders Lustgarten, Tarell Alvin McCraney, Martin McDonagh, Tom Morton-Smith, Rona Munro, Richard Nelson, Anthony Neilson, Harold Pinter, Phil Porter, Mike Poulton, Mark Ravenhill, Somalia Seaton, Adriano Shaplin, Tom Stoppard, debbie tucker green, Frances Ya-Chu Cowhig, Timberlake Wertenbaker, Peter Whelan and Roy Williams.

The Company today is led by Gregory Doran, whose appointment as Artistic Director represents a long-term commitment to the disciplines and craftsmanship required to put on the plays of Shakespeare. The RSC under his leadership is committed to illuminating the relevance of Shakespeare's plays and the works of his contemporaries for the next generation of audiences and believes that our continued investment in new plays and living writers is an essential part of that mission.

The RSC is grateful for the significant support of its principal funder, Arts Council England, without which our work would not be possible. Around 75 per cent of the RSC's income is self-generated from Box Office sales, sponsorship, donations, enterprise and partnerships with other organisations.

Supported using public funding by
ARTS COUNCIL ENGLAND

NEW WORK AT THE RSC

We are a contemporary theatre company built on classical rigour. Through an extensive programme of research and development, we resource writers, directors and actors to explore and develop new ideas for our stages, and as part of this we commission playwrights to engage with the muscularity and ambition of the classics and to set Shakespeare's world in the context of our own.

We invite writers to spend time with us in our rehearsal rooms, with our actors and creative teams. Alongside developing new plays for all our stages, we invite playwrights to contribute dramaturgically to both our productions of Shakespeare and his contemporaries, as well as our work for, and with, young people. We believe that engaging with living writers and contemporary theatre-makers helps to establish a creative culture within the Company which both inspires new work and creates an ever more urgent sense of enquiry into the classics.

Shakespeare was a great innovator and breaker of rules, as well as a bold commentator on the times in which he lived. It is his spirit which informs new work at the RSC. Erica Whyman, Deputy Artistic Director, heads up this strand of the Company's work alongside Pippa Hill as Literary Manager.

The work of the RSC Literary Department is generously supported by THE DRUE HEINZ TRUST.

These productions of *Imperium Part I: Conspirator* and *Imperium Part II: Dictator* were first performed by the Royal Shakespeare Company in the Swan Theatre, Stratford-upon-Avon, on 16 November 2017 and 23 November 2017. The cast was as follows:

Imperium Part I: Conspirator

CICERO, Consul	**Richard McCabe**
HYBRIDA, Cicero's fellow Consul, a drunk	**Hywel Morgan**

CICERO'S HOUSEHOLD

TIRO, his secretary	**Joseph Kloska**
TERENTIA, his wife	**Siobhan Redmond**
TULLIA, his daughter	**Jade Croot**
QUINTUS, his brother	**Paul Kemp**
SOSITHEUS, his slave	**Daniel Burke**
RUFUS, his young protege	**Oliver Johnstone**
CLODIUS, a young aristocrat	**Pierro Niel-Mee**
CLODIA, his sister	**Eloise Secker**
POMPEY, the Conquering General	**Christopher Saul**
CRASSUS, the richest man in Rome	**David Nicolle**
JULIUS CAESAR, an ambitious young Senator	**Peter de Jersey**
CATILINE, Cicero's aristocratic rival	**Joe Dixon**

CATILINE'S CONSPIRATORS

SURA, the urban praetor	**Guy Burgess**
CETHEGUS	**Patrick Knowles**
CAEPARIUS	**Jay Saighal**
CAMILLA, the mistress of a conspirator	**Lily Nichol**

THE PATRICIANS

ISAURICUS	**Patrick Romer**
CATULUS	**Simon Thorp**
LUCULLUS, a general awaiting his triumph	**John Dougall**
CELER, the Chief Augur	**Nicholas Boulton**
CATO, the stoic Senator	**Michael Grady-Hall**

Imperium Part II: Dictator

CICERO	**Richard McCabe**

CICERO'S HOUSEHOLD

TIRO, his secretary	**Joseph Kloska**
TERENTIA, his wife	**Siobhan Redmond**
TULLIA, his daughter	**Jade Croot**
MARCUS, his son	**Daniel Burke**
QUINTUS, his brother	**Paul Kemp**
DOLLABELLA, married to Tullia	**Patrick Knowles**
JULIUS CAESAR, dictator	**Peter de Jersey**
POPILIUS, his standard bearer	**Hywel Morgan**
CALPURNIA, his wife	**Lily Nichol**
PISO, her father	**Patrick Romer**
OCTAVIAN, Caesar's adopted son	**Oliver Johnstone**
AGRIPPA, his lieutenant	**Pierro Niel-Mee**

THE CONSPIRATORS

BRUTUS	**John Dougall**
CASSIUS	**Nicholas Boulton**
DECIMUS	**Jay Saighal**
HIRTIUS, a consul-elect	**Michael Grady-Hall**
PANSA, a consul-elect	**David Nicolle**
MARK ANTONY	**Joe Dixon**
FULVIA, his wife	**Eloise Secker**
LEPIDUS	**Guy Burgess**

THE SENATE

CALENUS, an Antony supporter	**Simon Thorp**
VATIA	**Christopher Saul**

All other parts played by members of the Company.

Imperium: Part I Conspirator and *Imperium: Part II Dictator* are recipients of an EDGERTON FOUNDATION NEW PLAYS AWARD.

The RSC Acting Companies are generously supported by THE GATSBY CHARITABLE FOUNDATION and THE KOVNER FOUNDATION.

Director	**Gregory Doran**
Designer	**Anthony Ward**
Lighting Designer	**Mark Henderson**
Composer	**Paul Englishby**
Sound Designer	**Claire Windsor**
Movement Director	**Anna Morrissey**
Fight Director	**Terry King**
Company Voice and Text Work	**Emma Woodvine**
Assistant Director	**Jennifer Tang**
Music Director	**Gareth Ellis**
Casting Directors	**Annelie Powell**
	Hannah Miller CDG
Literary Manager	**Pippa Hill**
Production Manager	**Carl Root**
Costume Supervisor	**Yvonne Milnes**
Company Manager	**Michael Dembowicz**
Stage Manager	**Suzanne Bourke**
Deputy Stage Manager	**Klare Roger**
Assistant Stage Managers	**Alice Barber**
	Christopher Carr
Producer	**Kevin Fitzmaurice**

MUSICIANS

Music played live by

Keyboard	**Gareth Ellis**
Trumpet	**Andrew Stone-Fewings**
Bass Trombone	**Andrew Clennell**
Tuba	**Ian Foster**
Cello	**Clare Spencer Smith**
Percussion	**Jim Jones**

This text may differ slightly from the play as performed.

LOVE THE RSC?

Become a Member or Patron and support our work

The RSC is a registered charity. Our aim is to stage theatre at its best, made in Stratford-upon-Avon and shared around the world with the widest possible audience and we need your support.

Become an RSC Member from £50 per year and access up to three weeks of Priority Booking, advance information, exclusive discounts and special offers, including free on-the-day seat upgrades.

Or support as a Patron from £150 per year for up to one additional week of Priority Booking, plus enjoy opportunities to discover more through special behind-the-scenes events.

For more information visit **www.rsc.org.uk/support** or call the RSC Membership Office on 01789 403440.

IMPERIUM

The Cicero Plays

Adapted for the stage by Mike Poulton

From the novels by Robert Harris

Contents

Adapting *Imperium*
Mike Poulton

I had been planning to adapt Robert Harris's Cicero trilogy –
Imperium, Lustrum and *Dictator* – even before he had finished
the final volume, or at least composing scenes in my head –
watching them play out on the stage of the Swan. Presumptuous
of me perhaps – but I had mentioned to Robert my ambition to
see a stage version of at least part of his epic achievement –
a work of astonishing insight and scope which – for me –
brought to life those all-absorbing moments when world
domination by a single person became a graspable possibility –
and then a political reality. Robert's books take us inside the
head of the only man capable of stopping Rome's headlong
slide from an imperfect democracy, with its human rights and
good laws, into a military dictatorship. We watch Cicero
succeed, and we are with him when he fails.

Fortunately, Robert was very keen on the idea of my adapting
his work for the stage. And, equally fortunately, Greg Doran
was up for directing it in, what for me, is the perfect theatre –
the RSC's Swan in Stratford-upon-Avon. It was something of
a challenge. I'd previously dealt with the Spanish Court of the
sixteenth century, had a couple of brief excursions into the
Courts of Elizabeth I, and Henry VIII, had fun with the England
of Chaucer, and the Britain of Thomas Malory – but this was
Rome – the place where, as far as we Westerners are concerned
– everything began. We are products of Rome. Shakespeare
knew far more about Roman history than he did about the
history of Britain – and he had better, and more accurate source
material. Like all schoolboys of his time, he owed a great deal
to Marcus Tullius Cicero.

The approach to adapting a literary epic is rather like adopting the
'slash and burn' approach to forest clearance. You have to brace
yourself for the destruction of a vast vista of natural beauty, awe
and wonder, in the hopes of creating something new. You can't

put thirty-odd years of Cicero's life into two evenings in the theatre. The starting point has to be to search out a couple of very strong plotlines – complete with beginning, middle and ending – that is going to have an audience on the edge of its seats for six hours. And you need an understanding – acquired over many years – of your audience.

An audience is a very different animal from the lone reader. The reader can set his or her own pace, take time, absorb, revisit long passages of stunning description, take meal breaks, and walk the dog. An audience is a sort of team, in the act of playing a team game – it brings a variety of communal skills into the theatre, and is prepared to deal with anything a company of actors throws at it. Language challenges are kicked back and forth between them. An audience wants to be surprised, amused, caught-out, frightened, thrilled – especially thrilled – all from the safety of a comfortable seat, over the space of two or three intense hours. And in the case of an adaptation, an audience wants to revisit the pleasures of reading the original novels, and experience the game from a different perspective.

The plays Robert, Greg and I identified, lying below the surface of the trilogy, concerned Cicero's destruction of the power-crazed and vicious Sergius Catiline, and Cicero's attempt to prevent Mark Antony from succeeding to Julius Caesar's dictatorship. The background to all six linked plays is Cicero's duel with Caesar, and its aftermath. It's a story of natural humanity, and good laws versus military ambition. Cicero succeeds in one case, and achieves a partial success in the other. But this flawed master of political oratory carries with him the seeds of his own destruction. He is, ultimately, brought low by young men – the next generation – he has trusted, taught and nurtured.

People seem obsessed with looking for 'relevance' in plays. A member of the cast pointed out to me that every time he turned on the global horrors of the evening news, he'd see parallels of what we'd spent the day exploring in the rehearsal room. These six plays deal with a period of history when the political values and certainties of local government were overwhelmed by a world in turmoil – does that sound familiar?

I'd like to acknowledge my enormous debt to Robert Harris and Greg Doran.

These six plays are for Bill and Joe.

And for Guy, Dan, Jade, Peter, Joe, John, Michael, Ollie, Paul, Paddy, Hywel, Lily, David, Pierro, Siobhan, Pat, Jay, Chris, Eloise, Simon, Nick, Suzy, Klare, Alice and Chris.

Mike Poulton

8

Characters

CICERO
TIRO
SOSITHEUS
OCTAVIUS
MOB 1
MOB 2
MOB 3
POMPEY
CRASSUS
CATILINE
CAESAR
TERENTIA
VERRES
NUMITORIUS
JUDGE
CATULUS
ISAURICUS
RUFUS
TULLIA
CLODIUS
RABIRIUS
ISAURICUS
POMPEIA
HYBRIDA
CELER
JUNIOR AUGUR
QUINTUS
CATO
CETHEGUS
SURA
PIUS
MARCUS

CAMILLA
LUCULLUS
SERVANT BOY
CLODIA
MURENA
SILANUS
VIRIDORIX
CAEPARIUS
STATILIUS
CAPITO
FULVIA
MARK ANTONY
DOLABELLA
MESSENGER
POMPEY'S OFFICER
FONTEIUS
YOUNG OFFICER
HIRTIUS
PANSA
DECIMUS
POPILLIUS
OCTAVIAN
BRUTUS
CASSIUS
LEPIDUS
PISO
CALPURNIA
SLAVE 1
SLAVE 2
SLAVE 3
TREBONIUS
TILLIUS CIMBER

CASCA
GLADIATOR 1
GLADIATOR 2
CINNA
SERVIUS SULPICIUS
MARCELLUS
CHIEF VESTAL
ACTOR CAESARS
SERVANT
AGRIPPA
SERVILLIA
NURSE
VATIA
CALENUS
JULIA
MESSENGER
OCTAVIAN'S SECRETARY

And MARINES, CROWDS, MOBS, SOLDIERS,
AQUILIFERS, SLAVES, THE PEOPLE OF ROME,
BEGGARS, PROSTITUTES, GANGS, SENATORS,
PRIESTS, VESTALS, SERVANTS, LICTORS, GUESTS,
BODYGUARDS, SUPPORTERS, GAULS, GUARDS,
OFFICERS, SECRETARIES, EUNUCHS, GLADIATORS,
MOURNERS, VETERANS, THUGS, SCRIBES,
CENTURIANS

*This text went to press before the end of rehearsals and so may
differ slightly from the plays as performed.*

PLAY ONE
CICERO

Prologue

A ship shed. Gloom. A liburnian under repair. Shaft of light on a boy's body, gilded, red fillets in the hair, looks asleep, half-covered by a sailcloth. CICERO and TIRO emerge out of the gloom. They look at the body. CICERO is at pains to hide his nausea. SOSITHEUS carrying a document case joins him, then the elder OCTAVIUS. MARINES on guard duty. Outside, a CROWD has gathered. OCTAVIUS steps forward, MARINES throw back the sailcloth. The body has been slit open from chest to groin, entrails removed. Shock.

OCTAVIUS. I would not have summoned you, Consul – on the eve of your inauguration – but –

CICERO. No, no – you were right to come to me –

OCTAVIUS. Let me show you.

He turns the boy's head, revealing the slashed throat.

CICERO. Gods!

OCTAVIUS. Felled from behind. By a hammer, I'd say.

TIRO. Throat cut… Eviscerated –

OCTAVIUS. It looks as if his killers – whoever they were – wanted to inspect the entrails.

CICERO (*shaken – hiding it*). A human sacrifice? Here in Rome?

TIRO. Who'd do such a thing?

SOSITHEUS. Gauls most likely –

CICERO. Has anyone claimed him?

OCTAVIUS. Not yet… But… I'm afraid there's worse to come – (*Turning over the body onto its stomach.*) Do you see?

TIRO. There's an owner's tattoo – above the left buttock.

SOSITHEUS. A slave.

CICERO. Can you read it, Tiro?

TIRO. 'C. Ant. M…' But surely? That's –

CICERO. Hybrida… the property of Antonius Hybrida.

OCTAVIUS. Your colleague in the Consulship. Sorry to land
you with it, Cicero. We fished the poor boy out of the river –
we couldn't just throw him back.

CICERO. You did what duty required of you. Who else knows
about this?

OCTAVIUS. The marines who found him – others who saw us
bring him ashore… There's a crowd gathering… They're
saying a ritual killing on the eve of your Consulship's a bad
omen – for you and for the City –

CICERO. They may be right. Have you informed Hybrida?

OCTAVIUS. No, I –

CICERO. Then don't. Leave Hybrida to me. Burn the remains –
let nobody see you doing it.

OCTAVIUS. What about the crowd?

CICERO. Deal with the body. I'll deal with the People.

> CICERO *and* OCTAVIUS *come out of the shed with* TIRO
> *and* SOSITHEUS. *The* MOB *is established as a force to be
> reckoned with. They crowd around* CICERO.

SOSITHEUS. Get back! Don't jostle your Consul –

MOB. The Gauls did it! Foreign scum – send 'em home – kick
'em out! It's Gauls! – Aliens – Savages – Human sacrifice –
Purify the City! We don't want 'em here, send 'em back
where they came from – (*Etc.*)

CICERO. Friends –

MOB 1. Only a Gaul would do that to a child –

MOB. Gauls eat human flesh – drink their blood – too many of
them here – (*Etc.*)

CICERO. Listen to me –

MOB. Not fit to live among decent people – We're Romans –
We don't want no aliens here – (*Etc.*)

OCTAVIUS. Citizens – let your Consul speak!

MOB 1. We want answers! Answer, Cicero! (*Etc.*)

CICERO *waits until he can be heard.*

CICERO. My friends... I have investigated this poor boy's
death... I'm satisfied it was an accident.

Jeers.

MOB 1. Don't take us for fools, Cicero – it was no accident! –

CICERO. There's nothing sinister here. Let's not trouble the
City with false rumours – go home to your families – enjoy
the New Year's festival –

MOB 2. It was a human sacrifice – I saw the body!

Supportive shouts from the MOB.

CICERO. It was nothing of the sort.

MOB 3. Gutted – throat cut – someone's put a curse on the City
– on your Consulship –

CICERO (*laughing*). Nonsense!

MOB 2. Purify the ground – fetch the priests –

MOB. The gods look down! Sacrifice! Exorcise us! Fetch a
priest – Lift the curse – (*Etc.*)

CICERO. My friends...

MOB 1. Hear him speak –

CICERO. There's no evidence – none at all – of foul play.

Howls of disbelief from the MOB.

The boy's been in the river for days – the fish have been
feasting on him –

MOB 1. Fetch a priest!

CICERO. Fetch a priest then...! But what do you imagine he
can do? Put a curse on all the fishes in the Tiber?

SOSITHEUS *giggles. Some laughter from the* MOB.

Now listen to me. It's New Year tomorrow – a new year
brings in a new government – and as your First Consul for
the coming year I'll do everything in my power to keep
Rome safe and secure… You – the People – have chosen me
to lead you… Do I have your trust?

Approval – mostly – from the MOB.

Now return to your homes.

MOB 2. Some of us don't have homes –

CICERO. May all the gods protect Rome!

TIRO, OCTAVIUS *and* SOSITHEUS. May the gods protect
Rome!

MOB. May the gods protect Rome!

Acclaim from the MOB.

CICERO. And for some days, my friends… I suggest you eat no
fish!

Laughter. Exeunt MOB, OCTAVIUS *and* MARINES.

TIRO. When the throat gaped open, the hairs on the back of my
neck spiked up –

CICERO (*shaken – hiding it*). Tiro – can we not…

TIRO. We were in the presence of evil.

CICERO. I felt it too… A palpable force – potent as lightning.
I am going to be… (*He is sick.*)

TIRO. Put your head down, Master – take deep breaths…

CICERO. Perhaps I should have fetched a priest.

Exit SOSITHEUS. CICERO *remains lost in thought*. TIRO
addresses the audience.

Scene One

TIRO. Welcome to Rome.

My name is Tiro… (*Studies the audience.*) Who are you?

I'm writing a life of the Roman statesman Marcus Tullius Cicero – the greatest orator of his age – some say of any age…

CICERO *turns.*

I was Cicero's confidential secretary – at his side for almost the whole of his life. People ask me what he was really like…

SOLDIERS *cross the stage.*

Given the current political climate, I hold my tongue…
You never know who's listening, do you? Throughout his life Cicero kept a record of everything he witnessed. We survived decades of political upheaval – a civil war… I have all his papers… But – at the end – Caesar forbade him to publish his account. Those in power were afraid of what he might say and write – they feared his voice – they feared his pen more. So, the task has fallen to me.

Checks he's not being overheard.

So far, I've dealt with his early years – his education in oratory and the law – his arrival in Rome from an insignificant town in the backwoods of –

CICERO. This is getting very expositional.

TIRO (*shrugs*). Very well. Let's go straight to the heart of the matter – let's talk about *power* –

Drum beats.

– men and power – those in pursuit of power – those *in* power, those *corrupted* by power… Romans have a word, '*Imperium*' – the power of life and death given by the State into the hands of a single individual… Our State was a democracy – Romans were all great voters – and to prevent any one man seizing *absolute* power we had checks and balances – we had two – *two* Heads of State – two Consuls. And the law was a major industry with us – we were all very litigious…

CICERO *looks impatient.*

The Consulship – to preside over the Senate – was the great prize of Roman politics. Cicero was proud of the fact that when – against all the odds – he was elected to his presidency –

CICERO. It was by the unanimous vote of the Roman People –

POMPEY, *in his General's kit,* AQUILIFERS, *and* CRASSUS *appear.*

TIRO. How did he manage it? He wasn't from the ruling class – he couldn't rely on privilege and political favour – he had no legions of soldiers to bully the People and sway an election, like this man – Pompey Magnus. He didn't have money – he couldn't bribe his way to high office – like Crassus here – the richest man in Rome at the time – who has six thousand amphorae overflowing with silver coins, and calls it loose change.

CRASSUS *waits for* CAESAR *and* CATILINE, *before he and* CATILINE *join the jury.*

TERENTIA (*studying* CICERO). He did have his wife's fortune. Had I not paid his election expenses he'd have got nowhere.

Enter CAESAR *and* CATILINE.

TIRO. He faced powerful opposition – from Catiline – mad as a baited bull... And from a young chancer called Gaius Julius Caesar.

All Cicero had was his *voice*... By a sheer effort of will he turned it into the most powerful instrument of political persuasion in the Republic... If only you'd seen him in action in the law courts at the beginning of his career!

Enter VERRES.

I wonder if I could show you? I don't like doing it – I prefer to set things down chronologically – but as you've turned up rather late in the story...

Blistering sunshine. TIRO *stands behind* VERRES. *The Court assembles.*

When a politician leaves high office, and returns to private life, his crimes sometimes catch up with him. Is it the same with you? Is there much corruption in the politics of your times? Documents are examined – accounts scrutinised – unsuspected evils and long-concealed frauds are brought to light. When the dossier of deceit is complete the accused is put on trial. This... is Gaius Verres – facing prosecution for corruption and extortion during his term as Governor of Sicily.

CICERO *stands behind* NUMITORIUS. *Tone shifts to grim.*

CICERO. Gentlemen of the jury, I'm going to question this witness –

NUMITORIUS. Gaius Numitorius –

CICERO. About the execution of one, Publius Gavius – a man who had knowledge of the criminal activities of Governor Verres there – and had made public his intention to expose them. Numitorius – tell the Court what happened to Publius Gavius.

NUMITORIUS. The Governor had him dragged to the marketplace. He shouted to the crowds that Gavius was a spy – and he was going to pay the penalty –

CICERO. A spy? For whom?

NUMITORIUS. Verres never said.

CICERO. And what was that penalty?

NUMITORIUS. Gavius was stripped naked and flogged.

CICERO. In front of the crowds – in the marketplace in Messina?

NUMITORIUS. Then they tortured him with hot irons.

CICERO. Did the victim speak?

NUMITORIUS. He swore he was innocent. Said he'd served in the Roman cavalry. He cried out that he was a Roman citizen.

CICERO. A Roman citizen! Mark that, members of the jury.

NUMITORIUS. A cross was set up overlooking the Straits of Regium so the prisoner could gaze upon Italy as he died.

CICERO. Gavius was crucified?

NUMITORIUS. He was.

CICERO. Without a trial… (*Advancing on* VERRES.) How did he meet his death?

NUMITORIUS. Bravely – like a Roman. While they were nailing him he never made a sound – but while they were whipping him – he cried out then. Every time a blow landed, he shouted, 'I am a Roman citizen!'

CICERO. Turn and face the jury, friend. Would you repeat what Gavius said? Speak up so they can all hear.

NUMITORIUS. He said, 'I am a Roman citizen!'

CICERO. A blow lands – (*Raising his wrists above his head, jerks forward as if lashed.*) and Gavius shouts through gritted teeth, 'I am a Roman citizen.' Another blow lands: 'I am a Roman citizen!' (*Repeats his act.*) Again, a blow: 'I am a Roman citizen!'

VERRES. That man's a liar –

NUMITORIUS. The whole town witnessed it –

CATILINE. Verres –

CRASSUS. Verres –

VERRES. He claimed he was a citizen to delay his just punishment –

CICERO. But he did say it…? You admit he said it?

VERRES. I…

CICERO (*triumphant*). You heard him say, 'I am a Roman citizen!' and you ignored his cries? Members of the jury, from his own mouth, Verres condemns himself. You heard Gavius claim his inalienable right to be tried before a jury, here in Rome –

VERRES. I tell you he was a liar and a spy!

JUDGE. Order!

CICERO. You crucified a Roman citizen!

VERRES *is restrained by* CATULUS *and* ISAURICUS.

JUDGE. Order – I'll have order in my Court!

CICERO. The poorest man of humblest birth knows himself possessed of one sure and certain hope and defence: it is that cry: 'I am a Roman citizen!'

SPECTATOR *concurrence*.

In every region of the known world it will gain him sanctuary. Except... except, it would seem, in a Court presided over by Governor Gaius Verres.

Anger from SPECTATORS.

You shame us, Verres – you have shamed Rome! What shall Rome say to you?

VERRES. Who was this Gavius anyway!

CICERO. He asks, 'Who was Gavius?'

CATILINE. He was a nobody!

CICERO (*advancing on* CATILINE). True! Gavius was nobody – an insignificant fellow no one had ever heard of...

VERRES. Why then! Why am I on trial?!

CICERO. Because it was not Gavius you nailed up on that cross, Verres... You nailed up – you crucified – the universal principle that a Roman citizen – any Roman citizen – is, and will always be, *a free man* – entitled to the protection of good government and the rule of law!

Uproar. A furious VERRES *is dragged to safety by* CATULUS *and* ISAURICUS, *pursued by a* LYNCH MOB. CATILINE *remains – flanked by* CAESAR *and* CRASSUS.

TIRO. That was the end of Gaius Verres, and the start of my master's rapid rise to high office... Er... My friends, there are a lot of characters in my story – quite a few of them are called Gaius – so try to keep up. When my master stood for Consul he topped the poll.

CATILINE (*through gritted teeth, to the audience*). How! A nobody! He has no people – all farmers, labourers, slaves...

TIRO. But Cicero was a man of integrity – something of a novelty among our politicians –

CATILINE. A man without honour – no valour, no breeding, no history… Yet he has the insolence to stand against me for high office? And the People vote him into power! The fools! What insolence… the insolence of the creature.

CATILINE *is led away by* CRASSUS *and* CAESAR.

TIRO. Bad loser. I must go home – we've still not finished writing Cicero's inaugural address… (*Exits*.)

Scene Two

CICERO*'s house establishes itself.* SLAVES *preparing for New Year, and inaugural celebrations.* RUFUS *and* CLODIUS *reading copies of the draft of the inaugural speech –* SOSITHEUS, *and* TERENTIA *studying accounts.* TULLIA *picks up* CICERO*'s copy.*

TULLIA. 'I have been elected Consul – not relying on the support of powerful individuals, nor through the influence of a few aristocratic families, but by a unanimous decision of the whole electorate – '

CICERO. Very good, Tullia. Give it back to me now –

TULLIA. Is it your speech for tomorrow? –

CICERO. Give.

TULLIA *gives him the speech, and goes out.*

CLODIUS. 'Roman People' would be better than 'the whole electorate' –

CICERO. Thank you, Clodius. 'Not through the influence of a few aristocratic families, but by a unanimous decision – *a unanimous decision* of the Roman People, that raises me far above men of the highest social standing…'

RUFUS. Oouff! Catiline won't like that –

CICERO. It's not my intention to give Catiline pleasure.

CLODIUS. Not much he can do about it – not during an inaugural address.

TULLIA *runs back in, followed by* TIRO.

TULLIA. It's snowing! Come and see!

TERENTIA. Not in here, Tullia – your father is working –

CICERO. Trying to.

TULLIA. He doesn't mind –

TIRO. There's a blanket of pure white over the whole City – it's a very good omen.

CICERO. No, Tiro – it's just snow. If Jupiter had wanted to congratulate me on my election he'd have sent an eagle with a letter in its beak.

TERENTIA. Don't mock the gods. You've a difficult year ahead – pray for their protection.

CICERO. Where was I?

TIRO. I'll go tell them to start shovelling. (*Exits*.)

RUFUS. 'In this office, and in the conduct of my life – '

CICERO. Thank you, Rufus. 'In this office, and in the conduct of my life, I am of the People.'

TERENTIA (*under her breath*). Pah!

TULLIA. After tomorrow – when you're Consul, Papa – will we be rich?

TERENTIA. Yes –

CICERO. No. Not especially –

TERENTIA. We'd better be!

CLODIUS. When your father's term of office is over –

TULLIA. After a year?

CLODIUS. Yes – after a year – they'll give him a province to rule –

TERENTIA. Then we'll be *very* rich –

TULLIA. What's a province?

CLODIUS. A small country.

TULLIA. Which country?

TERENTIA. Macedonia.

TULLIA. Will Papa be like a king?

TERENTIA. Yes.

CICERO (*horrified*). No!

CLODIUS. No – not exactly like a king – Romans don't approve of kings.

RUFUS. He'll be more like a judge.

TULLIA. That's a shame. I'd rather be a king than a judge.

CICERO. 'In the business of government, let me say, I wish to be known as the People's Consul…'

Enter TIRO.

What now?! No, don't tell me – the Tiber's running with blood? Ghosts are squeaking and gibbering in the streets?

SOSITHEUS *and* RUFUS *snigger.*

TIRO. It's a delegation from the Senate.

CLODIUS. That *is* ominous.

TULLIA. Are they very old, and incontinent?

TERENTIA. Tullia!

TIRO. I'll fetch them in.

Exeunt TIRO, TERENTIA *and* TULLIA, *hobbling like an ancient Senator.*

CICERO. How do I look?

RUFUS. Consular.

CLODIUS. Well… Getting there.

> CLODIUS *arranges* CICERO*'s toga. The delegation arrives – five or six, if possible.*

CICERO. Catulus – I'm honoured! Isauricus – Senators –

CATULUS. If they want a fight, we'll give them one! It's a declaration of war!

CICERO. I –

CATULUS. They've thrown down a challenge to the Senate – before you've even taken office –

CICERO. Who – who has?

CATULUS. Caesar, Crassus, Catiline – their gang of pleb-loving ruffians – I'll not stand for it –

RABIRIUS. I want to go home –

ISAURICUS. Pay no attention – his mind has gone –

CICERO. Rabirius? Senator Rabirius? Senator, do you know me? –

CATULUS. Well, of course he doesn't!

CICERO. What's this about –

ISAURICUS (*waving it*). This – this is what it's about.

CATULUS. They've served a writ on our Senatorial colleague here.

CICERO. What's the charge?

CATULUS. Murder.

CICERO. Murder! Rabirius! He can hardly stand.

RABIRIUS. I'm not a troublemaker…

ISAURICUS. Not now, Senator –

CICERO. Who's he supposed to have murdered?

ISAURICUS. A gang-leader – Lucius Saturninus. And, as Saturninus was killed in the sacred precincts of the Senate House, they're charging Rabirius with sacrilege as well as murder –

CICERO. But…! That was forty years ago!

CATULUS. Thirty-six years ago. I was part of it. Killing Saturninus was a public service. He rampaged through the City at the head of a mob – terrorising decent citizens.

CICERO. He was a Tribune of the People.

CATULLUS (*contempt*). The People!

CICERO. *Was* it Rabirius who killed him?

ISAURICUS. We *all* killed him – cornered him – pelted him with roof tiles –

CATULUS. Got to him before the public executioner, that's all. We were young then. We still had some juice in us.

RABIRIUS. I was young once…

CICERO. No jury would find this man guilty.

ISAURICUS. What jury? The charge is sacrilege – it won't come before a jury. It's to be heard before two judges. Julius Caesar's one – his cousin's the other.

CATULUS. A fix! A guilty verdict's a foregone conclusion.

RABIRIUS. Is this somebody's house? It's very small.

CICERO. I'm Consul – I won't let it happen. They can't execute a Roman citizen without a trial.

CLODIUS. If Caesar fetches the mob onto the streets, anything could happen. What's Caesar up to?

CICERO. Whatever it is, it has little to do with this poor fellow.

CLODIUS. He's sending you a warning –

ISAURICUS. No – he's punishing *us* for ditching his friend Catiline and making you Consul in his place –

CICERO. I was elected by the unanimous vote of the Roman People –

CATULUS. The People! Pah! 'Power to the People!' 'Bread for the People!' 'Land for the People!' Hang the People! Against our better judgement we made you Consul – do something!

CICERO. You'd have preferred Catiline as Head of State?

ISAURICUS. At least Catiline's one of our own –

CICERO. He disgraces you –

CLODIUS. He's barking mad!

CICERO. You say you performed a public service in killing Saturninus? If you really want to serve your country, bring your roof tiles and pelt Catiline.

ISAURICUS. Catiline's a Sergius – from one of the founding families of Rome –

CICERO. Had I not topped the poll, your Consuls for the coming year would have been Catiline and Antonius Hybrida – the dangerous lunatic and the hopeless drunk – both of them Caesar's creatures! As it is you've foisted the drunk on me –

ISAURICUS. It was Hybrida's turn – he's from one of the oldest –

CICERO. Families in Rome – yes, I know…

CLODIUS. What will you do?

CICERO. I'd better go and speak to Caesar – find out what he really wants.

CATULUS. You'll do no such thing!

ISAURICUS. The man's a traitor to his class! Does he imagine he can dictate terms to his betters?

CATULUS. I say we should call Pompey home – his soldiers would soon put Caesar in his place!

CICERO. I'm more than capable of dealing with Caesar.

CLODIUS. His bill for the redistribution of public land will be somewhere at the back of it.

CICERO. It wouldn't surprise me.

ISAURICUS. And what is that bill but shameless bribery? Free land for the poor in return for their voices and votes.

CLODIUS. Cunning.

CATULUS. They want to give away our property to the unwashed. Over my dead body!

ISAURICUS. Caesar's bill doesn't worry me – it could never pass in the Senate. Surely not? No Senator in his right mind would...

They all look at RABIRIUS.

RABIRIUS. Have we voted yet? Who must I vote for?

Scene Three

TIRO. So off we trudged through the snow to see *Gaius* Julius Caesar.

CICERO. The old guard will have to compromise – they'll resist it, but in the end everybody'll have to work together for the good of... for the good of... (*Kicks a pile of snow in anger.*) Is this what it's going to be like? A year spent running back and forth – carrying messages – trying to stop patricians and populists tearing each other to pieces...

TIRO. Probably.

CICERO *and* TIRO *try to avoid importunate* BEGGARS, *dangerous* STREET GANGS, *and female and male* PROSTITUTES. TIRO *speaks to the audience.*

Julius Caesar. People ask me what he was like. 'No – you actually met him! You conversed with a god!' Well, Caesar was no god... He wasn't even Caesar back then. He hadn't commanded legions – he was just another ambitious young politician...

CICERO. This is his house.

TIRO. Even so he had... *something*... How can I describe him? – An athlete's muscles under the silken tunic of a scented dandy – forever in debt – honeyed charm – pitiless ambition – The mob loved him. They gave my master their trust, but Caesar they *loved*.

CICERO. Ready?

TIRO. Sorry.

In the atrium, SLAVES *come and go – like Party HQ. Wax death masks of* CAESAR*'s ancestors – only three Consuls.*

Decayed grandeur in a slum. Why does he still live *here*?

CICERO. Look around. Catulus, or Isauricus, would see only beggars living in filth – thugs looking for victims – whores and rent boys. Caesar sees *votes*. He swims through the slums like some great shark – shoals of minnows in his wake – snapping up scraps. These down-and-outs – (*Re: the audience.*) are his power base. We sail in dangerous waters, Tiro.

TIRO. I'll look out for the rocks. (*Looks at the death masks.*) Caesar's ancestors.

CICERO. Only three made it to Consul.

TIRO. For one of the founding families of Rome it's not much of a showing.

CICERO. Especially not for one who claims to be descended from the goddess Venus.

TIRO. He doesn't believe that nonsense?

CICERO. The mob believes it.

TIRO. The mob will believe anything.

CICERO. Fortunately.

A WOMAN *hurries away adjusting her clothing.* CICERO *pretends not to notice her.*

TIRO. Was that his wife?

CICERO. It was *a* wife.

TIRO. Venus was a bit of a slut too, wasn't she? Must run in the family… You know what they say of him? 'Gaius Julius Caesar – Every woman's husband – '

CAESAR *is suddenly in the room – he appears from nowhere.*

CAESAR. 'And every man's wife.' Some exaggeration there, surely, Tiro? (*Laughs*.) Sorry to keep you waiting – I was discussing land reform with the wife of a client. How's your own wife – the formidable Terentia?

CICERO. I'm not here to discuss women, Caesar.

CAESAR. Pity. What *are* you here for?

TIRO *takes the writ from his satchel – hands it to* CAESAR *– he reacts as if it's red hot, hands it back to* TIRO.

No – no! I can't talk about the case – I'm to be one of the judges. (*Smiles*.) Are you trying to corrupt me?

CICERO. I want you to acquit Rabirius of these trumped-up charges.

CAESAR (*mirthless chuckle*). I'm sure you do!

CICERO. Your true purpose in bringing this prosecution is to intimidate the Senate. And me.

CAESAR. Why should a clique of patricians think they've the god-given right to rule over us for all eternity? It's time for a change. (*Thinks*.) Perhaps my purpose is to remind the Senate that if they oppose the will of the People, the People will revenge themselves. Even if it takes thirty or forty years.

CICERO. So, you'd demonstrate the moral superiority of the People by terrorising a helpless old man? Rabirius has lost his wits – he's no idea what's going on.

CAESAR. Then how can he be terrorised?

CICERO *fixes him with a stare. Even* CAESAR *looks unnerved.*

CICERO (*a different tone*). Let's not play games, Gaius. We've been friends many years…

CAESAR. I'd like to think so.

CICERO. You're still young –

CAESAR (*serious*). At my age, Alexander the Great had been three years in his grave –

CICERO. Why jeopardise your whole future? Set the People against their elected representatives – and there'll be riots – the innocent will die... Why d'you ally yourself with crooks like Crassus – ghouls like Catiline? It's a stain on your honour –

CAESAR (*a button has been pushed*). My *honour*... is inviolable! –

CICERO. Oh, it may play well with the mob today –

CAESAR. The mob? Do you mean the citizens of Rome? –

CICERO. A glittering career lies ahead of you... If only you'd start working within the laws and customs of the State – work with us – work with me –

CAESAR. Consider the forces ranged against you. As well as the people on the streets, we have support within the Government – the Tribunes, half the Praetors. Even your fellow Consul, Antonius Hybrida, will oppose you –

CICERO. If he can stay sober long enough –

CAESAR. Who are your faction – a few men of business, and the rags and tatters of our patrician elite? And they *despise* you! You're a 'nobody' – the 'new man'? Once the establishment has chewed you over they'll spit you out. As I see it – Consul – there's only one course open to you. (*Studies him.*) You can't beat us... Why not join us?

CICERO. I didn't see that one coming!

CAESAR. Look, I don't give a fuck for Rabirius – you'll think of a way to get him off... But I shall do whatever it takes to manoeuvre myself into a position where I can reform this tired old Republic – root and branch.

CICERO. If you acted within the law –

CAESAR. The People are sick of your system – nothing changes – nothing moves. Rome's destiny and mine are one and the same –

CICERO. Pompey and his legions might have something to say about that!

CAESAR. Pompey's away at the wars – half a world away! It'll be years before the fighting's over. In Rome I'm going to change everything – pull down what's old and worm-eaten – lay deep foundations – and build a new and better world... And I could use some help. Say you'll support me?

CICERO. How?

CAESAR. Back my campaign for land reform.

Pause.

CICERO. What do I get in return?

Enter POMPEIA – *she's young – twenty – and drunk.*

CAESAR. Ah – here's my wife. Where have you been, Pompeia?

POMPEIA (*embracing* CAESAR). Nowhere. Shopping.

CAESAR. Mother's angry with you –

POMPEIA. She's always angry with me. What have I done now?

CAESAR. Have you been drinking?

POMPEIA. No.

CAESAR. This is Cicero – he's our new Consul.

POMPEIA. Oh... I thought it was going to be. That... Cati... (*Grinds to a halt.*)

CAESAR. Shhhhh! Perhaps you should go and lie down. (*Pinches her behind.*)

POMPEIA. That Cat... Cati... (*Exit staggering, and giggling.*)

CAESAR. I fear you've formed a bad impression of me, Consul.

CICERO. No – my impression is unchanged, I assure you.

CAESAR. She's not at vacuous as you may imagine.

CICERO. I'm sure she couldn't be.

CAESAR (*laughs*). We're very much in love.

POMPEIA (*stumbling*). Whoops!

CICERO. I've a speech to write. Come on, Tiro.

CAESAR. Work with me – I could guarantee you a trouble-free year in office. When it's over you'll go to Macedonia – make your fortune! You'll buy a villa on the Bay of Naples – study philosophy – publish your memoirs. (*Pause*.) But if you oppose me…

CICERO. Oho – a threat? If I oppose you, what then?

CAESAR (*studies him*). My dear friend, it's nothing personal. We mean you no harm. Even Catiline wouldn't…

CICERO. Catiline wouldn't what?

CAESAR. He's prowling around like a rabid mastiff – howling on every street corner you rigged the election – cheated him of his Consulship! He's demanding a re-count! (*Laughs*.)

CICERO. I was elected by the unanimous vote of the Roman People. They may love you, Caesar – it's me they vote for.

CAESAR. For the moment… If ever you feel threatened – or find yourself in personal danger – I hope you know you can always rely on my protection.

CICERO. *I* can rely on *your* protection?

CAESAR. You have my word on it – the word of Caesar. I can control Catiline.

CICERO *and* TIRO *go out into the snow, among the* BEGGARS.

CICERO. I'm lost for words.

TIRO. That's a first… He seems very confident.

CICERO. Confident! I'm Consul – he treats me like his client!

TIRO. Don't take it personally – he treats everybody like that.

CRASSUS *arrives*.

CRASSUS. Consul.

CICERO. Crassus.

CRASSUS. Slumming it?

CICERO. Yes – I see you are.

CRASSUS *goes into* CAESAR.

Caesar will never get the better of me... No... The real problem we face is Pompey. If I lose control here, Pompey will march his army home 'to restore order', and we'll have another military dictatorship. How do I prevent that? My only weapons are words.

TIRO. Well... At least it would be the end of Caesar.

CICERO. It would be the end of the Republic – the end of me – the end of everything...

TIRO. What are you thinking about?

CICERO. That dead boy.

TIRO. Where are we going?

CICERO. To visit my befuddled fellow Consul – Antonius Hybrida...

Scene Four

HYBRIDA*'s house*.

HYBRIDA. Drink?

CICERO. No thank you.

HYBRIDA. Fellow Consuls, eh? (*Drinks.*) We'll have to find some way of working together, won't we? It's a problem – opposite sides of the House and all that... Doubt I could ever get on with a man who won't drink with me –

CICERO (*takes wine*). Tell me, Hybrida – did you lose a boy a few days ago?

HYBRIDA. A what?

CICERO. A boy. About twelve years old.

HYBRIDA. Oh, him! You heard about that then?

CICERO. What happened? (*Pause.*) If we're to serve together we'll have to trust each other.

HYBRIDA. Trust takes time – I can't go against Caesar and Crassus, can I? They pick up the bills… What about the slave?

CICERO. Tiro is utterly discreet.

HYBRIDA. I had nothing to do with it. (*Pouring*.) More?

> CICERO *puts his hand over the cup, shakes his head.*

> Never off-guard, are you? (*Pouring*.) Go on. (*Considers*.) He was a singing boy – a Smyrnan. I lent him to Catiline for a party.

CICERO. Catiline?

HYBRIDA. Gnawing himself away with hatred, isn't he? You've noticed how he never takes his eyes off you? Glowing red coals –

CICERO. I have.

HYBRIDA. That's a Sergius for you! Terrible people – old Roman princelings… (*Drinks*.) He can't bear the thought you cheated him of his Consul's chair – (*Drinks*.)

CICERO. I was elected by –

HYBRIDA. The boy was meant to be the entertainment – one way or another. Very beautiful – very musical… (*Studies him*.) I mean, who are you? Not even a true Roman – and now you're up there with the best of us. Who are your people – chickpea sellers in some shit-spattered village a country mile north of nowhere… Now you're Consul – next year you'll be ruling Macedonia – (*Rubs his fingers in a 'money' gesture*.) lucky bugger – how did you rig the ballot – who did you bribe? Wish I had your nerve. (*Drinks*.)

CICERO. The boy?

HYBRIDA (*drinks*). The boy was a sacrifice to seal an oath. Gods! I've seen some hair-raising things in my time… (*Shudders*.) Catiline painted the lad gold – tied ribbons in his hair – and when he started singing – got behind him… And bang!

CICERO. *Catiline* killed him?

HYBRIDA. Evil bastard! Smashed his skull in. Slit his throat –
   bled him white.

CICERO. Who else was present?

HYBRIDA. Usual gang – Senators – property speculators –
   bankers – Catiline's young thugs – your boy Rufus was one.

TIRO. Rufus!

HYBRIDA. I think so – maybe not – can't remember – I'd had
   a drink.

CICEERO. Who else?

HYBRIDA. No names.

CICERO. Let me be quite clear about this. A group of Rome's
   leading citizens sacrificed a child to ensure the secrecy of an
   oath?

HYBRIDA. He was only a slave! But such a sweet little singer.
   It was a *shame*! Cost me thousands. I could weep…

CICERO. What was the oath?

HYBRIDA. What do you think it was? Have a guess. No?
   Catiline made us swear a blood oath to kill you, Cicero.

   CICERO *is shaken*.

   Tell you something else – when he inspected the boy's
   innards – he found the omens unusually propitious. Before
   your year's out he'll have your guts too! Consul! (*Laughs*.)
   Long life, New Man! (*Drinks*.)

   CICERO *and* TIRO *leave*.

TIRO. Well, you wanted to be Consul –

CICERO. What sort of a slave are you? Why didn't you stop me!

Scene Five

Inauguration morning – dawn. A reception is being prepared.
TERENTIA *is unpacking boxes of clothes and jewels.* TIRO,
SOSITHEUS, TULLIA *trying on jewellery, with* CLODIUS.

CICERO. Terentia! Think of the expense –

TERENTIA. It's my money. Now you're First Man in Rome,
it's time I started dressing like Rome's First Lady.
Macedonia will pay.

CICERO. Well…

TULLIA. Look at these! We *are* rich!

She goes to her father.

CLODIUS. Macedonia will be like having your own private
gold mine –

TERENTIA. No longer a struggling politician living off his
wealthy wife. What do you think?

TERENTIA *tries on a necklace.*

CLODIUS. Very pretty –

CICERO. But superfluous… No ornament could make my dear
wife more adorable to me than she has always been.

TERENTIA. A rare compliment! I thought you preferred
making love to elderly Senators, these days –

CLODIUS. Really? Does he?

CICERO. That's not love, it's politics. I've had to make
promises.

TERENTIA. Well, now you're Consul you can break them.
That's politics.

TIRO. Then you really would need Caesar's protection!

TERENTIA. Caesar?

CICERO. He has great influence with the People.

TULLIA *has been dressing* CLODIUS *up with jewels.*

TERENTIA. I'd like to strangle the People – and Caesar with them.

CLODIUS. How do I look?

TERENTIA. I'd sooner be dead than popular.

CICERO. Is everybody turning against me? I'm beginning to wonder how I managed to get myself elected?

TIRO. You were the best of a bad lot.

CLODIUS. The alternatives were all so much worse.

CELER *and a* JUNIOR AUGUR *arrive.*

CELER. Morning, Consul. I've come to take the omens. What will the New Year hold for us, I wonder?

CICERO. You tell me, Celer – you're the Augur.

CELER. Clouds on the horizon. During the night, some fellow called Rullus posted up a Land Bill on the walls of the Temple –

TERENTIA. Who? –

CLODIUS. Gods, no – they can't have! Already!

CELER. Quite a crowd gathering to read it – troublemakers – laughing and whooping. Some fucking plebs' protest, is it? Who is this Rullus anyway?

CLODIUS. A Tribune of the People.

CICERO. It's Caesar's bill. Rullus is merely his errand boy.

TIRO. It's not unexpected.

TERENTIA. Surely, you'll conduct no business on your first day in office?

TIRO. They're trying to wreck your inauguration.

CELER. Looks like they're testing your mettle, Cicero. First day in office – no military experience – no family. I'd better take a look at the sky – which way's your roof?

Exeunt CELER *and the* JUNIOR AUGUR. QUINTUS *and* RUFUS *arrive*.

QUINTUS. Where is he? Where's the Great Man!

CICERO (*hurriedly*). Find out what's in the bill, Tiro. Make me a copy – every clause – hurry.

TIRO. Sositheus –

CLODIUS. I'll help.

Exeunt TIRO, CLODIUS *and* SOSITHEUS.

CICERO. Quintus!

QUINTUS. Marcus! My brother – Consul! Who'd have thought it!

RUFUS. Congratulations, Master – I'm proud to be your pupil.

CICERO. Thank you, Rufus. My friend too, I hope?

RUFUS. Is this your curule chair? What's it made of?

CICERO (*hiding his irritation*). Numidian ivory I'm afraid.

TERENTIA. Macedonia will pay.

RUFUS. Through the nose it would seem.

The house fills up with well-wishers.

They've published Caesar's Land Bill.

CICERO. I know. They've opened hostilities – lobbed their first slingshots –

RUFUS. I suppose you'll have to refer to it in your inaugural address?

TERENTIA. How can he? He doesn't know what's in it yet.

CICERO. I'll have less than an hour to study it. Extremely frustrating –

QUINTUS. They've not given you much time –

CICERO. Well, that was their intention. Obviously! Gods!

QUINTUS. Is it a problem for you?

RUFUS. If he speaks in its favour, his new patrician friends will abandon him.

CICERO. And if I oppose it the People will crucify me.

QUINTUS. Either way you're in the shit then, eh, brother?

CICERO. If I can't stop it, we all are. I might be able to delay it – lose it in some never-ending Senatorial inquiry –

RUFUS. Actually, I don't see what's so wrong with giving farms to demobbed soldiers and the City's poor? People are starving.

CICERO (*a withering look*). Who puts these ideas into your head, boy?

RUFUS. You're forever saying you're for the People – why not give them some useful work to do –

CICERO. It's food they want, not farms! Farming demands years of skill – backbreaking labour – I'd like to see those down-and-outs who squat in Caesar's doorway working the fields from dawn till dusk! If ever Rome has to rely on 'The People' for food, we'll starve to death –

RUFUS. At least Caesar's concerned for them –

CICERO. '*Concerned for them*'! Caesar's concerned for nobody but himself. And do you imagine his paymaster Crassus – the richest man in Rome – is *concerned* about the poor?

RUFUS. I –

CICERO. They want to dole out State-owned land – at no cost to themselves – to create an army of supporters so huge it'll keep them in power forever! Concerned? Really, Rufus! I sometimes think your political vision penetrates no further than the bottom of a wine flask, or the end of your overactive cock!

RUFUS turns away to hide his tears.

TERENTIA. A little harsh perhaps, husband?

CICERO. The boy has to learn.

More arrivals.

TERENTIA. People are walking in off the street now. Am I expected to feed them all?

CICERO. We've waited a long time for this day. Spare no expense.

QUINTUS. Macedonia will pay!

Re-enter CELER *and the* JUNIOR AUGUR.

CELER. Congratulations, Consul – lightning over the Capitol, and on the left side too. You saw it, didn't you, boy?

JUNIOR AUGUR. If you saw lightning, Augur, it must have been lightning.

CELER. The gods are on your side! By the way – General Lucullus sends his regards. Along with a gentle reminder that, in return for his block of votes, you've promised to make the Senate award him a Triumph.

CICERO. I'll do what I can for him –

CELER. He's been kept waiting a long time – five years now –

CICERO. I've not forgotten General Lucullus.

CELER. And he has soldiers he can call on. If this Land Bill nonsense ends in rioting and bloodshed – I tell you there's a mob down there in the Forum looking for trouble – you'll need a military man to restore order. Last thing we need's another civil war.

CICERO. You think filling Rome with Lucullus's drunken veterans a reliable way to keep order?

CELER. You were never a soldier, were you, Cicero? Well then, New Man! See you in the Temple.

Exeunt CELER *and his team. Enter* TIRO, CLODIUS, *and* SOSITHEUS *who hand* CICERO *their copies.*

CICERO. Caesar stirring up his mob – the People starving, a drunk for a consular colleague, Catiline ready to tear out my guts, and Pompey looking for an excuse to stage a military coup. And now there's talk of civil war! Allow me to wish you all a Happy New Year! Damn Caesar – damn his fu… Damn his bill! Well then, friends – to work!

Scene Six

Music. Temple of Jupiter. SENATORS, PRIESTS, VESTALS.
CICERO *briefing* HYBRIDA. *Enter* CATULUS, ISAURICUS,
CELER, CATO, *and other* PATRICIANS, *troubled.* CAESAR,
CRASSUS, SURA, CETHEGUS, *pleased with themselves.*
CATILINE *brings with him an air of menace. Trumpets.*
CICERO *covers his head with the folds of his toga and recites
the State prayer. A white bull is sacrificed. Trumpets. The
Pontifex Maximus,* METELLUS PIUS, *blind, feeble, carried in
on a litter, presides. Entrails inspected. A* BOY *presents them to*
CICERO *who hides his disgust and nods.*

PIUS. The omens are unusually propitious. The Consuls Marcus
Tullius Cicero and Antonius Hybrida are confirmed in office.
May all the gods protect Rome!

  CICERO *nervously acknowledges the crowd. A roar of
  response.*

ALL. May the gods protect Rome!

  PIUS *collapses in a heap.*

CATULUS. Consul... The Pontiff... He's fallen over.

  ACOLYTES *carry off* PIUS. SERVANTS *set the curule
  chair on a dais at the foot of the huge statue. While this is
  happening,* CICERO *takes* HYBRIDA *aside. An urgent,
  whispered conversation:*

CICERO. Do we have a bargain?

HYBRIDA. Absolutely! You'll not go back on your word?

CICERO. I never go back on my word.

HYBRIDA. I'm honest as the day is long – but I have to live.

  Hostile OPTIMATES *face* POPULISTS. CICERO, *nervous,
  prepares to address the Senate.*

TIRO. Nerves, Master?

CICERO. I'm shaking.

TIRO. Are you going to throw up? Shall I fetch a chamber pot?

CICERO. I've already thrown up.

TIRO. You haven't, have you?

CICERO. Yes – you're standing in it. I'll be all right once I get started.

CICERO stands – a long pause. The noise dies down. Starting quietly and hesitantly – an old trick.

Gentlemen… It's customary for a man elected to this great office to recall those of his antecedents who served as Consul before him – and pray he'll prove a worthy successor to his distinguished ancestors… In my own case – I'm pleased to say – such humility is not possible.

Laughter.

I have neither family nor wealth. I have never led Rome's legions. I owe my election victory to the will of the Roman People… Time out of mind the Consulship has been reserved for men of the highest birth – I've achieved the distinction through my own merit – and I wish to set a precedent for merit. The People raised me to these heights. As long as I hold office, I shall always be the People's Consul.

Support from CAESAR*'s faction, except* CATILINE *who stares with hatred at* CICERO, *mumbled discontent from the* PATRICIANS.

I mean to conduct my Consulship honestly – my affairs shall be open to public scrutiny – I shall publish my accounts – I shall accept none of the usual bribes, or the legitimate rewards that come with high office. And at the end of my term, I shall not seek the governorship of any province.

CATO. Praise the gods for an honest man!

CICERO. Now… During the night, the Tribune, Publius Servilius… er… *Rullus* posted a bill in the Forum proposing a redistribution of the public land. Here it is. I've examined it carefully, and formed a firm opinion of it.

Rullus – where is he? – (*Fixing on somebody in the audience.*) is a man of the People too… Well, he's doing his best to become one. No longer the bejewelled young dandy, he's growing a very serious beard. His conversation is grave, his voice has deepened, even his walk has altered... There's no longer the slightest suspicion of a mincing gait.

Laughter.

But it's the bill, not the man, we're here to discuss. Fellow Romans, I am not, nor was I ever, opposed to a fairer redistribution of land.

Horror from the PATRICIANS, *smugness from* CAESAR*'s faction.*

I shall support any law that benefits the honest citizen of Rome – the needy patriot – the demobbed soldier – who asks only the right to labour in the fields and help feed our hungry people. The poor have always been my chief *concern.*

Cheers from CAESAR*'s side 'Hear him – hear him', etc.*

But this law... (*Advancing on Rullus/member of audience.*) Rullus's law – I shall denounce. I *do* denounce.

Gasps – support from the PATRICIANS.

Gentlemen – this is not a land reform bill – land reform was never its purpose. What is it but a dagger pointed at the heart of our Republic? It's a conspiracy – an audacious attempt by a small group of malcontents to return our country to monarchical rule.

CATO. We'll have no kings in Rome! It's unthinkable!

CICERO. Is it, Cato? Ask yourselves, gentleman, what would be the consequences of passing Rullus's bill?

CATULUS. How can we know?

CELER. We've not had chance to read it –

CICERO. Then let me take you through it... Rullus is proposing to set up a commission of ten men – think of them as ten *kings* – with absolute power over the exchequer, the law, the military, our colonies – the rising and setting of the sun – the phases of the moon – over *everything* – Rome publically or privately possesses. A commission with dictatorial powers to give away free all our State-owned land and property.

CATO. Throw it out –

CATULUS. Throw out the bill – and Rullus with it!

CICERO. Rullus is a Tribune of the People – his person is inviolable.

CATULUS. What's Pompey's view? Has anybody informed Pompey what's happening here?

CICERO. A good question, Senator! Our loyal and embattled General is away defending Rome's Empire on its furthest borders – imagine Rullus giving orders to Pompey Magnus.

ISAURICUS. I say we recall Pompey – he'd soon sort out these *commissioners*!

CATULUS. Fetch him home – let the army deal with it!

CATO. Never!

RIGHT-WING SENATORS (*muttering*). Hear him! Yes! Pompey – Pompey Magnus – We need his strong arm! (*Etc.*)

CICERO (*nipping this in the bud – holds up the copy of the bill*). Who proposes the commission? Rullus.

Who selects the committee that will nominate the commissioners? (*Pretending to check.*) Rullus? Who convenes the assembly that will approve the commissioners?

PATRICIANS. Rullus!

CICERO. Who acts as returning officer and declares the results?

PATRICIANS. Rullus!

CICERO. Who is the only man guaranteed a place on the commission?

SENATE. Rullus!

CICERO. Who wrote the bill?

SENATE. Rullus!

Laughter.

CICERO. Rullus! Rullus wrote it… But there sit the architects who designed it – Caesar – Crassus – Catiline! No doubt, they were expecting to be its chief beneficiaries.

SENATORS. Shame! (*Etc.*)

CATO. Did they imagine we'd hand over *the whole of Italy*, unarmed and defenceless?

CICERO. Let's ask them. What was the plan, Caesar? Were you hoping to use public money to buy yourself the support you need to keep you in power forever? Anything to say? What about you, Crassus?

CATULUS *and* ISAURICUS. Answer! Answer!

CATO. Lost your voice?

Taunts, cries of 'throw them out', etc.

CAESAR *leans back and laughs.* CICERO *faces him.*

CICERO. I shall bow to no threats, open or veiled. I'll allow no man – no one man – whatever his rank, his abilities, his merits – to destabilise the institutions of the State. (*Looking at* CRASSUS.) I shall allow no man, whatever his wealth or his breeding, to threaten our constitution, or to undermine by bribery the rule of law. (*Looking at* CATILINE.) And I shall deal swiftly and severely with any man who incites violence on the streets of our City.

Astonishment.

CATILINE (*snarling*). You shall feel –

CATILINE *draws back his fist –* CAESAR *takes his arm, restraining him.*

CICERO. Senators, we have gone wrong. (*At* CATILINE.) There's evil here – an evil we shelter within our own walls. I mean to root it out. Lend me your support, gentlemen – together we'll restore the dignity, decency, and moral authority of Rome – the true Rome that existed in the time of our founding fathers.

Ecstatic applause from PATRICIANS, *led by* CATO, *hurried debate from* CAESAR*'s faction.*

SENATORS. Hybrida! – Let's hear Hybrida! – Hear the Consul! – Answer him! (*Etc.*)

HYBRIDA *stands – he's drunkish.*

CATILINE. Answer him, Consul – answer!

HYBRIDA. Well, I… er… From what I've seen of it… in my opinion – given the state of the Republic at this present time – well, this bill's not such a good idea… it's not been properly thought through – so I'm against it.

Uproar. CAESAR folds his arms, looks at the ceiling, and smiles. CATILINE is stupefied.

CRASSUS (*to CAESAR*). He's been bought. (*Exits.*)

CATILINE, letting out a roar, advances on CICERO. LICTORS close ranks to defend him.

CATILINE. You… You!

CAESAR. Catiline! Sit down –

CATILINE. You sit in a chair that's rightfully mine – cheating the People of land they were promised – and call yourself the People's Consul! You're nothing – no family, *no guts* – never cut down an enemy! The People's Consul? Let's see what you call yourself when the People have had their way with you – when I've had my way with you!

Storms out, some POPULISTS follow him. PATRICIANS surround and congratulate CICERO.

Scene Seven

Back home. Party. GUESTS arriving. CICERO embraces TERENTIA and TULLIA. SOSITHEUS with little MARCUS.

CICERO. My son! (*Picks him up and kisses him.*) One day he'll be Consul, like his father. (*Hands him back.*) Don't you think I was impressive – even for me?

TIRO. I'd call it foolhardy – to deliberately provoke Catiline like that. Gods! The man's taken an oath to kill you!

CICERO. This is Rome – not Scythia. I'm safe enough.

TIRO. What about the rest of us – you've a family – what about the children? You have your lictors until the end of the month. Then what do we do? Who'll protect the house?

CICERO. I wonder if we could get a spy into the enemy camp somehow. Who have we got?

TIRO. There's Rufus – he mixes with Catiline's boys. He's a likeable lad –

CICERO. Do you trust him?

TIRO. No.

CICERO. Nor do I. My dear Clodius!

   CICERO *moves away and embraces* CLODIUS.

QUINTUS. What could my brother have given Hybrida to make him turn coat like that?

TIRO. Macedonia.

QUINTUS. What!

CICERO. They were asking for a fight. It seemed like bad manners to refuse them one. Who do you think looked sicker – Caesar or Crassus?

CLODIUS. Catiline. You'll need a bodyguard. Seriously... I'd better look into it –

QUINTUS (*explodes*). You've given away our province! To Hybrida!

TERENTIA. What? What did he say?

   TULLIA *runs to* CICERO.

CICERO. It's my province – what I do with Macedonia is my business.

TERENTIA. Macedonia?

QUINTUS. No, Marcus, it's not *your* business, it's family business. How are we to repay the costs of your election – who'll pay all your other debts without the income from Macedonia?

CICERO. Oh, money just happens – it always does! I need a united Senate. How can I keep order if my fellow Consul's in league with my enemies?

QUINTUS. So Hybrida gets to plunder Macedonia? Where's 'the dignity, decency, and moral authority of Rome' in that? (*Storms out.*)

CICERO. If he plunders, I'll prosecute him. (*Seeing the look on* TERENTIA*'s face.*) Terentia?

She takes off her jewellery, drops it on the floor and exits. TULLIA *picks it up and tries it on.* CICERO *sighs, on the subsequent intake of breath he sniffs the air, is aware of* CATO, *who is arriving with* CELER, ISAURICUS *and* CATULUS.

CATO. Has something upset your wife?

CICERO. Of course not.

CATO. Women should keep themselves busy – spinning and weaving – supervising the household slaves – or all order breaks down... Fine speech, Consul... But anybody can make a speech. What are you going to do about Pompey? His soldiers call him Pompey Magnus now. What if he turns them against us? No one man should wield such power.

CICERO. Pompey's away at the wars – he'll not defeat Mithradates for years and years! He'll certainly not trouble us during my Consulship –

CATO. He needs reminding he's the Senate's servant – not Rome's master. The legions he commands are not some private army of his own –

CICERO. Might be difficult to persuade his soldiers of that.

CATO. You were never a military man, were you?

CELER. Shame we've lost our Pontiff.

ISAURICUS. He managed to struggle on through the ceremony – he was determined not to let us down. A true Roman!

Hypocritical grunts of agreement.

CATULUS. Well, the office is vacant, it's my turn now – I hope I can count on your vote, Consul?

ISAURICUS. I was hoping Cicero would support me.

CICERO. For Pontiff? You're both going to stand? Shouldn't you settle it between you? Don't, for the love of the gods, divide the vote!

RUFUS *appears looking miserable.*

Excuse me – I've an apology to make. Rufus! This morning I treated you like a boy – not as the fine young man you've become. (*Arm round* RUFUS*'s shoulder.*) You know, it's a failing in the old to see the young for what they were rather than for what they are. I'm truly sorry if I gave offence.

RUFUS. I can't agree with your views on the poor – but my respect – my love for you is unshaken.

CICERO. Hear that, Tiro? (*Pinches his cheek as if he were a six-year-old.*) He loves me! I never believed you wanted to kill me – did you?

TIRO. Rufus? Never!

RUFUS. What are you talking about?

CICERO. Friends of yours are plotting to murder me –

RUFUS. It's not true! Who?

CICERO. Catiline and his bully boys – they've taken an oath to kill me – on the body of a child they butchered –

RUFUS. I don't believe you.

CICERO. Hybrida assures me it's true. He said you were a witness.

TIRO. Well, to be fair to Rufus – Hybrida said he *thought* Rufus was there. He was too drunk to be absolutely sure.

RUFUS. *Had* I been there – which I was not – I'd have come straight round and warned you!

CICERO. Of course you would!

CICERO *embraces* RUFUS.

RUFUS. As if I'd involve myself in such a –

CICERO. Though if ever you *do* hear anything –

RUFUS. What *is* this? You're asking me to spy on my friends?

CICERO. I'm asking you to follow your conscience – to be what I know you are: a loyal citizen.

He embraces RUFUS *again.*

Say nothing of this to the others. Enjoy the celebrations – I'll join you shortly…

RUFUS *joins* CLODIUS.

That young man is on his way to repeat every word I've said to Catiline.

TIRO. If he is, it might be a good thing. When Catiline realises his plot's exposed, he'll have to pause and reconsider.

CICERO. And if Rufus stays loyal, we have our spy. First throw to me. I wonder what Caesar's next move will be.

TIRO. I expect it will be whatever we least expect.

Enter CAESAR *and* CRASSUS.

CAESAR. Consul! Many, many congratulations! That was the most entertaining inaugural speech I've ever heard. You shall certainly have my full support in your campaign to restore 'the moral authority of Rome – the true Rome of our founding fathers.'

CICERO. Thank you, Gaius – and welcome. Crassus.

He moves away with TIRO. CAESAR *and* CRASSUS *take wine and move apart.* CAESAR *doesn't drink his wine.*

CAESAR. Well, we lost that one – next time I'll win.

CRASSUS. You told me you'd won him over.

CAESAR. I said I'd made him an offer he'd be wise to accept.

CRASSUS. What shall we do now?

CAESAR. I need another loan.

CRASSUS. You already owe me five million – the interest is mounting. How much?

CAESAR. Another twenty.

CRASSUS. Thousand?

CAESAR. Million.

CRASSUS. You're a bad risk.

CAESAR. Yes, I am – can you get it for me?

CRASSUS. What's it for?

CAESAR. I have to get in among them – I need access to their innermost councils.

CRASSUS. How will you manage it?

CAESAR *raises his eyebrows.*

When do you need the money?

CAESAR. Now.

CRASSUS. How am I going to raise it?

CAESAR. Don't ask me – you're the banker. But raise it. Terentia – dear lady! Is this your lovely daughter?

TULLIA *is wearing all her mother's discarded jewels.*

TULLIA. Am I? Do you think I look lovely?

CAESAR. You're the prettiest little girl I've ever seen. (*Picks her up.*) I could eat you!

Everybody laughs. TULLIA *thinks it's funny.* CICERO *looks worried.*

CICERO (*to* TIRO). He wouldn't. Would he?

TIRO. Catiline might though…

Scene Eight

A street. CATILINE *in a rage, followed by* SURA, CETHEGUS, *others.*

CATILINE. What am I now? I'll not bow and scrape to the lowest of the low! They should tremble before me!

CETHEGUS. Be patient – Our friends in the north are raising and army of veterans – when we're strong enough to –

CATILINE (*not listening*). Power, wealth, patronage – everything's in their hands. Honest Romans left with nothing –

SURA. Catiline –

CATILINE. They've stolen Rome from us! How did we let it happen? I was born to rule! It was my turn – my right! We've become the slaves of weak old men. They tax us – chain us like dogs – while they plunder the State and pile up our gold?

SURA. All that will change –

CATILINE. I fought for my country – I shed my blood – they cowered at home – feeding their filthy appetites! I say – *I say* – let's seize their hoarded riches – get the wealth of this land flowing again? What have we to lose now? They've cheated us – men I thought my friends.

SURA. Stand again – you will be Consul – next year you'll win –

CATILINE. What is Cicero?! Doesn't know a sword from his prick – if he has a prick! These preening, simpering, eunuch *lawyers*! I'll crush him – crush him – crush him! I'll bring the People onto the streets – with swords and clubs and fire!

SURA. But not yet! –

CETHEGUS. Listen to Sura. We can't strike until our army is in place and ready to march on Rome. I am stockpiling the weapons we'll need here. But in the summer, you can stand again for election – next time you're sure to win! Next time – next time –

SURA. We'll make you Consul if it costs us ten million.

CATILINE. 'Next time, next time'! I'll kill him now – and nobody will stop me.

CETHEGUS. Where are you going? Come back – that's not the way!

SURA. If the fool betrays us… Gods – save us from our friends! Keep him on a tight leash – he'll get us all killed.

Scene Nine

PRIESTS *and* PEOPLE *assemble to hear the results of the Pontifical election.*

TIRO. How do I know what went on at meetings where I wasn't present? Research, friends, research for my book! Slaves have a network of information – a web spun all over the City – over the whole Roman world in fact. If you want to know who's plotting what – just ask a slave.

We held an election for a new Pontiff – High Priest of our State religion.

College of PRIESTS. ISAURICUS, *and* CATULUS, *waiting on the election platform for the results. Enter in a hurry* CELER *and* CICERO.

CICERO. In the election for Pontifex Maximus, the tribes have voted – and the votes have been counted. For Publius Vatia Isauricus –

TIRO (*aside*). Aristocratic Faction.

CICERO. There voted four tribes. For Quintus Lutatius Catulus –

TIRO (*aside*). Ancient Patrician.

CICERO. There voted six tribes. For… Gaius Julius Caesar…

TIRO (*aside*). People's Party.

CAESAR *appears from nowhere.*

CICERO. There voted seven tribes. I therefore declare that
Gaius Julius Caesar is elected Pontifex Maximus – supreme
judge in all matters of religion and morals – for life.

CAESAR *raises his arms, a moment's ecstasy, almost
demented with delight.*

CRASSUS. Twenty million well spent!

CATULUS. Shame on you, Caesar! You're plotting to
overthrow the State!

CAESAR *smiles as he goes.*

Your presence in this sacred place is an outrage!

CICERO *is joined by* TIRO *and* CLODIUS, SOSITHEUS
and other SLAVES. *A couple of* BODYGUARDS.

CICERO. You've only yourselves to blame.

CELER. Why in the name of all that's holy, didn't you settle it
between you! Either one of you would have had ten votes to
Caesar's seven –

CATULUS. It's Cicero's fault! He should never have let Caesar
stand – the office of Pontiff requires an incumbent of the
utmost moral rectitude –

CICERO. You tied my hands. You let him take the vote to the
People –

ISAURICUS. Damn the People! This is a holy office – not
popular entertainment!

CICERO. Well, the People have made him Pontiff now – he'll
have a voice in the innermost councils of the State –

TIRO. Not to mention custody of the Vestal Virgins.

CELER. You've shut the fox in your hen coop. Moral fucking
rectitude indeed!

TIRO. Word is, he paid out twenty million in bribes.

CELER. The balls of the man! Where'd he get that sort of
money? Had he lost he'd have been ruined. Well, his snout's
in the trough now – there'll be no stopping him.

TIRO. What kind of a man risks his whole political future – on a throw of a dice?

Scene Ten

Outside CICERO's *house, dangerous* PEOPLE *lurking.* CICERO *and* TIRO, CLODIUS, SOSITHEUS, *and* BODYGUARDS *arrive home – furious barking.*

CICERO. What's going on?

CLODIUS. Don't worry – I'll protect you.

They go into the house. MARCUS *crying, off.*

CICERO. What's that barking?

CLODIUS. Catiline! (*Laughs.*)

TIRO. It's Sargon.

CICERO. Who?

TIRO. I acquired a guard dog – his name is Sargon.

CICERO. What world are we living in?! Is the Consul no longer safe in his own home? That howling will drive me mad.

CLODIUS. Better than being murdered in your bed.

Enter TERENTIA *coming to meet them –* TULLIA *runs and clings to* CICERO.

CICERO. Terentia? What's the matter?

TERENTIA. There's a woman you must see –

CICERO. What woman? You're not still angry, are you? Macedonia was –

TERENTIA. If you ever – if you ever…! I'll settle your debts – but this is the last time – do you understand me? Angry? I'm furious… But I can't let them kill you –

CICERO. Let who – Tullia, don't –

TERENTIA. Though, I don't know why I should care. (*Exits*.)

CICERO. Irritating woman! What's got into her?

TIRO. Don't ask me – she's your wife –

Re-enter TERENTIA *with* CAMILLA, *who is nervous, she's been weeping.*

TERENTIA. Her name is Camilla.

CAMILLA. I'll not speak in front of slaves –

TERENTIA. Tiro has more common sense than his master. Tell the Consul what you've heard from Senator Curius –

CAMILLA. Quintus Curius –

TERENTIA. She's his mistress.

CAMILLA. My husband doesn't –

TERENTIA. Doesn't know. And he's about the only man in Rome who doesn't.

CICERO. My dear –

TERENTIA. Quintus Curius is one of Catiline's cronies –

CICERO. Terentia, please! Let the lady tell her own story.

TERENTIA. Go on! Tell him.

CAMILLA. I've loved Curius since our childhood – but our families wouldn't let us marry.

TERENTIA. He was a very rich man –

CAMILLA. Not any more. He's deeply in debt. Catiline's cheated him of everything... It's the man who is supposed to provide, isn't it? Now I pay for everything –

TERENTIA. Imagine that, husband!

CAMILLA. Last night Curius confided in me... He was drunk... He told me our financial worries will soon be over – Catiline's going to make him rich again. (*Gathering courage*.)

TERENTIA. Go on.

CAMILLA. It's a conspiracy. They're plotting to seize the City by force. They're secretly mustering an army of veterans in the north – preparing to march on Rome. Catiline's going to call an Assembly of the People – have your election declared invalid – and grant him emergency powers.

CICERO. When?

CAMILLA. When the rebels are ready to attack, Catiline will promise the People cancellation of all debts and taxes – he'll confiscate the property of the rich, and divide the great Offices of State among his supporters. Any Senators who oppose him will be executed...

TERENTIA. And the signal for the uprising is to be your murder. Tell the Consul about the boy.

CAMILLA. Catiline made his supporters swear a blood oath on the body of a child.

CICERO. I know.

TERENTIA. You know! Why didn't you tell me!

CICERO. I didn't want to alarm you. I'm only now beginning to realise how serious –

TERENTIA. They kill and disembowel a child! They swear to do the same to you – and you didn't think it serious!

CICERO. I knew about the plot – but I didn't have the evidence I need. I can't move against them without evidence. I need names –

CAMILLA. Don't ask me to name names!

TERENTIA. You must! It's treason to withhold them!

CICERO. Gently, gently –

CAMILLA (*weeps*). They'll kill me! What Catiline did to that boy... (*Tears.*)

CICERO. I'll see you come to no harm.

TERENTIA. Their names!

CAMILLA. Where to start – there are so many of them! Cethegus, and Cassius Longinus... Your fellow Consul, Antonius Hybrida – and Lentulus Sura.

CLODIUS. Sura! Impossible!

CICERO. No! Sura's Urban Praetor – charged with keeping law and order –

CAMILLA. He took the oath.

CICERO. Dear gods! What's been going on in this City! Under our very noses –

TERENTIA. Arrest them.

CICERO. On what grounds?! What's the word of one woman – against so many Senators –

CAMILLA. There are others involved –

TULLIA. Papa –

TIRO. Julius Caesar?

CAMILLA. Yes – I've heard Caesar's name mentioned – and Crassus.

CICERO. While Catiline reduces the City to chaos – Caesar will watch from the side-lines –

TIRO. Waiting to swoop down and seize the spoils.

TULLIA. Papa –

TIRO. And the call to arms is to be your murder.

TULLIA. Papa –

TERENTIA. I'd a mind to do it myself when you gave away Macedonia.

CICERO. Terentia… Please can we just call a truce over Macedonia? Take Tullia – she shouldn't be hearing this –

CAMILLA. What's to become of me? I can't go back to Curius after this.

CICERO. You must. And pass on to Terentia every scrap of information you hear.

CAMILLA. Can you protect Curius?

CICERO. I'll do what I can for him, but… If he's guilty of treason…

CAMILLA. When Catiline comes into your life, the warmth
goes out of it… From the day he fell in with Catiline… He
was corrupted by evil – a terrible change came over him…
Evil… I sense it on Curius… It's in his eyes, on his breath –
even his clothes whenever he come back from Catiline's
house…

TERENTIA. You've behaved very well – like a true Roman.
Come –

Exeunt TERENTIA *and* CAMILLA.

CICERO. If the gods made all things for the benefit of mankind,
how do we explain evil, Tiro? How do we explain
cockroaches, snakes, and Lucius Sergius Catiline? Tell me that.

CLODIUS – *a little apart – turns and studies the two of
them.*

End of Play One.

PLAY TWO

CATILINE

Scene One

Drums. CATILINE *enters in armour, followed by his*
AQUILIFER. *He addresses the audience.* SURA, CETHEGUS
and other CATILINE SUPPORTERS. CAESAR *and*
CRASSUS *a little apart –* CRASSUS *looking worried.*

CATILINE. Citizens! Are you with me?

> *A roar of approval from his* SUPPORTERS. *His*
> AQUILIFER *hands him the silver Eagle.*

> The right to rule is enshrined in the minds and impulses of
> our nobility. Lesser men must entrust the protection of the
> State to those fit to lead them – good men from Rome's
> founding families – men who, from time immemorial, have
> defended Rome's borders, nurtured her growth, honoured her
> gods, lifted her, carried her, and placed her at the very centre
> of the world...

> You – the People – are the sinew and muscle of the State –
> you are the will and unconquerable force of Rome! Into
> whose hands will you commit Rome's unimaginable power?
> I am Catiline – your last hope of freedom! I share your
> poverty – I feel your anger. Awake! Fight – for honour, for
> glory, and for the prizes of victory! Make me your Consul.
> Help me tear down the corrupt and moribund order of
> privileged tyranny! I shall cancel your debts, and give you
> their riches – I shall give you bread – I shall give you land!
> I shall give you liberty!

MOB. Land and Liberty! Bread! Freedom! Freedom! Freedom!
(*Etc.*)

> CICERO *working in his study.* SOSITHEUS *and other*
> SLAVES *hard at work.*

TIRO (*addressing the audience*). Election time is here again! In
Rome, elections for Consul are held mid-term. It's beginning
to look as if Catiline might succeed Cicero in the office, and
win the popular vote without resorting to violence – relying

instead on intimidation, blackmail, promising the unaffordable and the downright impossible, and, as is the custom here, massive amounts of bribery and corruption. Sound familiar? (*Reading his mansucript.*) 'Like a man in the condemned cell, Cicero waits for the blow to fall… Expecting it any day – any moment – and forces himself to go on with the business of governing the country.' It takes courage… And my master was never a courageous man.

CICERO. Imagine… Catiline as Consul – Caesar and Crassus the real power in Rome! All my hopes of reforming the Republic are dying with me. What can I do, Tiro?

TIRO. Call it a day. Walk away. Retire to Athens – become a teacher.

CICERO. It would have been better for the State if he'd sent his thugs to murder me – tried to seize the City by force… An open rebellion I can deal with – but while he keeps within the law –

TIRO. Keeps within the law! He's bankrupted himself to buy votes. Even so, the People are beginning to say, 'It's his turn'.

CICERO. The People! If the gods had destined Catiline for the Consulship they'd have given him a brain.

TIRO. If you try to stop him again – he'll tear your flesh with his own teeth…

CICERO. Who could we put up against him? Clodius thinks Murena might stand.

TIRO. Murena!

CICERO. What's wrong with him?

TIRO. He's away with the legions in Gaul. Nobody remembers who he is. And he's an idiot.

CICERO. Stupid people tend to vote for stupid people. Sometimes a most unlikely candidate plays well with the mob. Hybrida got in, didn't he? And look at… Well, I could give you a long list.

TIRO. Murena couldn't fund an election campaign – he has no money.

CICERO. I had no money.

TIRO. Your wife had – and you had a brain – and a persuasive voice. Murena has neither.

CICERO. I know… He's a soldier. It's a problem… I wonder if I could find some rich old fool who'd put up the cash?

TIRO. No – you should retire to Athens – write your memoirs –

CICERO. You're right as usual, Tiro – that's what *I should* do… Abandon every principle I've ever fought for – run away – hide my head in dishonourable exile… But could I live with myself? What would be left of Cicero?

Starts to go, then turns.

So I think I know what I *must* do.

TIRO. Oh? What?

CICERO. Go and pack a bag.

Scene Two

TIRO. So… We travelled down to the Bay of Naples to see one of the richest men in the world – General Licinius Lucullus. Do you remember Lucullus?

LUCULLUS – *languid, mid-fifties, Greek dress – is feeding his fish. A* SLAVE *holds a silver bucket of fish food. Enter* CICERO *and* TIRO.

He's the one who's been waiting five years for the Senate to award him a Triumph… Behind the scenes, his enemy – Pompey – jealous of all military honours but his own – has been using his considerable influence to prevent it.

VOICE (*off*). What's a Triumph?

TIRO. A Triumph? It's a parade. A victorious General enters Rome in a big chariot at the head of his whole army – the soldiers sing filthy songs and get a huge bonus in gold coins – and everybody gets drunk. A national, monumental hangover is the highest honour Rome can award. I don't really see the point – but that sort of thing seems to appeal to soldiers.

LUCULLUS. Consul.

CICERO. General.

LUCULLUS. Give me a moment... I'm just feeding my eels.

CICERO. My! Aren't they big ones!

LUCULLUS. I give them all names. See that fat one – gold rings in his fins – isn't he repulsive! I call him Pompey Magnus. Do you want to feed him his supper – he'll let you tickle his belly? Come here, Pompey – good eel, good eel...

CICERO. I'd rather not.

LUCULLUS. What brings you all the way to Misenum?

CICERO. I had to come to you – since you no longer come to Rome.

LUCULLUS. Sore point! How can I come to Rome? I can't enter the City, unless I give up my Imperium – that would mean I can't celebrate my Triumph.

CICERO. Yes – difficult for you. I sympathise –

LUCULLUS. Five years – five years I've waited! Pompey's cronies keep me out. Bastards! I've earned my Triumph – I deserve the applause of my country – they should heap honours upon me... I have everything I could wish for – except the one thing in the word I want most...

CICERO. It's your Triumph I'm here to discuss.

LUCULLUS. Hoped it might be. Hungry? I take it you like fish?

CICERO. Once it's on a plate...

Dozens of SLAVES *bring wine, and elaborate fish dishes on gold plates. Instant luxury.*

Is this how you dine every day? Even when you're on your own?

LUCULLUS. What else have I to spend my money on?

CICERO. I'm going to lay a motion before the Senate awarding you your Triumph.

LUCULLUS. Hmmm... But will it pass?

CICERO. I don't call votes I can't win, General.

LUCULLUS. What's in it for you?

CICERO. Catiline is standing for Consul again. I need your help to keep him out.

LUCULLUS. Consul! He should be chained up. The man's barking!

CICERO. In my experience, that's never been an impediment to high office.

LUCULLUS. He'll never get in.

CICERO. His support among the People is growing. With Caesar's backing and Crassus's money, I think he could scrape into second place. Once they're in power they'll seize land and property from the rich and redistribute it among the poor.

LUCULLUS. And I am rich. I have land.

CICERO. All this – the silks, the gold – your fish ponds – will be taken from you and given to the beggars who hang around street corners, waiting to do Caesar's bidding. It's easy to incite men who have nothing, to plunder the wealth of the industrious rich.

LUCULLUS. Catiline! Dear gods, have the Roman People lost their senses!

CICERO. They'll make him Consul unless you stop him,

LUCULLUS. Me! How?

CICERO. By celebrating your Triumph at just the right moment... This is delicious – what is it?

LUCULLUS. Turbot.

CICERO. Did he have a name?

LUCULLUS (*looks at* CICERO *as if he's an idiot*). Just turbot. What have you in mind?

CICERO. Stage your Triumph on the eve of the consular elections... We'll put on the biggest show Rome's seen for years. You'll enter the City – a conquering General – at the head of tens of thousands of veterans.

LUCULLUS. Imagine the spectacle!

CICERO. A victory parade of voters! And you'll shower your soldiers in gold.

LUCULLUS. Naturally. They've waited as long for their bounty as I have for my Triumph.

CICERO. So they'll vote the way you tell them?

LUCULLUS. They'd better.

CICERO. The candidate we'll put up against Catiline is your old legate – Murena. With your money, and the votes of your army, he might just push Catiline into third place.

LUCULLUS. Hmmmm... Murena... Well...

CICERO. What's the matter?

LUCULLUS. I don't care for his friends. His right-hand man is a young fellow so corrupt – so depraved –

CICERO. Ah – young Clodius!

LUCULLUS. Clodius did his military service under me – caused me endless problems. He has a gift for insubordination, so naturally he was adored by the rank and file – to say nothing of his disgraceful sexual excesses – the swine's insatiable –

CICERO (*amused*). I know! He'll seduce anything that moves –

LUCULLUS. He seduced my wife.

CICERO (*the slightest of all hesitations*). Yes – but he was very young!

LUCULLUS. She was his sister!

CICERO. Boys will be boys, you know – but he's grown up into a mature, and responsible citizen. I'm something of a mentor to him. Look, General, to save the Republic you should be prepared to support an old comrade. Fund Murena's campaign – leave me to deal with Clodius. At all costs, we must keep Catiline and Caesar out of power.

LUCULLUS. No – there must be some other way.

CICERO. If there were any other way, d'you think I'd not have thought of it? If you've no stomach for politics, Lucullus, you'd better stay down here in Misenum, complaining to your fish of the injustices your country has done you.

LUCULLUS *goes and feeds, contemplatively, his fish.*

TIRO (*aside*). It was going so well!

CICERO (*aside to* TIRO). They flaunt their wealth – and then they wonder why they're so hated.

LUCULLUS. Five years – five years I've waited…

CICERO. Shameful!

LUCULLUS. Five years… (*Pause.*) I suppose Murena might make a decent enough Consul if he were willing to take advice…

CICERO. The Senate would vote you Rome's greatest honour.

LUCULLUS. My Triumph…

CICERO. So long overdue.

LUCULLUS (*almost tearful*). Long overdue… Just warn that little shit Publius Clodius to stay out of my way… Goodnight, Pompey. Sleep well… You ugly… ugly… fish… (*Exits.*)

TIRO. Well, you have the funds you needed.

CICERO. All I have to do now is win the election for Murena.

TIRO. And stop young Clodius ruining his chances.

CICERO. Oh, the boy will do as I tell him. He always has, he always will.

TIRO. I wouldn't be too sure. He's growing up.

CICERO. We'll see.

TIRO. He's staying with his sister – on the Palatine.

CICERO. How would you know a thing like that?

TIRO. I know everything. I'm a slave.

Scene Three

CELER*'s house on the Palatine*.

TIRO. They say Clodius's sister is very beautiful – and very dangerous.

CICERO. Clodia? I can't imagine how she came to be married to our old friend Metellus Celer – a most unlikely match… All this shameless luxury! When Lucullus threw her out she certainly landed on her feet.

TIRO. Or her back.

CICERO. What did you say?

TIRO. Nothing.

Enter a pampered SERVANT BOY.

CICERO. The master of the house?

BOY. He's not at home.

CICERO. The Lady then?

BOY. I'll see if the Lady Clodia has finished dressing. (*Exits.*)

TIRO. At this time of day?

CICERO. I'll tell you a story about Clodia. There was a young man called Vettius who failed to satisfy her as a lover. She spread stories about his inadequacy. In revenge, he began to say of her that though she was witty, well-read, charming, and seductive in the salon, in bed she was dry, repetitive, and prosaic – his exact words were, 'It's like fucking a public library'… So she had two of her other lovers beat Vettius to a pulp and then – to make the punishment fit the crime – they buggered him half to death – dear Lady Clodia!

CLODIA (*entering, half-dressed*). Marcus Tullius Cicero! The Consul under my humble roof – you do me great honour!

CICERO. Hardly a humble roof, Clodia – what gardens – what a glorious view of the City!

CLODIA. D'you like it? The house next door is for sale – why don't you buy it? It would be wonderfully amusing to have Cicero as my neighbour.

CICERO. A house on the Palatine is way beyond the resources of a poor lawyer, I fear. Who owns it?

CLODIA. Crassus. Doesn't he own everything? I'm afraid my husband's not at home.

CICERO. Dear lady, it's your brother I've come to see – I was told he's here.

CLODIA. Clodius? Yes – he's just returned from Gaul… He's… resting. Won't I do instead? Is there no little service I can perform?

CICERO. Politics, I'm afraid.

CLODIA. Oh, how very dull! (*To* BOY.) Go and wake my brother.

BOY. Lady. (*Exits*.)

CLODIA. He stays out all night – gets up to all sorts of mischief. Dreadful boy! We're very close. People say terrible things about us – but we rather like it. Notoriety can be a wonderful stimulant – sexually speaking – don't you find?

CICERO. I'm a lawyer, lady.

Enter CLODIUS *and* RUFUS, *both nearly naked*.

CLODIA. It's you he wants not me.

CLODIUS. Everybody wants me. My dear old mentor and friend!

CLODIUS *embraces* CICERO.

CICERO. Dear boy –

CLODIUS. I've been visiting my regiment. Did you miss me? Here's Rufus too –

RUFUS. Master.

CLODIUS. I've been in training – (*Re: his muscles.*) feel.
Without me to protect you, I've been worrying Catiline
might sneak up on you some dark night, and beat your brains
out! (*Laughs.*)

CICERO. Tiro's guard dog stood in for you.

CLODIUS. Oh, I remember Sargon. I've been visiting Murena.

CICERO. It's Murena I'm here to discuss.

CLODIA. Is this your famous secretary?

CICERO. Tiro – yes.

CLODIA. They say he can write as fast as one can speak? How
much do you want for him?

CICERO. He's not for sale. I couldn't manage the Consulship
without him. Ask again next year – I might be open to an
offer if the price is right.

CLODIA. Ah well! If you're going to talk politics... Rufus –
come and make love to me.

Exeunt CLODIA *and* RUFUS.

CLODIUS. My sister's such a flirt. I'm a flirt myself – must run
in the family.

CICERO. I hear your friend Murena wants to stand for Consul?

CLODIUS. He does. That's why I went to see him.

CICERO. He's been away three years, hasn't he? Who
remembers him – who'd *vote* for him, I wonder? There are
two consular seats – the patricians will back Silanus – he'll
get in easily – so it's a fight for second place. Caesar, and
Crassus will back Catiline. Where does that leave Murena?

CLODIUS. Well... Give us time –

CICERO. Murena should have been out canvassing all year.
Who's running his election campaign?

CLODIUS. I shall run it.

CICERO. My dear boy! (*Laughs.*)

CLODIUS. What's wrong with that?

CICERO. Well… Do you think you have the experience? You've never held office – never even –

CLODIUS. Well, damn you, Cicero! If you're so sure we're going to lose –

CICERO. *Lose?* (*Putting his arm around* CLODIUS.) No – Murena's going to win – he's the only man who can beat Catiline. Of course he'll win!

CLODIUS. Ahhhhh. I see! This is not about getting Murena in, is it? It's about keeping Catiline out.

CICERO. How well you know me!

CLODIUS. And love you – and trust you –

CICERO. That's why I've come to give you a tutorial in the gentle art of electioneering. Together we'll beat Catiline – if, *if* you do exactly as I tell you. Agreed? Are we friends?

CLODIUS. Get Murena the Consulship – and you'll not need Sargon. I'll be your faithful dog forever…

CICERO. Woof!

CLODIUS. Woof!

Scene Four

Night. Storms. MEN *with torches.*

TIRO. It was the most corrupt – violent – vindictive election campaign in living memory… What are you up to, Sositheus?

SOSITHEUS. Nothing – running errands. Election business…

SOSITHEUS, *carrying a bulging satchel, puts up his hood and crosses the stage – exits through the audience.*

TIRO. Canvassing gave way to street-fighting –

The election campaign. Slogan-shouting and street-fighting.
On the steps of the Senate House, CATO, CELER,
CATULUS, ISAURICUS, HYBRIDA, CICERO,
CLODIUS, MURENA, *etc., coming out, are confronted by*
CATILINE *and his* SUPPORTERS. CAESAR *and*
CRASSUS *present but not quite part of it.*

CATO. Stop this! Out of my way! Let me pass! Is this Rome?
Am I Cato?! I've never known such corruption!

CATILINE. Corruption! Look at the men who surround you,
Cato!

Jeers.

CATO. Millions – paid out in bribes! Rioting in the streets –
demobbed soldiers – brigands – gladiators –

Jeers, threats.

CATILINE. Do you hear their anger? That glorious sound is
called 'The Will of the People'! (*To the* MOB.) Citizens! Our
Republic has two bodies – one frail, and sickly with an
empty head – look at them! The other is healthy – full of
vigour – but it has no head at all. I shall be your head! Give
me your votes! Make me your leader!

MOB. Change! Change! Change! The People demand change!
Change! Change! Change! The People will have justice! The
People's voice will be heard! Freedom! Freedom! (*Etc*.)

CATILINE. The People's voice *shall* be heard! Freedom!

MOB. Freedom! Freedom! Freedom! Throw out the old corrupt
order! (*Etc*.)

CATO. Catiline – are you mad! Men are being hacked to death
– you are to blame – you I accuse! You brought this evil into
our City! Fit to stand for Consul? You – Head of State! It's
beyond belief!

CATILINE. I am the champion of the oppressed… You started a
fire to consume my fortunes… but I shall put out the flames
– I'll demolish the whole rotten structure –

Shocked gasps 'Oh! Oh!', etc. Then angry protests.

CICERO. You heard him, friends – you heard that threat!
Sergius Catiline would overthrow our sacred institutions –
burn down your City! Abandon him! Reject his mad
ambition! Chose Murena for your Consul!

Drums drown him out. CATILINE *and his* SUPPORTERS
swarm off, drums beating, flags flying. CICERO *and* TIRO
*go home – heavily guarded – they run the gauntlet through
a hostile crowd, protected by* CLODIUS, QUINTUS, *and
a couple of big* BODYGUARDS.

CRASSUS. We've kicked over a nest of hornets. I don't know
which would be worse – a defeat for Catiline or a win.

CAESAR. But don't you find it exhilarating? Politics at its
rawest and best! Hold your nerve, man. Hold your nerve!

CAMILLA *is chased across the stage by a* GANG.

Scene Five

Triumphal music. The whole cast cast their votes. Then
CICERO*'s house.*

CELER. What a glorious sight! Lucullus's Triumph – thousands
upon thousands of veterans casting their votes – surely it's
enough?

CICERO. I fear the gods might have given me what I prayed for.

TIRO. A victory for Murena?

CICERO. A defeat for Catiline.

TIRO. It's only a matter of time before he comes to kill you –

TULLIA. Why does Papa have to go out? Is he in danger?

CLODIUS. It's election day. The Consul oversees the vote –
presides over the count – declares the result.

TULLIA. *Is* he in danger? I mean real danger – I mean his life –

CLODIUS. No, Tullia. We'll protect him –

CELER. Here – put on this breastplate.

CICERO. Certainly not – I'd look ridiculous. I may not have
the physical courage of other men – but I'll not look like
a coward –

CELER. Better ridiculous than dead – my guess is they'll try to
stab you in the confusion.

TIRO. Of course, if an assassin's determined enough, he's
bound to get through – a madman with a knife – if he's
prepared to die in the attempt you're helpless against him.

Sargon barking. Enter TERENTIA *and* SLAVES.

CICERO. Thanks for that, Tiro. Now what's happening?
Terentia? What's wrong?

TERENTIA. They've found a body – in the street – in front of
our door –

TULLIA *clings to her father.*

TULLIA. A dead body!

CICERO. Where's my son?

TERENTIA. Marcus is safe. It's Camilla – she must have been
coming to warn us –

CELER. Who? Warn you? Of what?

TERENTIA. Her head has been smashed in by a hammer blow
– her throat has been cut – her entrails removed.

CICERO. I promised to protect her… I gave my word… I'm
helpless against… against…

TULLIA. Papa, I'm afraid – don't go out – stay here with me.

TERENTIA. He'll do no such thing. He'll be brave, he'll do his
duty, and no harm will come to him. The gods are looking
down – they'll protect the righteous and punish the evildoers.

CICERO *kisses* TERENTIA.

CLODIUS. Still – you'd better put on the breastplate.

CLODIUS *and* CELER *force him into it – under his toga.*
CICERO *improvises a protest.*

CICERO. I feel so foolish –

CLODIUS. I'm not surprised. You look ridiculous.

TIRO. But it may save your life –

CELER. Keep still!

> *They go to the vote. Drums, trumpets.* LUCULLUS, *as a Triumphing General – leads* MURENA *to the rostra.* CICERO *and* CLODIUS, *backed by the* PATRICIANS, *present* SILANUS *and* MURENA *to the cheering* PEOPLE.

CICERO. The Tribes have voted. The People have made their choice. I, your Consul, give you your Consuls for the coming year – Junius Silanus, and Lucius *Murena*!

CROWD. Murena! Murena! Murena!

> *Wild cheering from the fickle* MOB. CATILINE, *a grim smile, and his* SUPPORTERS *leave. Last out are* CAESAR *and* CRASSUS.

Scene Six

CICERO*'s house, in darkness. Gloom. Tension.* CICERO *with* TERENTIA, CLODIUS *and* BODYGUARDS. *Weapons lying about.*

CLODIUS. Now you've wounded him he's at his most dangerous…

CICERO. Damn this thing!

> *He takes off the breastplate – and flings it down.* TULLIA *tries it on.*

I wish I could goad him into action – flush him out…

> SOSITHEUS *guiltily hangs his head.* CICERO *flashes a warning look at him.*

TIRO. Until he makes his move we're helpless.

CICERO. The irony! The very laws made to protect our freedom tie our hands. What defence can we ever have against conspiracy? We know what he's done – we know what he's planning to do... But...

CLODIUS. Sooner or later he'll strike.

TERENTIA. The disease is reaching its crisis – it will be 'kill or cure.'

CICERO. Am I to stay trembling behind locked doors – a prisoner in my own house for the rest of my life?

CLODIUS. No. Only for the rest of Catiline's life.

A pounding at the door.

TIRO. Here they come.

CLODIUS *positions* BODYGUARDS *by the door. They draw swords.* TULLIA *picks up a pilum. Sargon barking.* SOSITHEUS *goes to the door.* TIRO *holds a torch.* CLODIUS *nods to* SOSITHEUS.

SOSITHEUS. Who's there?

CRASSUS (*off*). Crassus.

TIRO. Who?

CRASSUS. Crassus.

TIRO. He says it's Crassus.

CICERO. And is it?

TIRO. Sounds like him.

SOSITHEUS (*aside to* CICERO). Master – I think it's working.

CICERO (*aside*). Shhh.

TERENTIA. Tullia!

TERENTIA *takes* TULLIA *to safety.*

CLODIUS. I'm ready for them. Open the door.

SOSITHEUS *lets in* CRASSUS, *he has a document case, and two young* PATRICIANS.

CRASSUS. Ah… Consul… Is there somewhere private we can talk?

CICERO. I feel safer with my friends around me.

CRASSUS. I'm no assassin.

CICERO. You keep company with assassins.

CRASSUS. Well… No longer. I've received a warning –

CICERO. From whom?

CRASSUS. We're not sure. Catiline is planning to declare the election invalid – bring his gangs onto the street – and take the City by force.

CICERO. Go on.

CRASSUS. They've raised an army in Etruria – it's preparing to march south to seize Praeneste – as a base for operations against Rome. Word is they're hoping to form an alliance with a tribe of Gauls –

CICERO. You *are* well informed.

TIRO. Praeneste's only a day's march away.

CRASSUS. I keep a foot in both camps.

CICERO. That's supposed to reassure me, is it?

CRASSUS. Consul – we've had our differences, but first and last, I'm a loyal citizen. If Catiline starts a war we'll have Pompey Magnus descending on us with his legions to stamp it out. It's the excuse he's been waiting for. The last thing Rome needs is a military dictatorship – especially one headed by Pompey. It's to be avoided at all costs.

CICERO. That, at least, is something we can agree on.

CRASSUS. Here's proof of my good faith. (*Takes a bundle of letters from a document case.*) We've been sent warning letters – this one's addressed to me – these to my friends here – others for Catiline's supporters in the Senate…

TIRO. Who delivered them?

CRASSUS. No idea. They were handed in to my doorkeeper. At night. By a hooded messenger.

CICERO. Of course they were. (*Reading*.) 'The time for debate is over. Catiline sends warning there will be bloodshed in Rome. Save yourself. Leave the City secretly. You will be informed when it is safe to return.'

TIRO. Naturally it's unsigned?

CRASSUS. It's treason in the highest degree. I want no part of it. I believe you've driven him out of his mind.

CICERO. Catiline was insane long before I set out to bring him down.

CLODIUS. Where is he?

CRASSUS. I imagine he's gone north to join his rebel army.

CICERO. Why should Catiline single you out as his messenger, Crassus?

CRASSUS. Your guess is as good as mine... I owe you an apology, Consul... You've never wavered in your distrust of Catiline, have you? Few heeded your warnings. Will you call an emergency meeting of the Senate? You know you can always count on my full support? You'll need to raise an army –

CICERO. Yes. It looks as if we'll have to declare a state of emergency – adopt the Final Act.

CRASSUS. You're not a military man, are you? If you need someone to take command, I'd be willing to volunteer?

CICERO. My plans are in place. I've been expecting this for some time. Metellus Celer will organise the defence of the State.

CRASSUS. Celer? But the Senate –

CICERO. If I'd waited for the Senate to act, Catiline and his thugs would be in the Forum by now, slitting throats.

CRASSUS. My dear friend... I can't tell you how pleased I am that any past misunderstandings between us are laid to rest.

CICERO. Goodnight, Crassus.

CRASSUS. Goodnight.

They shake hands. Exeunt CRASSUS *and young*
PATRICIANS.

CICERO. What a complete and utter lying shit!

TIRO. You don't believe him?

CICERO. Do you?

TIRO. I think he might have written those letters himself.

SOSITHEUS *catches* CICERO*'s eye – and exits, worried.*

But Caesar will be at the back of it. In the People's eyes, he
can do no wrong – he's Pontiff now. He's climbing the
political ladder. A clean break with his disreputable past
would be a great advantage.

CLODIUS. Perhaps Caesar thinks it's time to come into the fold
– start behaving responsibly.

CICERO. Ha! The fox in the hen coop promoted to wolf in
the fold!

TIRO. Catiline's a political liability – couldn't it be that
Caesar's decided to cut him adrift? And sent Crassus here to
betray him?

CICERO. Possibly – but I don't think so.

TIRO. Why?

CLODIUS. Wouldn't Caesar have come himself?

CICERO. No – Caesar will be where he always is – waiting in
the wings… I'd be surprised if Caesar even knows Crassus
has been here –

TIRO. But they plot everything together. Why do you say –

CICERO. Isn't it obvious?

CLODIUS. Is it?

CICERO. Think, boy, think! Have I taught you nothing? Work
it through.

CLODIUS. Er…

CICERO. Say they succeed in killing me – overturn the election
result – and throw out Murena. Who replaces him as Consul?

TIRO. The candidate who came third –

CLODIUS. Catiline.

CICERO. What happens next?

CLODIUS. Oh – the usual, I suppose, riots, looting, a city in flames –

CICERO. Good – then what?

CLODIUS. Well... Er...

CICERO. How is order restored? And by whom?

CLODIUS. Pompey?

CICERO. Pompey! Pompey Magnus restores order – he dashes home with his army – the streets run with blood, for a day or so – then what?

CLODIUS. Pompey makes himself Dictator.

CICERO. Rome becomes a military dictatorship! And the Republic – everything I've worked for is finished. *Everybody* loses. But think... Who has the *most* to lose?

CLODIUS. Er...

CICERO. Tell him, Tiro.

TIRO. Crassus.

CICERO. Crassus! There's no place for Crassus in Pompey's Rome – they loathe each other! Crassus would lose everything – all the silver and gold he's carefully salted away, year after year. I wouldn't mind betting it's Crassus who's decided to betray Catiline – Crassus acting on his own.

CLODIUS. Of course! Obvious, isn't it? It's like having an endless private tutorial in the art of politics. I'm learning so much.

CICERO. We must get to work. Celer must call up his soldiers.

TIRO. So, you won't give Crassus the command?

CICERO. Do I look like an idiot? Do you think you can keep me alive until tomorrow's Senate meeting?

CLODIUS. It won't be easy... I'll do my best.

They go to the Senate meeting. Uproar and confusion in the Senate. Enter CICERO, CRASSUS *and* HYBRIDA – *drunk.* CRASSUS *reads his letter.*

CRASSUS. 'Catiline sends warning there will be bloodshed in Rome. Save yourself. Leave the City secretly. You will be informed when it is safe to return.'

Shock.

CATULUS. In view of this appalling discovery, I propose the Consuls be empowered to take all necessary measures for the defence of the nation, under the provisions of the Final Act. These powers shall include the authority to levy troops, to conduct war, and to exercise supreme command both at home and in the field.

CICERO. Does anyone oppose it?

All look at CAESAR, *who looks at the floor.*

The motion is carried.

I propose that Metellus Celer be invested with full military Imperium, and be given the authority to raise an army for the defence of the City. Celer, are you willing to accept this command?

CELER. I am.

CICERO. Gentleman – are we agreed?

SENATE (*except* CAESAR. *Very loud*). Aye!

TIRO. All we can do now is wait.

Scene Seven

Night. Late. CICERO's house. CLODIUS's BODYGUARDS lying about. Doors barricaded. TULLIA reading by candlelight. Enter CICERO, TIRO, CLODIUS and CATO from the study – CATO has been lecturing CICERO.

CICERO. Can we continue this discussion another time, Cato? I'm tired.

CATO. Very well. But I must tell you I'm considering bringing an action against Murena for malpractice during the election –

CICERO. Not now, I hope – not while Catiline –

CATO. Whose idea was it to flood Rome with Lucullus's veterans? –

CICERO. Lucullus has a perfect right to celebrate his Triumph – his veterans are entitled to their votes –

CATO. The charge will be bribery.

CICERO. Feasting and entertainment – kissing a few babies – has always been part of an election campaign – and always will be –

CATO. Kissing babies! Murena and Lucullus have been shamelessly coercing the electorate –

CICERO. I'd rather say *enthusing* them.

CATO. Who put them up to it?

CICERO. These are poor men – they need to imagine their votes have value – they like to feel that Rome's great and good are paying them attention. It only happens once a year –

CATO. Cicero! I never thought I'd hear a Roman Consul say such a thing. Power has completely corrupted you –

CICERO. Oh, Cato – you're such a… *lawyer*! Always the lawyer, never the politician!

CATO. Then we'd better see what the law has to say on the matter.

CICERO. You'll take it to Court?

CATO. It's what the Courts are for.

CICERO. Have you considered this – if you bring a case against Murena and win it, Catiline will be Consul? He took third place in the election.

CATO. Let the law take its course.

TIRO. Whatever the outcome?

CATO. Whatever the outcome.

CICERO. *But not now!* Not while Catiline's trying to destroy the law, the constitution, the Courts, everything we hold dear –

CATO. Many in the Senate believe you're overplaying that particular threat –

CICERO. And why would I do that? Do you think your Consul enjoys doing time as Rome's most closely guarded prisoner?

CATO. You've become obsessed with Catiline – your fears for your own personal safety are making life intolerable for everybody else –

CICERO. You heard Crassus read the warning letter.

CATO. There are those who say Catiline knew nothing about it.

CICERO. What else do they say?

CATO. That you're a coward. That you always wear a breastplate under your toga –

CICERO. Well, damn them then – whoever they are!

The BODYGUARDS *unbarricade the door to let him out. Sargon barks.*

CATO. I think they're right. You are a coward. Goodnight, Consul.

SOSITHEUS *sees him out.*

CICERO. What's the point of going on with it all, Tiro? I'm finished – a year from now no one will remember my name.

TULLIA. I didn't like that man. Doesn't he ever wash? Phew, what a stink!

CICERO. He thinks bathing is an affront to nature.

TULLIA. Well, he's an affront to my nose.

TIRO. You should be in bed. Come on. I'll light the way.

TULLIA. I don't feel safe in bed.

Exit TIRO *and* TULLIA.

SOSITHEUS. Master, Metellus Celer is here.

CICERO. Not now! At this time of night? When am I supposed
to sleep?

CLODIUS. I'll fetch him. (*Exits.*)

SOSITHEUS. Master – what if they find out?

CICERO. They won't. How could they? You mustn't worry. It
was an honourable part you played, Sositheus – Rome is in
your debt.

Enter CELER *with* TIRO *and* CLODIUS.

CICERO. Ah – Rome's sword and shield never sleep! What's
the matter now?

CELER. Are you sure all these measures are necessary, Cicero?

CICERO. Necessary! Catiline and his rebels are probably
encircling us as we speak.

CELER. I mean… the Final Act? Seems all very… *final* to me.
And these letters… They've scared the few remaining wits
out of those Senators who had any to start with – but there's
something suspicious about them… To my way of thinking
anyway.

CICERO. Oh, Celer! –

CELER. Catiline swears he knows nothing about it – he's
willing to take an oath –

CICERO (*laughing*). An oath! Quick! Hide the children!

CLODIUS. Are you saying Catiline's still in Rome?

CELER. He is. He's offered to surrender himself into my
custody until talk of this conspiracy is proved groundless.
I've brought him to see you.

CICERO. What! He's here? *In my house!*

CELER. I think you should talk to him –

CICERO. It's gone beyond talking –

CELER. He's a Sergius, Consul, descended from the royal blood of Troy – one of the City's founding families – that should count for something?

CICERO (*sighs*). Never let it be said that I rejected any chance of peace – however remote.

CELER. Good man. (*Exits.*)

TIRO. Is this wise?

CICERO. No.

CLODIUS. Perhaps he's come to apologise.

An ironic laugh between CICERO *and* CLODIUS.

TIRO. It's beyond me.

Enter CATILINE, *menacing, with* CELER.

CATILINE (*raising his hand in mock salute*). Consul. Why are you spreading these lies about me?

CICERO. This is pointless –

CELER. Just hear him out!

CATILINE. Who in his right mind would lay himself open by such an act of folly? On the bones of my ancestors, I swear I did not write those letters… Good enough for you?

CICERO. You've plenty of acolytes reckless enough to write them for you.

CATILINE. They're forgeries! I've thought long and hard about it… Do you want to know who wrote them?

CICERO. Go on.

CATILINE. You did. You wrote them.

CICERO. We've thought about it too. Our money is on Crassus – he has the most to gain. They give him the perfect excuse to turn his back on your treasons.

CATILINE. Treasons! (*Lunges at* CICERO, *then backs off.*) No
– I'll not let you provoke me… I see it in your eyes… You
did write them.

CICERO. And these rebels in the north? I suppose you had no
hand in that either? Is that my doing too?

CATILINE. They're not rebels – they are poor, starving
wretches driven to desperate lengths by moneylenders,
extortionists, and land-grabbers. You call yourself the
People's Consul? You manipulate the People – mislead them
with your fine voice and lying arguments – but it's to me
they look for leadership.

CICERO. To incite rebellion?

CATILINE. They have my sympathy – not my support. (*Pause.*)
I'll make you an offer, Consul – the same offer I made Celer
here. I'll surrender myself into your custody. If you are a
moral man – if you love justice as you claim – sooner or
later you'll be forced to accept my innocence.

CICERO. I don't feel safe living in the same city as you – I'd
hardly welcome you into my home.

CATILINE. How else can I satisfy you of my good faith?

CICERO. Leave Rome – remove yourself from Italy – never
return.

CATILINE. This is my City! My ancestor Sergestus came with
Aeneas to lay its foundations – my family built its temples –
gave it just laws –

CICERO. Oh, spare us the family folklore!

CLODIUS *sniggers.*

Put the good of the State before your ambition for once.
Make your noble ancestors proud of you.

CATILINE (*fury*). I'll take no lecture on nobility from the runt
of a shit-shovelling chickpea-farmer!

CLODIUS *explodes with laughter.*

He'll be giving you orders next, Celer!

CATILINE is getting too close to CICERO – CLODIUS *interposes himself.*

You do know they despise you? They all laugh at you – use you for their dirty work. They've lifted you up – up to the heights – but when you've served their turn they'll drop you.

He strides out, shoving GUARDS *out of his way.*

CLODIUS. Well! I never heard the Sergii did much for Rome – it was my family built the roads, the aqueducts, the temples and the fountains. Twenty-eight Consuls in my line – not that I'd ever boast of it.

CICERO *manages a smile – but he's shaking.*

TIRO. What do you think he'll do now?

CELER. He's a cornered rat – he'll fly at the throat of anyone who goes near him. (*Starts to go.*) And... All that nonsense about despising you – there's not a word of truth in it, you know.

CLODIUS. I'll stay with you tonight. We'll get you safely to the Senate in the morning.

CICERO. Dear gods – will I ever feel safe again!

Lightning and thunder.

Scene Eight

A violent storm. Howling wind. Rain. Lots of rushing about in the darkness – torches. CATILINE *with his* AQUILIFERS *leads* SURA, VIRIDORIX, CETHEGUS, CAEPARIUS, STATILIUS, CAPITO – *and other shadowy figures; one being* CAESAR – *across the stage.* RUFUS *hangs back. Exeunt all but* RUFUS. *He goes to* CICERO*'s house and beats on the door – where he is grabbed by* CLODIUS, *and the* BODYGUARDS, *and brought before* CICERO.

CICERO. Rufus, dear boy. Come in out of the rain. I was beginning to think you'd deserted us.

RUFUS. Get your hands off me! They're going to kill you –
you'll never make it to the Senate tomorrow.

TERENTIA. What's happening?

RUFUS. Catiline's at the house of Marcus Laeca – the whole
gang is with him – Sura, Cethegus, Caeparius – all of them.

CLODIUS. We're ready for them.

CICERO. Is Caesar with him?

RUFUS. He has been. They talk all the time – I'm certain he's
giving the orders –

CLODIUS. What's his plan?

RUFUS. To kill Cicero. Then they'll arm the mob, and set fire
to the City. Cethegus will lead them up to the Palatine and
butcher any Senators who've opposed them. Then they'll
open the City gates to the rebel army.

Noise of an attack. Enter SOSITHEUS *and* QUINTUS.
Sargon barking.

SOSITHEUS. They're here.

QUINTUS. We're under attack. I've come for the fight.

CICERO. I'm very glad to see you, brother.

Enter TULLIA *carrying* MARCUS.

TULLIA. Marcus woke up. Are we being killed?

CICERO. Come with me, Tullia.

TERENTIA (*picking up a candlestick*). Where are you going?

CICERO. To the library – I must protect my books.

Exeunt CICERO, TULLIA, *and a* SLAVE *carrying*
MARCUS.

RUFUS. Give me a sword.

TERENTIA. The door will hold them for a while –

CLODIUS. At last! What an adventure! I'm going to enjoy this.

TIRO. I'm not… Sositheus – get up on the roof – fetch water –
they'll try and burn us out.

TERENTIA. My ancestors gave Hannibal a thrashing when he came knocking at our door – let them do their worst!

TIRO *picks up a torch and an unlikely weapon. Noise and confusion. A battle.*

Scene Nine

TIRO. Thanks to Clodius, Quintus, and – I'm proud to say – we slaves, the assassins were driven off – and their leaders made prisoner – by Celer and his men, who arrived in the nick of time...

Hushed conversation. CICERO *takes the chair.*

CICERO. May all the gods protect Rome!

ALL. May the gods protect Rome!

CICERO. Cato has informed me there are those among you who feel I have exaggerated the threat posed by Catiline to the security of the State.

Now judge for yourselves. Last night, a group of desperate men – led by two members of this Senate – attempted to murder me and my family, set fires in the suburbs, and to...

CICERO*'s mouth gapes open in astonishment.* CATILINE, *with his* AQUILIFER, *makes a long entrance, sauntering through the audience, and calmly takes his place. The* AQUILIFER *waits at the door. Gasps and then outrage from the* SENATORS.

CATILINE. Don't let me interrupt the proceedings.

CICERO (*advancing on* CATILINE). Has there ever been such arrogance! How much longer, Catiline, will you try our patience? How much longer must we put up with your madness?

Your conspiracy is exposed – can't you understand that? These Senators know all your secrets – I, their Consul, have

tracked your every move. Why do we sit here and take no
action against you? Oh, what times are these – and oh what
morals! Why is this creature still alive, gentlemen? Alive?
Not just alive – he walks calmly into our meeting – and all
the time he's watching us – deciding which of us he'll spare
and which of us he'll kill! Has the law no sword –

CATILINE. What do you know of swords!

CICERO. In the midst of this most sacred council sit men who
have plotted to destroy us – destroy our City – destroy
everything that binds us together as a nation! What more can
we say to you, Catiline? The gates of Rome stand open – for
the love of the gods, go! In the north, a legion of traitors
awaits its General – go – take your men with you – you'll
remain here no longer – I cannot, I will not, I must not
permit it.

CATILINE. You! 'Permit'!

SENATORS (*uproar*). Throw him out! Arrest the traitor! Go!
Go! Go! (*Etc.*)

CATILINE (*advancing on* CICERO). Back in the days when his
people were up in the mountains fucking goats –

SENATORS (*drowning him out*). Kill him! Stone him! Throw
him down the Rock!

CATILINE. This alien – this – this –

*He runs to the door and seizes his silver Eagle from one of
his* SUPPORTERS.

I never wanted this – it's not my doing! You're bringing
destruction on yourselves!

Exeunt CATILINE *and a few* SUPPORTERS. *Drums, etc.
Calm. Enter* VIRIDORIX *and a group of* GAULS.
VIRIDORIX *hands letters to* TIRO.

TIRO. Property was searched. Arrests were made. Among the
documents found were letters to a tribe of Gauls – Rome's
ancient enemy – urging them to join Catiline's rebellion and
rise up against their Roman masters.

TIRO *gives* CICERO *the letters*.

It wasn't difficult for Cicero to persuade the Gauls to turn State's evidence – on the promise of freedom from prosecution. And a large sum of gold… This is Viridorix, a prince of the Gauls.

CICERO *leads* VIRIDORIX *into the Senate*.

At last, Cicero had the evidence he needed –

CICERO. There stands Viridorix – envoy of the Gauls, whom the traitors vainly attempted to draw into their conspiracy. This loyal friend of Rome willingly informed against them.

Murmuring.

CATO. Do the traitors have names?

CICERO. Let them name themselves.

CETHEGUS *saunters in, escorted by* CLODIUS *and* GUARDS.

CETHEGUS. Gaius Cornelius Cethegus.

CICERO. See that pile of letters? You wrote one of them.

CETHEGUS. This one's mine.

CICERO. Hand it to me.

CETHEGUS. It's the height of bad manners to open another gentleman's mail, you know.

CICERO. It's worse manners to conspire against the Senate and People of Rome.

'To the Chiefs of the Gauls – greetings! If the Gauls rise up against their oppressors in Rome, you will find us loyal allies.'

Howls of protest.

Your signature? Speak up.

CETHEGUS *nods*.

We discovered at your house a veritable armoury – hundreds of swords and daggers.

CETHEGUS. Some men collect art, others mistresses – I collect weapons.

Violent response, CETHEGUS *is shaken.*

CICERO. Bring in the others.

CLODIUS *and* SOLDIERS *bring in* CAEPARIUS, STATILIUS, *and* CAPITO.

These have confessed their guilt... Caeparius there tried to escape and failed. Tell the Senate why do you wish to ruin your country.

CAEPARIUS. I hoped to reclaim it. I want a Rome fit for Romans – not the pigpen you're reducing it to. I've confessed everything – so kill me – get it over with. I'll not live in a City ruled by the tyrant Cicero.

Exit, guarded.

CLODIUS. Lentulus Sura.

Gasps of disbelief.

CICERO. Sura, you are Urban Praetor – responsible for good order in the City. You've served as Consul, your ancestry is noble – for twenty-five years you've served on the innermost councils of the Republic –

SENATORS. Shame! Shame on you!

CICERO. Did you write Catiline this letter? Read it to us.

SURA (*reluctantly, reading*). 'Be a man. At this moment of crisis, everything depends upon your intervention. Enlist aid wherever you can find it – even from the lowest of the low...'

CICERO. Who do you mean by 'the lowest of the low'?

SURA. Poor people – oh, I don't know – shepherds, tenant farmers –

CICERO. No – you mean slaves!

Shock.

SENATORS. Slaves?! Slaves?!

CICERO. You're inciting another revolt of slaves.

Fury.

SENATORS. Slaves? Slaves!! Resign!

SURA *is beaten up*.

CICERO. Step forward, Viridorix… Your loyalty to Rome has exposed five dangerous conspirators. Are there more? Do you have names?

VIRIDORIX. Some. There was Autronius Paetus, Servius Sulla, Cassius Longinus, Marcus Laeca, Lucius Bestia –

CICERO. A familiar roll call!

VIRIDORIX. There were others… Marcus Licinius Crassus – and I heard the name Julius Caesar.

Shock, whistles, etc. CAESAR *and* CRASSUS *shake their heads.*

CICERO. Caesar and Crassus? Where's your evidence? Have you spoken to them – seen them with the other traitors?

VIRIDORIX. No – but their names were often mentioned. It was rumoured –

CICERO. I don't deal in rumours… (*Thinks.*) Strike from the record the names Crassus… and Caesar. Evidence, not rumour, is what's needed.

Anger – CAESAR *and* CRASSUS *protest their innocence.*

Gentlemen, it's late. We cannot settle the fate of these traitors today. Who'll volunteer to guard them overnight? Celer – will you take Statilius?

CELER *nods*.

Silanus – Caeparius?

SILANUS (*from the audience*). If I must.

CICERO. Crassus, you'll take Capito?

CRASSUS *is stunned*.

And… Caesar, perhaps you will keep Sura locked up in the House of the Pontiff?

CAESAR *is unreadable.*

The Senate stands adjourned until tomorrow.

CATULUS. A moment, Consul! I feel this House should recognise that one amongst us has been constant in his policy, and consistently attacked for it. As events have proved, he has been wiser than any of us. I propose that in view of the fact that Marcus Tullius Cicero has saved Rome from burning, and its citizens from massacre, this House decrees three days of thanksgiving, at every shrine and temple, for having favoured us at such a time with such a Consul. From henceforth he shall be called 'The Father of the Nation'.

Cheering – CICERO, *in a state of semi-collapse, is escorted to his house by the* PATRICIANS, TIRO, CLODIUS *and a* BODYGUARD. ISAURICUS, CATULUS, LUCULLUS, *and other* PATRICIANS. CAESAR *is left frozen to his seat.* TULLIA *runs to greet* CICERO, *who embraces her.*

CICERO. Tullia! You're safe now – we're all safe. A good day's work for the Republic.

LUCULLUS. This is just the start.

ISAURICUS. You must arrest Caesar.

CATULUS. I can't think why you missed your chance when that Gaul named him –

ISAURICUS. Lock him up in the Carcer –

CICERO. For what offence?

ISAURICUS. Treason of course!

CATULUS. You cannot doubt he's part of this conspiracy?

CICERO. I have no doubts.

CATULUS. Arrest him then!

CICERO. I have no evidence –

CATULUS. Then *make the evidence*!

LUCULLUS. He must die – along with the others.

CICERO. Execute the Pontifex Maximus? The People's favourite? Start a civil war?

LUCULLUS. Start a war! Catiline, with an army of slaves and veterans, goaded on by Julius Caesar, is marching against Rome!

ISAURICUS. *Start* a war? You're in the middle of one!

CATULUS. Act! Be a man. We made you Consul to keep these people in their place – so fucking well put them in their place!

TULLIA. How rude!

TERENTIA. I'll not have your barrack-room language in my house – control your tongue, old man, or get out!

CATULUS. I –

CICERO. I wasn't elected Consul – by a unanimous vote of the Roman People – named Father of the Nation –

ISAURICUS. Oh, here we go! –

CICERO. So I could butcher my political opponents! I've just been granted a public thanksgiving –

CATULUS. You were granted it because I proposed it! –

CICERO. I'll not do it! Even a traitor is entitled to the protection of the law until he breaks it – you're so consumed with hatred, Catulus, you're no longer thinking straight. It's because Caesar beat you to the Pontificate, isn't it? Now listen to me – all of you! I have my enemies where I want them. Caesar knows I know he's as guilty as the others – so I can make him obey me... He won't dare show his face during the remainder of my Consulship.

CATULUS. A snake's not dead till you cut off its head.

LUCULLUS. Well... What do you intend to do with the other traitors?

CICERO. The Senate will decide.

CATULUS. They'll look to you for a lead.

TERENTIA. Dear gods, hasn't he done enough!

CICERO. I've denied Catiline the Consulship – driven him from Rome – saved your lives, and your homes from the flames – and delivered the traitors into your custody...

Must I lay myself open to the opprobrium of executing them as well? I won't do it. It's time some of you got your hands dirty. You'll stand up in the Senate tomorrow and sentence these traitors. If it's to be death then you'll say so – loud and clear. When I go before the People, I'll address them as the voice of the Senate – not as the public executioner.

CATULUS. You're wrong about Caesar. If you don't put him down now… you may live to regret it.

Exeunt PATRICIANS. *The* CHILDREN *go to their father.*

TERENTIA. Such dreadful people… But it doesn't stop them being right.

CICERO. What am I to do, Tiro?

TIRO. Your Consulship has less than a month to run. I'd lock them away. Let your successor decide their fate.

TERENTIA. A coward's way out?

TIRO. It's a way out.

Exeunt TERENTIA *and* CHILDREN.

CLODIUS (*when she has gone*). Formidable lady… I'm thinking of taking a wife myself.

CICERO. Good. Time you settled down.

CLODIUS. I've learned so much from you. I'll always be grateful. As I follow in your footsteps – climbing the political ladder.

TIRO. Who knows – Clodius might be Consul one day.

CLODIUS. All I need now is a rich wife.

TIRO. Do you have a woman in mind?

CLODIUS. Yes… Lots… But it's time I had one of my own. Fulvia – heir to the Gracchi estates – fabulously rich…

CICERO. Then what are you waiting for?

FULVIA *crosses the stage. Exeunt* CICERO *and* CLODIUS.

Scene Ten

The PRISONERS *are led across the stage, some calm, some terrified.*

TIRO. The next day's events were to trouble our lives ever after –

Senate assembles. CICERO *takes his place.*

CICERO. I have never presided over such a solemn assembly – I hope I shall never again face so unpleasant a duty. Every man who wishes to speak may do so. I shall express no view myself –

Cries of protest.

Whatever punishment the House decides must be carried out swiftly. Catiline is with his rebel army. I have sent my fellow Consul, Hybrida, with the Senate's legions to intercept him. Should Rome come under attack, Metellus Celer stands ready to defend the City.

CAESAR *enters the Senate.*

Murena, as Consul-elect you have the right to speak first.

MURENA. Gentlemen… I am by nature inclined to mercy – Sura was one of my closest friends – but the security of the State must override any considerations of friendship. Who would have believed that a man charged with the security of our City should plan its destruction? There can be no other sentence but death.

CICERO. Catulus?

CATULUS. Death. These men would have murdered us in our beds – what more is there to say? Let the public executioner strangle them.

CICERO. Isauricus?

ISAURICUS. Death.

CICERO. Lucullus?

LUCULLUS. Death.

> *A chant of 'Death! Death! Death!' begins.* CICERO *restores order.*

CICERO. The sentiment of this House is clear. The sentence –

CAESAR. Wait! I wish to speak.

> *'Traitor! Traitor! Traitor!', etc.*

> I am opposed to the death penalty... (*Outrage in the Senate*) Calmly – calmly... How shall we come by the truth if we let emotion govern our reason?

SENATORS *rage and jeer.*

> You may ask why –

CATULUS. Because you're a traitor too – you were behind this conspiracy from the start!

CAESAR. These men were my friends – they deserve to die – no torture is sufficient punishment for treason... But consider the future. Their crimes will quickly be forgotten – what will be remembered forever will be the penalty this Senate decrees for them. In adopting the Final Act, we have granted Cicero the power of life and death over us – over Roman citizens. I doubt absolute power will make a tyrant of Cicero. But what of those who come after him? Who shall restrain them? Think carefully. Should we set so dangerous a precedent?

CICERO. You're suggesting I release these men to swell the ranks of Catiline's army?

CAESAR. No – I'm not. In order to spare Cicero the opprobrium of ending his term as Consul with the blood of Roman citizens on his hands, I'm proposing a harsher punishment than death. Life imprisonment is my sentence. Banish them from the City – imprison each of the traitors in a separate town – deny them the right of appeal. And let life mean life...

MURENA. I withdraw my proposal of the death sentence in favour of life imprisonment.

> *Approval.*

CICERO. I had determined not to speak… Now I feel I must. Let me put a case to you. If one of you returned home to find your wife and children killed by a slave – and out of compassion you pardoned that slave, would your neighbours approve your mildness? Or would they condemn you – for not making certain the murderer committed no future outrage? Reluctantly… I must cast my vote for death –

CAESAR. The cases are not alike. A murderous slave ought to die – but in the case of these conspirators the crime may have been *intended* but it was not committed.

CATO. Exactly!

CICERO. Cato?

CATO. Caesar is right – we're not dealing with crimes that have been committed but with crimes that were *intended*. Isn't that the point? A conspiracy has been nipped in the bud… (*Advancing on* CAESAR.) Does that wash away the guilt of the conspirators? Wake up! Wake up, Senators, and defend your Republic! Our liberty – our lives are at stake!

He fixes on members of the Senate in turn.

A plot was hatched, by citizens of the highest rank, to demolish by fire and slaughter the City of their birth. They called to arms enemy tribes – Gauls, veterans, and *slaves*! Yet here we sit as Catiline's rebel soldiers – flags flying, drums beating – advance towards us… And still you hesitate? You can't decide how terrorists captured within your own walls should be treated? 'Oh, but they're young men!' you'll say – they've been led astray – they're as much Catiline's victims as the rest of us – let them off with a caution! (*Studies their faces*.) Are you mad? Are *all of you* mad! How can any community thrive and grow if it has no means to cure the diseases it nurtures in its healthy body? – If it has no law to counter conspiracy? I'll give you a law. Write down this motion: 'By testimony and confession the accused stand convicted of planning massacre, arson and other foul atrocities against their fellow citizens. Having admitted their criminal intention – they should be treated as if they had been caught in the actual commission of capital crimes and – in accordance with ancient custom instantly put to death.'

Wild acclaim. 'Death! Death! Death!', etc.

CAESAR. I wish to reply – let me speak –

SENATORS. No! No! Silence him! –

CAESAR *is attacked by a group of* SENATORS, *prefiguring his assassination – they pull knives on him.* CICERO *interposes himself and protects* CAESAR.

CICERO. This is sacrilege – in this sacred place – leave him! Go back to your places!

CAESAR *is released.*

The sentiment of this House is clear. Cato's motion passes. The sentence is death.

CONSPIRATORS *led away.*

CETHEGUS. Where are they taking us?

CAEPARIUS (*to the audience*). Citizens – remember us – we fought for your freedom – fight on! Fight against these men who would enslave you!

SURA (*to the audience*). We are Roman citizens – denied our right to a trial. Remember us! We are Roman citizens!

They are hurried away. MARK ANTONY (*sixteen*) *bursts in and throws himself on his knees.*

MARK ANTONY. Pardon, Consul! Pardon my stepfather, Sura. I beg you, citizens – let him live!

CICERO. Remove him.

LICTORS *remove* MARK ANTONY, *protesting.*

Who was that boy, Tiro?

TIRO. Nobody. His name's Mark Antony.

Scene Eleven

Mountains. Snow. Drums, flags and trumpets. Eagles.

CATILINE. Good men must stand ready to die for truth, justice, love of the gods – or they're no better than sheep. A hero is judged by the manner of his death. Sell yourselves dearly – let our enemies count the cost in widows and orphans – let bloodshed and mourning be the price they pay for their victory. Sound trumpets – forward, forward!

A battle. HYBRIDA, *in armour, staggers through the battle to* CICERO, *carrying a bucket with a lid.*

HYBRIDA. Well, fellow Consul, you have your victory. I return covered in glory. Got anything to drink?

CICERO. Tiro.

TIRO pours him a drink.

HYBRIDA. Say what you like about Catiline, there can be no doubting his bravery. The carnage was terrible – he was in the thick of it – they fought to the last man. You should have been there!

Gives TIRO *the bucket.*

A gift. First of many. I'm off to Macedonia – and, don't worry, you'll get your twenty per cent. I say – this isn't bad. (*Holding his cup out for more wine.*) You live well these days. Macedonia! (*Raises his cup and drinks.*) Could have gone either way. But I sent in a crack praetorian cohort under Marcus Petreius – that finished 'em – hacked 'em to bits.

CICERO. You were not in the fight yourself?

HYBRIDA. No – I stayed in my tent. Bit of a runny tummy – must have been a bad oyster – but Petreius is a capable fellow. Aren't you going to open it?

CICERO. Thank you. Tiro?

TIRO takes the lid off the bucket. He looks horrified.

What is it?

HYBRIDA. You're not squeamish, are you, Cicero? Look at it this way. If I'd not warned you of the plot – if I'd not won this famous victory, Catiline'd be Consul now – and you'd have ended up in the bucket. Good day to you, Marcus Tullius. (*Exits*.)

CICERO. Let me see.

TIRO. Are you sure?

CICERO. Give it to me.

He takes out the head, pickled in salt water and spirits, he forces himself to stare at it. Slime spills everywhere.

End of Play Two.

PLAY THREE

CLODIUS

Prologue

Music. Darkness. Incense. Stage full of WOMEN. *Rites of the Good Goddess led by* THE CHIEF VESTAL *and* TERENTIA. *Cries of alarm, off.* CLODIUS, *dressed as a woman, carrying a lyre, runs on with* CAESAR's *wife* POMPEIA – *they've been caught in the act.* TERENTIA *and other* WOMEN *chase them with torches, grab* POMPEIA. CLODIUS *exposes himself to them – runs off laughing.* POMPEIA *is left to face the music. Darkness.*

TIRO. The fool in a comedy cracks an egg… and out of the egg hatches tragedy… That so farcical an episode could have such devastating consequences will surely strike future generations as absurd. However – let's not get ahead of ourselves… (*Produces a scroll.*)

Scene One

CICERO's *house.* CICERO *emerges, with* CRASSUS, *and* RUFUS.

TIRO (*reading from his biography*). 'At the end of his year as Consul, everyone clamoured to hear how my master had foiled the conspiracy of Sergius Catiline…' The Father of His Country never missed an opportunity to lecture anyone who'd listen on how he'd saved the Republic.

CICERO (*to the audience*). As we thank the gods for the Divine Romulus – blessing the day he founded our City – so you and your descendants will surely give thanks to Jupiter the Protector – honouring the Consul who preserved Rome from destruction…

TIRO. In short – and whoever would have imagined saying this of Cicero? – he began to turn into a crashing bore.

CICERO, SOSITHEUS, CRASSUS, RUFUS, *etc., and* TIRO *in the study.*

CRASSUS. Stirring stuff… But now I really must go.

CICERO. Just listen to this letter I've written Pompey –

TIRO. Worse – he was losing his political surefootedness –

CICERO. 'At a crisis in Rome's history, the gods gave us two men – you, Pompey Magnus, and myself – who while you campaigned abroad, preserved at home the heart of our Empire.'

TIRO. Perhaps his greatest folly was to buy a house on the Palatine –

CICERO. By the way, Crassus – that empty house on the Palatine –

CRASSUS. House? It's a palace. Next door to the beautiful Lady Clodia? Why? Do you want to buy it?

TIRO. *Don't do it!* I tried to warn him there was something fishy about the deal – there was always something fishy about any deal with Crassus –

CICERO. How much is it?

CRASSUS. Fourteen million.

CICERO. Ouch! Too expensive for me –

TIRO. Way out of your range –

CRASSUS. I'd let you have it for ten –

CICERO. That's generous but –

CRASSUS. Eight?

CICERO. No really – I should never have brought the subject up –

CRASSUS. Six? Four? You'd be close to Lady Clodia – we hear you're getting close to her in other ways…

CICERO. Nonsense! (*Thinks*.) I could possibly manage three.

CRASSUS. Let's settle on three-and-a-half and you've got yourself a bargain. A house fit for the Father of the Nation. I'm robbing myself.

CICERO. Indeed.

CRASSUS. I suppose you've heard the rumours? They say Pompey's on the point of winning a great victory in the east.

CICERO. There are always rumours.

CRASSUS. Last thing we need's an over-mighty General dictating terms to us. You must be relieved your term's over.

Exit CRASSUS, *followed by* RUFUS. RUFUS *gives* TIRO *a 'Has the master gone mad?' look as he goes*.

RUFUS. Master.

TIRO. If Pompey *does* come home –

CICERO. I can handle Pompey. In the eyes of the City I'm his equal now. I'll persuade the Senate to flatter him a little… Then I'll use him to keep Caesar in his place.

TIRO. You're not going to buy that house?

CICERO. I might.

TIRO. You don't have three-and-a-half million.

CICERO. I'll take out a loan. (*Reads a letter*.)

TIRO. At a crippling rate of interest?

CICERO. Don't nag, Tiro! Money just happens…

TIRO. Ha! What about Tullia's wedding? You can't even raise the money for her dowry –

CICERO. Don't remind me! I don't want to think about my daughter's marriage. That girl is my whole existence – what will my life be without her? And the husband they've chosen – Dolabella! What is one to do?!

TIRO. Refuse permission.

CICERO. How? Tullia's set her heart on him – and Terentia! I think she's half in love with the fellow herself.

TERENTIA *and* MAIDS *enter.* TULLIA *runs to* CICERO.

TERENTIA. It's an absolute scandal. Somebody should do something.

CICERO. What's happened? (*To* TULLIA.) My darling girl!

TERENTIA. A *man* has profaned the ceremonies of the Good Goddess – sacred rites that since the founding of Rome, have only ever been witnessed by women. And in the house of the Pontiff!

TULLIA. The Chief Vestal was forced to abandon the ritual – sent us all home.

CICERO. How dreadful! Was the intruder caught?

TERENTIA. Yes – in the act – with Caesar's wife and her maid – all three of them drunk. He'd disguised himself – as a lyre player.

CICERO. Outrageous!

TERENTIA. He'd put on rouge and lipstick, but there was no mistaking him. It was your friend – the loathsome Clodius.

CICERO. Surely not! Your ceremonies are held in darkness – can you even be certain it was a man?

TERENTIA. Of course it was a man!

TULLIA. He exposed himself to the Vestal Virgins –

TERENTIA. He waved his private parts at the mother of the Pontiff.

CICERO. Did she wave back?

TERENTIA. You may laugh – Clodius won't find it funny. The punishment for sacrilege is to be flogged to death – and the Vestals will insist on the full rigour of the law.

TULLIA. It's no joke, Papa.

Exeunt TERENTIA *with* TULLIA.

CICERO. It is, though, isn't it! Idiot! He's nearly thirty, not thirteen! But oh, how wonderful! Think of the trouble it will cause Caesar – his wife shamed – Rome's cuckolder-in-chief cuckolded by our boy Clodius!

TIRO. Poor Caesar.

Enter SOSITHEUS.

SOSITHEUS. Master – Publius Clodius is waiting in the atrium.

CICERO. No! Go and send him away, Tiro.

Exeunt with SOSITHEUS. TIRO *goes to* CLODIUS.

CLODIUS. Ah, Tiro! It's the funniest thing ever. I suppose
you've heard? I've come to see the master – may as well get
my punishment over and done with.

TIRO. I'm afraid he isn't in.

CLODIUS. Oh, come on! I've worked the whole thing up into
a hilarious story – I've had some women in my time but
Caesar's wife! Phwoar! My sister still has the edge, of
course, but… Where's he hiding?

CLODIUS *pushes past* TIRO.

TIRO. Crassus was here – I think they left together –

CLODIUS. Crassus! I don't believe you. Surely he's not angry
with me? Look, Tiro… I think… fact is… I might be in all
sorts of trouble. If anybody can get me off, it's Cicero. And
he owes me… I saved you all from Catiline. Put in a word
for me?

TIRO. Of course.

CLODIUS. Well… Tell him I called… I really need him…
(*Exits.*)

CICERO (*appearing*). I can have nothing more to do with that
young man – I've my reputation to think of. If he calls again,
I'm not at home.

Scene Two

Music. Preparations for wedding ceremony. Enter GUESTS.
Then TULLIA *and* DOLABELLA. TULLIA – *in white, with
a flame-coloured veil. She and* DOLABELLA *throw grain and
incense on an altar.*

TULLIA. *Ubi tu Gaius, ego Gaia.*

DOLABELLA. *Ubi tu Gaia, ego Gaius.*

They kiss, CICERO *winces.* DOLABELLA *drinks, offers the
cup to* TULLIA, *who drinks.*

CICERO. Dolabella – I give you the best I have to give… The
better part of myself – my life, my soul – no temper sweeter,
no nature kinder, no…

TULLIA. Papa?

CICERO *throws incense on the altar. He goes to* TIRO.

CICERO. May all the gods, if they happen to be listening – if
they happen to exist – send me no more days as terrible as
this… My poor child… No father ever lost such a
daughter… I've never been so depressed.

Enter LUCULLUS, CATO *and* CELER, *with a*
MESSENGER.

TIRO. You'll have me in tears – it's her wedding not her funeral.

CICERO. Don't…

CELER. Sorry to intrude upon so joyful an occasion, my friend
– the Consul Murena has sent for us. Pompey has landed at
Brundisium – he's on his way to Rome.

LUCULLUS. It's an outrage!

CELER. He can't enter the City, so they're preparing the Villa
Publica for his arrival.

CICERO. Just when I thought the day could get no worse –

CATO. What are you going to do about it? Pompey's a servant
of the Republic, not its master. He'll take over the entire
State if you don't stop him –

CICERO. I suggest you speak to the Consul, Cato.

CATO. Murena! What use is Murena?

Scene Three

Military march. Villa Publica. Music. POMPEY, *absurd Trump hairstyle, in armour, with* OFFICERS. *Applauding* SENATORS *queue to be received.* POMPEY *carries an ivory swagger stick, and his* OFFICERS *laugh.*

CICERO. For the love of the gods, Tiro – don't laugh at the hair.

POMPEY. Gentlemen. I've put an end to the Republic's greatest enemy! Mithradates King of Pontus, and Armenia is dead... Cicero? Is that you? Lurking at the back there? Come – embrace me! But for this man, gentlemen, I'd have no country to come home to. I know it's true, because he never stops telling me it is – in letter after letter, after letter.

Crushes CICERO *in an embrace – laughter.*

Well then... Let's get down to business. The war is over. I have captured a thousand fortifications, nine hundred cities, and fourteen countries – including Palestine, Arabia, Mesopotamia, Judea, and... er...

POMPEY'S OFFICER. Syria.

POMPEY. Syria. I have established thirty-nine new cites – and to three of them I have given my name: Pompeiopolis.

TIRO stifles a laugh. CICERO *gives him a look.*

The taxes I've imposed on the east will increase the State Revenues by one third – let me repeat that – *one third* – and from my *personal* wealth I shall make a donation to the Treasury of two hundred million. I've doubled the size of our Empire, gentlemen!

Applause.

Rome's frontier now stands on the Red Sea.

Applause.

Of course, I'll require the Senate to pass a retrospective bill making everything I've done legal.

CATO. Just one bill!

POMPEY. Yes – let's keep it simple – one sentence: 'The Senate and People of Rome approve all decisions made by Pompey Magnus in his settlement of the east.' You may add a few lines of congratulation.

CATO. But – this is – it's… I… You… (*Speechless for once, grinds to a halt.*)

LUCULLUS. Anything else?

POMPEY. I want the Consulship. Next year – ten years after my first. All perfectly legal.

CATO. But to stand for election you'd need to surrender your Imperium – give up your Triumph –

POMPEY. I shall Triumph on my birthday –

CATO. But how? If –

POMPEY. Simple. Another bill. One sentence: 'The Senate and People of Rome permit Pompey Magnus to seek election to the Consulship *in absentia*.' I won't bother to canvass – I imagine people know who I am.

Sycophantic laughter. Exit CRASSUS, *angry,* RUFUS *follows him.*

LUCULLUS. And your soldiers?

POMPEY. Disbanded, and dispersed to their homes. They'll need rewarding, of course. I've given them my word.

LUCULLUS. We hear you've promised them land.

POMPEY. That's right. Listen, gentlemen. You know very well I could have marched my army to the gates of Rome and demanded whatever I liked… That's not Pompey's way – Pompey Magnus is a good Republican. I shall serve the Senate – not to dictate to it… (*A gesture of dismissal.*) That's all. Off you go, now. You, Cicero – walk with me. (*Aside.*)

You're a clever fellow, aren't you? You'll steer my bills
through the Senate.

CICERO. Shouldn't you talk to the Consuls, General?

POMPEY. I'm talking to the Father of the Nation.

CICERO. I'm one of six hundred Senators – you've plenty of
opposition among the rest –

POMPEY. Name them.

CICERO. Difficult to know where to start: Crassus – Lucullus –
Cato – Celer – Catulus – Isauricus – Piso –

POMPEY (*exploding*). I don't want to hear it! I won't have it!
I've done more for Rome than any man living – I demand
the respect due to me. D'you hear? I demand it! D'you hear!

CICERO. I imagine the dead in Hades can hear you, General.

POMPEY. And what about this Catiline nonsense? Why didn't
you call me home? I could have finished him like *that*!

CICERO. Not before he'd murdered me and half the Senate –
burned Rome to the ground –

POMPEY. I don't want to hear it! But let me tell you this, my
friend – get me land for my soldiers – make the Senate
reward my legions or… Well, let's just say I'll find *friends*
elsewhere. Have I made myself clear?

Exit POMPEY *and* ENTOURAGE.

TIRO. Well, that went well.

CICERO. He's a great ox. He bellows – but he's harmless.
I believe I have sufficient wit to outmanoeuvre a clown like
Pompey.

TIRO. Friends elsewhere? He means Caesar, doesn't he? If
Caesar and Pompey join forces –

CICERO. Impossible! Caesar's up to his ears in debt to Crassus
– he can't afford to offend him – and nobody hates Pompey
more than Crassus.

TIRO. Why? Why does Crassus hate him?

CICERO. Jealousy. He longs for Pompey's military glory.
It should be easy to set them at each other's throats – I see
endless opportunities for making mischief –

TIRO. But if he's Consul –

CICERO. I doubt he could do much damage. He has all those
qualities I value most in my political opponents – no
imagination, no intellect, no cunning, no oratorical skills.
I wonder who he'll choose as his running mate? His
hairdresser perhaps? Or maybe just his hair?

    CATO approaches.

CATO. The Republic is drifting, Cicero – drifting towards
disaster on the winds and currents of easy compromise.
Where's Pompey's authorisation for all these cities he's
founded – these countries he's occupied? Has the Senate
approved it? Have the People voted? We are meddling in
places about which we know nothing. Syria! What business
do we have in Syria –

CICERO. Oh, Cato – let's not pick fights we can't win –

CATO. You realise that these countries will have to be
permanently occupied by standing armies – and whoever
commands those armies will be a constant threat to Rome?

CICERO. I've told you – speak to the Consul.

    They go home.

Scene Four

They arrive home, the house is in darkness. SOSITHEUS *is waiting.*

TIRO. Let's hope for a better day tomorrow. Goodnight then. (*Exits.*)

CICERO. Has my wife gone to bed?

SOSITHEUS. Yes. But –

CICERO. Good.

SOSITHEUS. But –

CICERO. What is it?

> CLODIA *waiting in the study – she kneels and grasps* CICERO*'s knees like a Greek supplicant.*

Clodia!

CLODIA. I've come to plead with you. My poor brother is beside himself with fear and remorse –

CICERO. I can't –

CLODIA. Clodius has been a faithful friend to you – he saved you from Catiline – now you shut your doors in his face. He's too proud to beg – so I've come to beg for him. It's no little thing for a Claudian to kneel – but you see me at your feet –

CICERO. Get up off the floor, Clodia – my wife's a light sleeper –

CLODIA. Defend my poor brother!

CICERO. I'll not speak a word until you stand up.

> *She does, and bows her head – kisses his hand.*

Now listen to me. You want me to help Clodius?

CLODIA. Don't let them kill my poor, frightened, innocent boy –

CICERO. He must write to every woman whose honour he outraged – swear it was a fit of madness – he's no longer worthy to breathe the same air as them – that sort of thing. He can't be too obsequious, believe me. For the present, he'll have to abandon his political ambitions and go into exile –

CLODIA. Exile! To leave Rome would kill him! –

CICERO. Rome will kill him if he stays.

CLODIA. You could easily get him off.

CICERO. Look… After a few years the affair might be forgotten –

CLODIA. Years! –

CICERO. When things calm down he'll be able creep home and start again…

CLODIA. Claudians do not creep!

CICERO. I'm afraid it's the best advice I have to offer.

CLODIA. At least swear not to join the attacks on him –

CICERO. Of course! I want nothing to do with it. I'll keep out of it if I can.

CLODIA. The People love Clodius – everybody loves him – you love him, don't you? It was only a childish prank – he deserves to be punished – but not with death! Say you'll defend him –

CICERO. No! –

CLODIA. Surely you can't believe he's guilty?

CICERO. Clodia, the whole world *knows* he's guilty!

CLODIA. He wasn't even in Rome on the night of the Festival of the Good Goddess –

CICERO. Oh! – (*Laughs.*)

CLODIA. Why do you imagine my beautiful, beautiful brother – who can have any girl he likes, or any boy for that matter – would want to spy on a herd of chanting frumps?

CICERO. He was fu…! He was caught with Caesar's wife!

CLODIA. No – he was visiting friends – a day's journey away.

CICERO. He was in my house! He boasted of it! If they put me on oath I shall be forced to give evidence against him.

CLODIA. You wouldn't dare! Clodius says you've promised to defend Hybrida when he comes home – and Hybrida's the biggest thief who ever lived – you know *he's* guilty. And Hybrida's fat and old and ugly – he deserves to be punished... But Clodius is so lovable and charming – don't let them condemn him. Help us! I'll do anything.

She drops her cloak. She's naked. CICERO *puts it back on her shoulders.*

CICERO. Go home, Clodia.

CLODIA. He'll come himself if you'd prefer it? You could have us both –

CICERO. Clodia!

CLODIA. Don't make an enemy of me!

CICERO. Clodius must leave Rome tonight. When the time is right I'll argue in the Senate for his return. That's the only comfort I have to offer. Now goodnight.

CLODIA. If you abandon us I swear we'll revenge it.

CICERO. You're speaking to the man who destroyed Catiline. I believe I've little to fear from... from a pair of... Well, what are you? Now go tell your brother what I say.

Scene Five

The Forum. Enter CLODIUS *and his* SUPPORTERS.

TIRO. My master's prosecution of Verres set his foot on the first rung of the political ladder. Two other trials threatened to topple him down – the first was the prosecution of Clodius for sacrilege.

Enter the PATRICIANS *and the* WOMEN *on the other side, protesting.*

The People were for Clodius – why should a popular young man die for a childish prank? The old guard, together with most women of good family – demanded vengeance.

LUCULLUS. Flog him! –

TERENTIA. Strip him naked and flog him!

CICERO. Dear gods! I'm married to a Fury!

TERENTIA. The women of Rome demand his death! (*To* CICERO.) This is your fault – you encouraged him – you sponsored his political career –

CLODIUS *jumps on a cart.*

CLODIUS. Citizens! Listen to me! I am the victim of a conspiracy. Because I am a friend of the People, my own class is deserting me – I need your help! I am being persecuted by a group of corrupt Senators who hate the People. They're determined to cling on to their wealth and power – and silence me! I have lived among them – I know their secrets – their lies – their schemes. I was not even in Rome on the night of the Festival of the Good Goddess – I shall bring witnesses to prove I was a full day's journey from the City. I am a god-fearing man – I would never profane the ceremonies of the deities that protect us! Be afraid! If this can happen to me – a member of one of Rome's founding families who gave our City twenty-eight of her Consuls – it could happen to any one of you!

Uproar. The MOB *carries off* CLODIUS *on their shoulders.*
CAESAR *and* CRASSUS *are talking to* RUFUS. CAESAR
has his arm round RUFUS – *an animated conversation.*

CICERO. Rufus?

RUFUS. Master. (*Moves away with* CRASSUS.)

CAESAR. Cicero?

CICERO. This must be humiliating for you, Caesar. Your wife –

CAESAR. She's no longer my wife. Are you going to give
evidence?

CICERO. I've done everything I can to avoid it. Terentia is
insisting I destroy the young fool's alibi. Clodius swears he
was nowhere near Rome during the festival – he's lying – he
was at my house.

CAESAR. He's a man without honour – a parasite. Even so
he'll be acquitted. I can tell you – in confidence: in spite of
my strong opposition, our friend Crassus has bought the jury
for him.

CICERO. Why? What can Crassus possibly hope to gain…?

CAESAR. He likes to keep a foot in both camps, doesn't he?
Listen, old friend… Sooner or later I shall be Consul – it's
my destiny.

CICERO. And when you are Consul, I shall do everything in
my power to make you obey the ancient laws and customs of
the Republic.

CAESAR. The People want land – Pompey's soldiers are
demanding land – they've shed their blood for Roman soil –
it's their right. You must see that? You're going to have to
bow to the inevitable and support me.

CICERO. I've contrived the worst of all possible worlds for
myself, haven't I? If I speak in favour of your bill my friends
will denounce me as a turncoat – and my wife will make my
life a living hell. If I oppose you, I'll be howled off the stage.
Fine politician I turned out to be!

CAESAR. Your reward will be my gratitude – my undying
friendship. You'll be my guide and mentor – how could

I survive without Cicero to keep me up to the mark? But...
You do know, don't you – if you speak against Clodius at
this trial, he'll make it a point of honour to hound you out of
Rome? Imagine! The Father of his Country thrown out of the
City he saved! I've heard he's planning to renounce his class.
As a plebeian, he could stand for Tribune.

CICERO. But surely – no Claudian would ever stoop so low!

CAESAR. As Tribune he'd be undisputed leader of the Roman
mob. The People love him, you know? All Catiline's young
men – those who survived – are encouraging him. You really
would be in trouble – if Clodius brings a prosecution against
you – before an Assembly – for executing Roman citizens
without a trial...? You'd be lynched.

CICERO. After all I've done for them...

CAESAR. I had a lucky escape, didn't I? When you had the
conspirators strangled? You had me worried for a moment or
two –

CICERO. Worried? You? I don't believe it.

CAESAR. Look... if ever Clodius becomes a threat, never
forget that I'll always protect you.

CICERO. Thank you...

CAESAR. When I'm given a military command, I'll need a
legate to handle the civil administration. I could put you on
my staff.

CICERO. But I've no –

CAESAR. It would give you immunity from prosecution –
Clodius wouldn't be able to touch you. Think about it.
You've only to ask.

CAESAR *rejoins* RUFUS *and* CRASSUS.

TIRO. A handsome offer!

CICERO. He never ceases to amaze me.

RUFUS *and* CLODIA, *and a cheering* MOB, *carry*
CLODIUS *out of Court.*

TIRO. Never, in the history of the Republic, has a jury been so bribed – and not just in gold.

Sound of creaking beds.

On the eve of the verdict, beds were creaking in noble houses all over Rome. They say both brother and sister were enthusiastically lending a hand.

CLODIUS (*sadly, to* CICERO). You should have defended me, old man – as I defended you from Catiline – not tried to destroy me. Why are you siding with my enemies?

CLODIA. I begged you – I knelt at your feet. One day I'll make you'll kneel at mine.

Scene Six

TIRO. The second trial which brought my master into great danger was… Well, see for yourself.

CICERO*'s study.*

CICERO. Sositheus? You look as if you've seen a ghost.

SOSITHEUS. I've seen something worse. Antonius Hybrida's back from Macedonia.

CICERO. Hybrida! Oh, not now! I've not deserved this! Pompey bullying me – Clodius and his ghastly sister threatening revenge – and no daughter to comfort me!

TIRO. Our past comes back to haunt us.

CICERO. Am I the plaything of some malicious god!

TIRO. Don't worry. Things are sure to look up when they make your friend Caesar Consul.

CICERO. I don't find that funny, Tiro.

SOSITHEUS. Shall I show Hybrida in?

CICERO. No!

TIRO. Yes – best get it over with.

> HYBRIDA *stands in the doorway – a bloated wreck. He shakes. He is holding a writ.*

HYBRIDA. Cicero! Well, I can't say you look pleased to see me!

TIRO. How was Macedonia?

HYBRIDA. Read this.

TIRO. A writ? When was it served?

HYBRIDA. This morning.

CICERO (*reading*). Do you understand what this is?

HYBRIDA. No – it's Greek to me. Is it serious?

CICERO. They're charging you with treason.

HYBRIDA. That's a relief! I thought they'd come after me for corruption. Phew!

CICERO. Did you hear what I said? A writ for *treason* –

HYBRIDA. But I'm not guilty of treason, am I? Corruption's different – I'm in it up to my neck – and so are you, Cicero. You've had your cut –

CICERO. It says you lost an army?

HYBRIDA. I never did!

CICERO. In Histria – a year ago –

HYBRIDA. Not true –

CICERO. Can you have been so drunk you lost your army and didn't notice?

HYBRIDA. No – well, yes – but it was only the infantry. Nice place you've got here – Corinthian bronzes on the terrace, gold basins in the lavatory –

CICERO. Dear gods! Who's to lead for the Prosecution?

HYBRIDA. Aha! A bit of luck there! It's one of your boys – young Rufus! He's twenty-three – still wet behind the ears – you'll run rings round him – easy! And if you just have a quiet word beforehand –

CICERO. Are you seriously suggesting I bribe the State Prosecutor in a treason trial?

HYBRIDA. Why not! I've got the money – so have you… Got anything to drink?

CICERO (*throws the writ into* HYBRIDA*'s lap*). Find somebody else to defend you.

HYBRIDA. No! I'm having you. You taught this boy Rufus – you know his weaknesses –

CICERO. He may know a few of mine!

HYBRIDA. We made a deal. You've taken a hefty percentage of everything I squeezed out of Macedonia – and you swore, if ever I got caught, you'd defend me –

CICERO. Yes – against corruption charges – this is treason!

HYBRIDA. You'd have had your work cut out if it was corruption, I can tell you!

TIRO. Something's not right. Why Rufus? It smells of Caesar – it reeks of Crassus.

HYBRIDA. Rufus was your boy –

TIRO. And then he was Catiline's boy –

CICERO. And now I think he may be Caesar's.

HYBRIDA. Come up in the world, haven't you? Forgotten your old friends and colleagues? Clearly you've come into money – and this house… How much did it cost – eight – ten million? Do people know where you got the money to pay for it? Go fetch us some wine, Tiro. Things always seem clearer after a drink.

Scene Seven

The Court assembles.

TIRO. Nervous?

CICERO. Well, of course I am. What a question!

Enter POMPEY *and* CAESAR.

POMPEY (*aloof*). Cicero.

He takes his place.

CAESAR. I wish you the best of luck, old friend.

CICERO. Thank you, Caesar.

CAESAR. I imagine our young Rufus won't make much of an impression on your dazzling oratory.

CICERO. I taught him well. I'm sure he'll acquit himself with honour.

CAESAR. Ah, honour… And Hybrida… Yes… Oh, it will interest you to know, Marcus Tullius, I've reached an agreement with my son-in-law. It's time we settled this Land Bill once and for all.

CICERO. What agreement? What son-in-law?

CAESAR. I have betrothed my daughter Julia to Pompey Magnus.

CICERO. I… It's…

CAESAR. Good news, isn't it?

CICERO. I –

CAESAR. How's your own son-in-law, by the way? Has that excellent youth, Dolabella, made a grandfather of you yet?

CICERO. I…

CAESAR. My wedding gift will be land reform – our lands in Campania will be divided between Pompey's demobbed soldiers, and the poor of Rome who wish to become farmers.

CICERO. I opposed your bill at the beginning of my Consulship – I'll do everything in my power to stop you again.

CAESAR. I doubt that – not when you hear what I have to offer.

CICERO. You're in no position to make offers –

CAESAR. I soon will be. When I'm Consul –

CICERO. If you're Consul –

CAESAR. Hear me out! I've redrafted the bill. This time the managing commission will consist of just four men –

CICERO. What four men?

CAESAR. Myself, and Pompey – and I would be honoured – most honoured – if you would agree to join us.

CICERO. Would you indeed! Who would be the fourth?

CAESAR. Crassus.

CICERO. *Crassus!* Crassus and Pompey can hardly bear to be in the same country – let alone sit together on a committee –

CAESAR. Crassus is my good friend, Pompey will be my son-in-law – they'll set aside past differences. The matter is settled.

CICERO. Then why do you need me?

CAESAR. As Father of the Nation –

CICERO. I'd provide a mask of respectability to disguise your headlong rush for power –

CAESAR. I wish only to serve – I always put the good of my country before personal ambition –

CICERO. The Consuls would be your puppets, the Senate an impotent gossiping-shop –

CAESAR. No change there, then! My scheme would bring strength and stability –

CICERO. Or civil war… I value your friendship, Caesar, but I'll not be part of your conspiracy.

CAESAR. Well… Think it over… Anyway, best of luck with your defence of Hybrida. I hope I haven't put you off your stride?

The MOB. *The Court.*

TIRO. My master was twice Rufus's age. When he went to wish the young man luck, he looked stooped and careworn. I sensed he was faltering. I wasn't worried – once he began to speak I knew his confidence would come flowing back.

Rufus's opening speech was devastating. By the end of the first day things were looking grim for Hybrida.

The audience is the Court of Law – RUFUS *addresses them.*

RUFUS. Members of the jury, let me go over what we've heard today. Many of us expected that, on his return to Rome, Hybrida would face prosecution for corruption. All his energies during his year as Governor were given to extorting as much money as he could from the people of Macedonia. I've shown how revenues raised to pay his soldiers disappeared into his own pockets. But corruption is not the charge. The charge is treason. My witnesses – his advisers, his centurions – the common prostitutes he took with him on campaign – have spoken of Hybrida's drunkenness, incompetence, and cowardice. During his term of office, rebellious tribes flourished unchecked – Rome lost hard-won territories around the Lower Danube and Histria – on the field of battle, as his leaderless legions faced disaster, Hybrida snored in his tent. I say Antonius Hybrida has betrayed his army. He has betrayed his class, he has betrayed Rome.

A break in proceedings.

HYBRIDA. Not exactly going well, is it?

CICERO. Flee while you can – that's the best advice I can give. Voluntary exile is preferable to being jeered out of the City. Rufus is humiliating you –

HYBRIDA (*tears*). What did I ever do to that young man?

CICERO. He's ambitious to rise in the world, that's all. The law's never personal. At least it shouldn't be.

HYBRIDA. You trained him too well.

CICERO. Verres's trial made my name – yours, I fear, will make his.

HYBRIDA. Damn him! Let him do his worst – you're still the best. You'll have young Rufus for breakfast.

PRAETOR. Antonius Hybrida, do you swear to tell the truth?

HYBRIDA. By the gods that protect the City and our Republic, I solemnly so swear!

CICERO. Gentlemen… My young colleague accuses my client of cowardice in the face of the enemy. But what does this boy know of war?

CLODIUS (*from the gallery*). What do you know, Cicero!

CICERO. In the hour of Rome's greatest peril – I refer to the conspiracy of Catiline – you, Hybrida, led the Senate's legions north to crush the traitor?

HYBRIDA. I did.

CICERO. You sent back Catiline's head as proof of your victory?

HYBRIDA. I did.

CICERO. Is that, gentlemen, the action of a traitor?

Mixed response from the SPECTATORS.

No, it is not! In those difficult days, young Rufus there was a rebel himself – a supporter of Catiline – you wouldn't attempt to deny it, would you, boy? He fled Rome to escape a traitor's fate – *now* he comes creeping back to charge with treason the very man who, next to myself, did most to save the Republic… Hybrida, this money you're supposed to have extorted from the Macedonians – what became of it?

HYBRIDA. I can account for all of it – down to the last copper coin. I spent that money to raise and equip two legions. I led those legions east to punish the rebel tribes – it was an extremely hazardous journey… We were harried all the way by savage tribesmen – yet I was able to maintain the strictest discipline.

CICERO. Rufus says that when your scouts warned you of
    enemy columns ahead, you split your forces – leading your
    cavalry to safety, but leaving your infantry undefended. True?

HYBRIDA. False – absolutely false. I led my cavalry by
    a roundabout route – to engage the enemy.

CICERO. What Rufus calls panic and flight was, in fact, a
    military stratagem?

CLODIUS. Laughable!

HYBRIDA. Yes, it was – and it would have succeeded. But as
    I charged ahead, other forces crossed the Danube and
    attacked our infantry in the rear.

CICERO. Nothing you could do?

HYBRIDA (*tears*). Nothing...

CICERO. Your infantry was commanded by the same officers
    Rufus has brought here to accuse you of cowardice?

HYBRIDA. They were the cowards! My faith in them was
    misplaced.

CICERO. You could hardly be in two places at the same time –
    leading a cavalry charge against impossible odds, while
    defending the infantry you'd ordered to stand firm. You lost
    many friends in the action?

HYBRIDA. A great many – too many...

CICERO. Members of the jury, some of you have served
    bravely in Rome's legions – I don't need to remind you the
    fortunes of war can be cruel and capricious. A General in the
    field sometimes takes a difficult decision that leads to
    disaster. *That* is not the same as treason.

    Applause.

HYBRIDA (*aside to* TIRO). He's swung it, hasn't he? Did I do
    all right?

TIRO. You were unbelievable.

HYBRIDA. Gods, I need a drink.

RUFUS *saunters over to the witness stand, completely relaxed.*

RUFUS. Antonius Hybrida… Would you say you have a good memory?

HYBRIDA. Yes – I do.

RUFUS. Good – then you'll remember a slave who was murdered a short while before you began your term as Consul?

HYBRIDA. A slave… (*Looking to* CICERO *for help*.) I'm not sure…

RUFUS. One of your slaves?

HYBRIDA. Over the years I've had many slaves. I can't be expected –

RUFUS. A boy – a singing boy about twelve years old? His body was fished out of the Tiber –

HYBRIDA. No…

RUFUS. Cicero there was summoned by the Urban Praetor to inspect the remains.

HYBRIDA. No – I…

RUFUS. His throat had been cut – intestines removed? –

CICERO. Surely this can have no relevance to a battle on the Danube.

PRAETOR. We don't know that. I find, in life, all sorts of things are linked.

RUFUS. Well?

HYBRIDA. I have some vague memory –

RUFUS. Oh, come on! Even in the depraved circles in which you move, I can't believe it's every day you take part in a human sacrifice! Catiline performed the ritual – the slitting of the throat – the removal of the child's entrails –

HYBRIDA. Well, if he did I've no memory of it –

RUFUS. He made you swear an oath – a blood oath –

HYBRIDA. Catiline did? I think you've been misinformed, boy –

RUFUS. You thrust your hands into the boy's warm body… D'you remember what that oath was about?

HYBRIDA. It was over four years ago – how could I?

CICERO (*wincing*). Oh!

RUFUS. Let me remind you. A dozen Senators – yourself included – swore to kill your fellow Consul. Cicero. Remember Cicero? Look to your right – he's the one conducting your defence – he's sitting over there on the bench.

Laughter.

CICERO. Really this is a *pity*. Until now my young friend wasn't doing a bad job – many of you here know he was my pupil. Now he ruins his case by introducing an absurd fiction. You should go back to the classroom, boy.

RUFUS. You claim it's untrue?

CICERO. A human sacrifice – of course it's untrue!

RUFUS. But it was you who told me about it, Master… Back in the classroom.

CICERO (*a flicker of a hesitation*). You ungrateful wretch!

RUFUS. You say I was a supporter of Catiline? On the first day of your Consulship – you called me to your house and asked me if Catiline had ever, in my presence, spoken of a plot to kill you. You told me Hybrida had confessed it –

HYBRIDA. What's that! –

RUFUS. You begged me to return to Catiline and keep my ears open –

CICERO. It's a lie!

RUFUS. You knew what a rogue and a thief Hybrida was – yet you unleashed him on the long-suffering people of Macedonia – why was that, Cicero? How was it a man who hated you so much he once swore to kill you suddenly became your friend and partner in crime? What sort of pact – what agreement did you make with him?

CICERO. There was no agreement!

RUFUS. No? What of the agreement you made on the day of your Consulship – to split the plunder between you?

CICERO. I don't have to answer this – I am not on trial –

RUFUS. Oho – I think you are!

HYBRIDA. No! This isn't right! I may have sent Cicero a gift or two from time to time –

RUFUS. A gift? A *gift*? Look up there, members of the jury – do you see a golden glow over the Palatine – it's the sun shining down on the white marble of Cicero's house. How much do you think such a house is worth? I see Senator Crassus there – he knows about the price of property. Senator – please tell the Court – what, in your estimation, might a house like that sell for?

CRASSUS (*calling out*). I'd guess about fourteen million.

RUFUS. Fourteen million – *fourteen million*! Some gift! Ask yourselves, where Cicero – who prides himself on his humble origins – got fourteen million? Can he deny that it came from his partner there – the man he blackmailed and protected – Antonius Hybrida? Hybrida – the coward who abandoned his army and fled the field of battle – Hybrida – the thief who pillaged and abused the defenceless people of Macedonia – Hybrida – Rome's disloyal servant who could not have committed his crimes without the collusion of his consular colleague – Marcus Tullius Cicero. Let's not waste the rest of the day. I'm confident I've done more than enough to prove Hybrida guilty of extortion, incompetence, and treason. Let's go straight to a vote – send him into exile tonight – remove him from our City.

CAESAR *and* POMPEY *join* CRASSUS *in the audience.*

PRAETOR. The Prosecutor has made his closing speech. Senator? Cicero – do you wish to sum up for the defence?

CICERO. Yes, I do… (*Waits for silence.*) I made common cause with Hybrida – I won't deny it.

CLODIUS. He admits it! You heard him admit it!

CICERO. I sought him out – I overlooked differences in the
way we conduct our lives – my morals, his lack of them...

Jeers.

Yes – I overlooked too many things – because my mind,
through every waking hour, was fixed on a single object.
Somebody had to restore law and order to this City! I alone
could save the Republic! I was desperate... I needed allies –
and I couldn't afford to be too particular where they came
from.

CLODIUS. This is the man who swore he'd restore the decency,
dignity, and moral authority of Rome!

CICERO. Cast your minds back to those terrible times. Who
among you honestly believes Catiline acted alone in plotting
his revolt? Could one madman – even a fanatic as depraved
as Catiline – have brought Rome to the brink of destruction,
had he not had powerful backers?

Gasps.

MOB. Who were they? Name them! Name them! (*Etc.*)

CICERO. Oh, I'm not talking about Catiline's ragbag following –
bankrupt Senators, gamblers, drunks, lechers, and perfumed
youths – our young prosecutor there was one of them!

RUFUS. That's a lie –

CICERO. I'm talking about men of great influence – who saw
an opportunity in the terrors Catiline was about to unleash –
to further their own ambition. It's the old, old story: silence
the law, terrorise the people, burn and pull everything down
– then step in to 'restore order' by force of arms.

Approval and protest mixed.

The men who lurked in Catiline's shadow didn't flee into
exile. Today – these men – these same men – by bribery,
corruption, and the threat of military action – have gained
a stranglehold on the institutions of our Republic.

Look around you. We're governed, now, by secret conclaves
– while gangs riot in our streets –

POMPEY (*standing*). I think we've heard enough.

CICERO. Members of the jury, shall I tell you a terrible truth?
As Consul I stamped out the conspiracy of Sergius Catiline,
but a second conspiracy – by far the deadlier of the two –
lives on, festers and grows stronger by the day. (*Pointing at*
RUFUS.) Do you imagine Rufus there is the author of this
prosecution? Rufus is a child!

CLODIUS. A child who's got you by the balls!

CICERO. Who put him up to it? The whole purpose of this trial,
members of the jury, is to discredit me. Why? Because in
order to seize power, the enemies of freedom know they'll
first have to silence me. Dear gods – you accuse Hybrida of
corruption! He is an innocent – a helpless baby – when
compared with the sleazy venality of Gaius Julius Caesar,
Marcus Licinius Crassus, and the evil they are planning to
unleash in our Republic –

Gasps.

CLODIUS. Sit down!

CICERO. That Hybrida made mistakes, I've no doubt. That he
indulged himself more than is wise, I concede. But think
back upon the man who stood at my side in the hour of
Rome's peril. Look beyond his sins. He may have played the
fool, but he is not guilty of treason.

A buzz of amazement.

CAESAR (*aside to* CICERO, *as he leaves, puzzled and hurt*).
I offered you the hand of friendship.

Exeunt POMPEY, CRASSUS, CAESAR, RUFUS *and*
CLODIUS.

CICERO (*to* TIRO). Did you get it all down?

TIRO. What have you done?

CICERO. Cleared my conscience.

TIRO. Caesar will never forgive you – Clodius will set the mob
on you –

CICERO. Clodius! D'you think I'd let that giggling, puerile little pervert get the better of me? I could snap his spine with a single well-aimed epigram.

PRAETOR. There voted in favour of condemnation forty-seven. In favour of acquittal twelve.

Huge cheer.

Hybrida is stripped of his rights of citizenship and property. From midnight, he is denied fire and water anywhere throughout the lands, colonies, and cities of Italy. The Court stands adjourned.

The MOB *goes wild.*

HYBRIDA. Not your fault, my friend. I knew the game was up even before I called on you. I've plenty hidden away – and they say the south coast of Gaul is very like the Bay of Naples. But if I were you – after that speech – I'd get right away from Rome. Caesar will have your guts for lute strings. Come on – let's find a drink.

They are jeered at by the MOB *as they leave the Court.* CELER, LUCULLUS, ISAURICUS, CATO, *etc., come to meet them.*

CELER. By all the gods, Cicero – what have you done!

CATULUS. What did you just say in Court?

CICERO. I told a few home truths –

LUCULLUS. Caesar's exacting a terrible revenge –

CELER. He's in Senate House – turning that *pustule* Publius Clodius into a plebeian!

CICERO. He can't!

CATO. He can! He's our Pontiff!

CICERO. Clodius seduced Caesar's wife – humiliated and dishonoured him! Caesar wouldn't work with Clodius – it's impossible!

TIRO. It's what Caesar does, isn't it? The impossible.

LUCULLUS. You should have beheaded the snake when you had the chance.

ISAURICUS. If Clodius becomes Tribune, he'll wreck the Constitution.

CATO. He'll bypass the Senate and rule over us through Assemblies of the People –

CELER. Come with us to the Senate House – we have to stop them.

CICERO. But how? How? How?

TIRO. You should never have bought that house –

CICERO. Oh, for…

Exeunt.

Scene Eight

CAESAR, *flanked by* POMPEY, *and* CRASSUS, *like a priest at a wedding ceremony.* CLODIUS *and a spotty male prostitute,* FONTEIUS, *kneel in front of him holding hands.*

CAESAR. Publius Clodius Pulcher, I, Gaius Julius Caesar, by the sacred powers vested in me as Pontiff declare that you are now the adopted son of Publius Fonteius, and will be entered into the State records as a plebeian.

CLODIUS. Father! (*Kisses* FONTEIUS.)

CAESAR. You are now eligible to stand for Tribune of the People in the coming election. Thank you, gentlemen.

CELER, CICERO, CATO, TIRO, *etc., arrive at the door.*

CELER (*bellowing*). What's going on here!

CAESAR. Metellus Celer, remember where you are! This is a religious ceremony – you stand on holy ground.

CELER. Then what's this shit doing on it? Have you forgotten – he's fucking your wife!

CAESAR. Ex-wife.

CELER aims a kick at CLODIUS who, laughing, runs and crouches at CAESAR's feet. CELER grabs the terrified, pimply youth.

CELER. Who the fuck are you?

CLODIUS. Metellus Celer – (*Giggling.*) Show some respect for my aged father!

CELER advances on CLODIUS, raised fists, he's held back by CAESAR's MEN.

CICERO. Don't give them an excuse to arrest you.

CAESAR. Wise advice.

CELER. How! How by any law of reason or morality – could *this* be your father? He's half your age! Religious ceremony? It's shaming –

CLODIUS. He was the best money could buy at short notice. Come along, ancient Father – lean on me – (*Laughs.*)

CAESAR. We're finished here.

CELER. You may be finished, Caesar – I haven't even started! And I command legions!

CAESAR. I'll have an army of my own before long. The People will vote me whatever province I ask. Don't threaten me, Celer – that's how wars start.

(*To CICERO, as he exits.*) Now look what you've made me do.

CELER (*to CLODIUS*). You – a Tribune? Over my dead body!

CLODIUS. Well, there's a thought... (*Gives him the pointed-fingers sign.*)

Exeunt all but CICERO, TIRO, CATO and CELER.

CICERO. For years I've held Caesar in check. But with Pompey at his side – Clodius controlling the streets – the People granting his every wish... How will I survive?

They leave, hooted and jeered at by CLODIUS's GANG.

Offer them no provocation! Give them no excuse –

CLODIUS *blocks their way.*

You should have taken my advice – gone into exile. The downward path you've chosen can only end badly.

CLODIUS. Long after you're forgotten, Cicero, I'll be remembered in Rome's annals as one of her greatest heroes. Her People will put up statues to me –

CICERO. In women's clothing – flashing your little prick no doubt? Get out of my way.

CLODIUS (*takes* CICERO *by the arm, meaning it, hurt*). All I wanted was to be your friend.

CICERO. Claudians make unreliable friends –

CLODIUS. And merciless enemies.

CICERO. Do you imagine the man who destroyed Sergius Catiline incapable of seeing off his bastard son? Let me pass.

CLODIUS. Hear that, citizens? Did you hear him admit it? (*Appealing to the* MOB.) Yes – you destroyed Catiline – a noble Roman – and butchered his innocent friends! Roman citizens – executed without trial! Walk away, tyrant – the People will have their revenge – blood will have blood!

CICERO*'s party walk away.*

My fellow citizens, I was born a patrician, but my own class turned against me. You have supported and followed me. I am of you – I wish to serve you – until the end of my days I shall dedicate myself to you. I have today become a plebeian. I shall begin my political career – not in the Senate – filled as it is with corrupt, bloated, self-serving despots – but as your faithful representative – the People's Tribune! If elected I shall feed the poor and the dispossessed, I shall give you bread, I shall cancel your debts, I shall give you land! And I make you this pledge, my friends: once I am in power, those who have taken the lives of Roman citizens without trial will learn what it is to taste the People's vengeance!

Cheering. The MOB *takes over. They occupy the Temple of Castor, which they cover with slogans.*

Scene Nine

TIRO. Caesar was elected First Consul by the unanimous vote of all the tribes – the only candidate to achieve this since Cicero… Caesar Head of State, Clodius a Tribune – his mob terrorising the streets. Waking up – the morning after the elections – imagine the shock felt by all good men?

CICERO (*aside to* TIRO). How did we let it happen!

The Senate. CAESAR *as Consul in the chair.*

CAESAR. A bill for the redistribution of State lands to army veterans and Rome's poor. Who wishes to speak?

POMPEY. I'm in favour of the bill.

CRASSUS. As am I.

A SENATOR. And I.

ANOTHER SENATOR. And I.

ANOTHER SENATOR. I am in favour.

CATO. I am opposed. (*Takes out a sackful of documents and, taking his time, takes the floor.*) I can show many precedents – going back to the foundation of the City – demonstrating that the common land is held in trust for all the nation, and is not to be parcelled out by unscrupulous 'here-today, gone-tomorrow' politicians for their own gain –

CAESAR. Just say whether you are in favour or opposed, Cato, and sit down.

CATO. Any Senator has the right to speak for as long as he wishes –

CAESAR. I said sit down, you sanctimonious windbag!

CATO. If you wish to preside over this House you should study its rules and procedures –

CAESAR. Sit down!

CATO. In the Consulship of Quintus Fabius Maximus –

CAESAR. Remove him! I'll not let him talk out my bill –

CATO. I'll not be intimidated –

CAESAR. Throw him out!

> LICTORS *remove* CATO, *protesting*.

> Cicero – what have you to say?

CICERO. Only this –

POMPEY. Oh, there can only be one possible outcome! – Why prolong the debate –

CRASSUS. Aye! Agreed – I propose we move to a vote.

CAESAR. All in favour?

SENATE (*a roar*). Aye!

CAESAR. The bill passes. Next business?

POMPEY. In view of the sudden death of our dear friend and colleague, our Chief Augur Metellus Celer –

SENATORS (*consternation*). What? Is Celer dead? When did he die? How? Not Celer? Surely not! (*Etc.*)

CAESAR. Silence!

POMPEY. In view of Celer's death, I propose that the province – Further Gaul – allotted to Celer be transferred to Caesar...

LUCULLUS. But – gentlemen – Caesar has already been granted Bithynia. And he has prevailed upon the People's Assembly to grant him Nearer Gaul –

POMPEY. Precisely. If Caesar commands both Further and Nearer Gaul – his unified command will make it easier to crush any future rebellion. Therefore, I propose that, in view of the unsettled nature of the region, Caesar should be given an extra legion –

LUCULLUS. *Five!* Caesar would command five legions?

CAESAR. Are there any objections to the proposals of Pompey Magnus?

LUCULLUS. And do you also intend to retain command of Bithynia?

CAESAR. I do.

LUCULLUS. Bithynia is a thousand miles from Gaul! (*A contemptuous laugh – nobody joins in.*)

CAESAR. We all know our geography, Lucullus –

LUCULLUS. And you'll remain in post for five years?

CAESAR. Five years – the People decreed it. Are you opposed to the will of the People?

LUCULLUS. Gentlemen, we can't allow any one man to control twenty-two thousand soldiers, on the very borders of Italy, for *five years*! What if he were to move against Rome?

A chill descends.

POMPEY. Perhaps General Lucullus should go home and discuss his faded military glories with the fishes. Times have changed.

LUCULLUS. Clearly. And not for the better…

CAESAR. In his time, Lucullus commanded more legions than I have been voted. Yet still he failed to bring Mithradates to heel. That task was left to my gallant son-in-law, Pompey Magnus. What can Lucullus have been doing out there in the east, at such great cost to the public purse?

LUCULLUS. I –

CAESAR. I think the People would be interested to know how he acquired his great wealth. And since he has insulted me – called my honour in question – this House thinks he should offer me an apology.

Loud approval, from CAESAR's SUPPORTERS *– horrified silence from the others.*

LUCULLUS. If my words have offended you, Caesar –

CAESAR. On his knees…

LUCULLUS (*bewildered*). What?

CAESAR. The Senate wants to hear you apologise to me – *on your knees*!

LUCULLUS, *with difficulty, gets down on his knees before*
CAESAR. *He extends his arms and bows his head.*
CAESAR *exits in a rage.* CICERO *and* TIRO – *ashen – help*
LUCULLUS *to his feet.*

Scene Ten

An Assembly of the People.

CLODIUS. A Law – of the Tribune Publius Clodius against
Cicero.

Whereas Marcus Tullius Cicero has put Roman citizens to
death unheard and uncondemned – and abused the authority
and decrees of the Senate, it is hereby ordained by the People
that he be forbidden fire and water to a distance of four
hundred miles from Rome – that nobody should harbour or
receive him, on pain of death – that all his property and
possessions be forfeit – that his house be demolished and
a shrine to Liberty consecrated in its place – and whosoever
shall speak, vote or take any step towards recalling him shall
be treated as a public enemy... Unless those whom Cicero
unlawfully put to death should spring back to life.

Cheers, jeers, laughter.

Is it the wish of the People that this bill should become law?

OMNES. Aye! Aye! Aye! (*Cheers, noise, drums, etc.*)

Scene Eleven

CICERO's house. Family and SUPPORTERS. The SENATORS are dressed in mourning. Sounds of a distant MOB throughout.

TERENTIA. Why are you dressed in black?

LUCULLUS. We're in mourning for the Republic –

CATO. And in defiance of Clodius, who had forbidden all gestures of support for your husband.

TERENTIA. Gestures of support! We need action – we need armed men to go down there and destroy Clodius! It's time some of you showed some leadership –

Enter TIRO *with* TULLIA.

TIRO. My master has turned his face to the wall. He won't speak to me – he won't even speak to Tullia...

TULLIA. They've robbed him of his voice... What is my father without his voice?

TERENTIA. Voices! Listen to them! The voice of the People! The howls of the mob. The Senate and People of Rome – they're as bad as each other.

TULLIA. Papa must leave Italy before Clodius's law comes into force.

TERENTIA. Clodius! Who is Clodius to give Rome laws!

LUCULLUS. Nobody can control him. Even Caesar's abandoning the City – he's off to conquer the world – it's 'All power to the People!'

CATO. The Republic lies on its deathbed.

TIRO. Athens would welcome us.

TERENTIA. Men! My husband shall stay and fight. I'll defend this house myself.

CATO. I don't see how he can survive –

TIRO. There may be one last hope. In the summer, Caesar offered him an appointment as his legate.

CATO. Cicero in the army!

TIRO. He wouldn't have to fight. The point is – it would give him immunity from prosecution… As long as Caesar holds his Imperium, any law Clodius passes against my master would be legally unenforceable.

TERENTIA. Lawyers' tricks!

CATO. It's unthinkable. He'd be just another of Caesar's lackeys – that's not Cicero! He'd never demean himself –

TIRO. But if it saves his life –

TERENTIA. Would you all go now? I must try and speak to my husband.

TULLIA. It's no use – I've tried – best leave him alone.

LUCULLUS. Tell him he has our full support.

They start to exit.

TERENTIA. Goodnight, friends.

CATO (*turning back*). He could always kill himself. That would be a noble act.

Exeunt SENATORS. *Enter* SOSITHEUS, *very sick.*

TERENTIA. Somebody has to take charge. Have the contents of this house packed up and removed, Tiro. Send the valuables to Lucullus for safekeeping – it will have to be done secretly – the house is watched.

TIRO. I've made a start. His books are the most precious things he owns.

TULLIA. I'll help.

TERENTIA. I wonder if I should go and speak to that woman? Our neighbour – his sister –

TIRO. Clodia? No! I'd advise against it –

TERENTIA. She has influence with her brother. I've heard they're close – indecently close.

TIRO. Yes but –

TERENTIA. But what? To save my husband I'd be prepared to swallow my pride – talk to her – woman to woman. What have I to lose now? (*Exits.*)

SOSITHEUS. Do you think they'll attack the house again? This time I won't be much help...

TIRO. They'll not make their move until Clodius's law takes effect. We've a few days grace.

TULLIA. You shouldn't be out of bed, Sositheus. (*Exits.*)

TIRO. Give me your arm –

SOSITHEUS. I'm dying.

TIRO. Sit here – it's just a fever –

SOSITHEUS. That's not true... Tiro... There's something you must know... I can't carry this burden to my grave. The letters... I copied out the letters.

TIRO. What letters?

CICERO *appears, unnoticed, dressed in mourning, broken and frail.*

SOSITHEUS. The warning letters Catiline was supposed to have written... Our master wrote them... Cicero dictated them to me. I was the hooded messenger. Crassus knew – he beat it out of me when the master sent me to collect the title deeds of this house. Don't be angry.

CICERO. Poor boy – you must have been terrified.

SOSITHEUS. Master!

CICERO. Why didn't you come to me? I'd have forgiven you – put your mind at rest... It was my fault – I should never have involved you. Go and sleep – poor boy...

He embraces SOSITHEUS, *who goes.*

It should have been you... I should have asked you to do the copying

TIRO. Why didn't you?

CICERO. Have I hurt your feelings?

TIRO. A little.

CICERO. You've too many scruples, Tiro. Politics is a dirty business. I could never have carried off such a deception under your disapproving gaze. Is he dying?

TIRO. He doesn't have long. The cancer will take him.

CICERO. I've made a decision. I'm going to ask Caesar for that legateship. Then I'll stay – and fight on. Dare you come with me?

TIRO. If you want me to.

CICERO. I must defend what's left of the Republic... Somehow... Terentia's put backbone into me. Her ancestors –

TIRO (*echoing*). Saw off Hannibal –

CICERO. Saw off Hannibal...

Scene Twelve

CAESAR*'s camp on the Field of Mars. A* STANDARD-BEARER. *A bright, enthusiastic* YOUNG OFFICER.

YOUNG OFFICER. Wait here, Senator. I'll ask if he'll see you.

YOUNG OFFICER *goes in to* CAESAR.

CICERO. He likes to keep his visitors waiting.

TIRO. Do you remember – we visited him when you were Consul – and he was a nobody living in the slums?

CICERO. How could I forget?

Young SOLDIERS *come out of* CAESAR*'s tent, laughing.*

YOUNG OFFICER. You can come in now.

CAESAR *– first time in military uniform – at a campaign table, signing documents and handing them to* SECRETARIES.

CAESAR. Out.

TIRO, SECRETARIES *and* OFFICERS *leave*.

My dear Cicero… (*Studies* CICERO.) It distresses me greatly to see you reduced to this condition. How can I help?

CICERO. I've come to accept your offer – to serve as your legate.

CAESAR. Have you indeed! I must say you've left it rather late. So! Clodius's law takes effect at midnight?

CICERO. It does.

CAESAR. It's immunity from prosecution you're after then? The choice comes down to an alliance with me, or to be strangled by the public executioner?

CICERO (*uncomfortable*). Or exile.

CAESAR. Well, that's hardly very flattering! (*Laughs.*) In the summer, when I made the offer, you were in an infinitely stronger position than you are now.

CICERO. You promised that if my life were in danger, I could come to you.

CAESAR. Six months ago, Clodius wasn't much of a threat. Now he's master of Rome. Yes – I'd say you're in danger. Considerable danger.

CICERO. Caesar – if you're asking me to beg –

CAESAR. I'm not asking you to beg. I would, however, like you to explain. How would I benefit by appointing you to my staff? What have you to offer me?

CICERO (*grim*). Well… Since you press me – I'd say that while you still enjoy huge support among the People, you've lost what little influence and respect you had in the Senate. My position is the reverse. I've lost the confidence of the mob – my support in the Senate remains strong… The more Clodius persecutes me, the more it increases.

CAESAR. You're offering to protect my interests in the Senate?

CICERO. I would represent your views… When the need arose
  – I could relay their views back to you.

CAESAR. Your loyalty would be exclusively to me?

CICERO. My loyalty has always been, and will always be, to
  my country. In reconciling your interests with those of the
  Senate, we'd both be loyally serving the State –

CAESAR. But I don't give a fuck for the Senate – or their
  interests… My interests are Rome's interests. My interests
  come first and the State benefits from my achievements…

  I once marched through a village in the foothills of the
  Pyrenees – can't remember its name – I doubt it had one –
  a complete shithole. Pouring with rain – the most miserable
  place I've ever been in – and one of my officers said to me –
  I suppose he was trying to make a joke – 'You know, I'll bet
  even here there are men jostling for power – and there's fierce
  competition and bitter jealousies over who wins first place…'
  I said to him, 'I'd rather be First Man here than second man in
  Rome.' And I meant it, Cicero – I really meant it. True story.
  You see? Do you understand at last… who I am?

CICERO. I believe I do. You've always been a puzzle to me.
  I think I've just solved it. Thank you for your honesty.
  (Suddenly laughs.)

CAESAR. What's funny?

CICERO. Here are the two of us – and I'm the one they're
  driving out of Rome for seeking to make myself a tyrant.

CAESAR (grins). You're right… it really is very funny.

CICERO. There's no point in going on – you're off to conquer
  the world – I must go into exile –

CAESAR. Don't say that! You can be my legate – of course you
  can. Come, Cicero – really! (Extends his hand.) I'm
  surrounded by soldiers, and dreary old bores – we're the two
  cleverest people alive – just think what we could accomplish
  for Rome if we work together! Come!

CICERO. We could never work together.

CAESAR. Why? Why ever not?

CICERO. I'd want to be First Man in your village... If I couldn't be first, I'd still want to be free – free from fear – free to speak out against corruption wherever I encountered it... I'd want to be safe – to feel I was protected by strong laws... This need you have, Caesar – to set yourself above us all chills me... You're more brutal that Catiline, more vicious than Clodius...

CAESAR (*prepared to consider the possibility for the first time*). Am I?

CICERO. You'll not rest until you have the whole world grovelling on its knees.

Scene Thirteen

TERENTIA, *a* SLAVE *holding little* MARCUS *in his arms,* TULLIA, SENATORS, FRIENDS, SLAVES.

TERENTIA. Caesar offered you his protection?

CICERO. He did... I turned him down.

TERENTIA *lets out a howl – sinks to her knees.* CICERO *kneels and holds her.*

TERENTIA. Why! Why are you putting your family through this? Give me my life back – my home – go back to Caesar – beg – beg! –

CICERO. I can't do it –

TERENTIA. Why – in the name of all the gods? Why!

CICERO. What is a life? I'd move – I'd breathe – I'd speak – I'd laugh sometimes, or weep... But Cicero? An empty shell. Whatever thing Cicero *is* – would cease to exist...

TERENTIA *clings to him weeping silently.*

Terentia... What's become of my brave wife – a woman who could see off Hannibal?

TERENTIA. Don't speak... Just...

CICERO. Marriage to me has reduced you to this… this misery… I'm sorry.

TERENTIA. I have lived only for you. What is there for me now? (*Exits.*)

TULLIA. Where will you go?

CICERO. South – to Brundisium. We'll find a boat – who knows… As my homeland rejects me, I'll trust the winds and currents to decide my fate… My dearest daughter…

CICERO and TULLIA – a long embrace. Nothing is said. Exeunt all but CICERO and TIRO. Drums and noise. MOB approaching.

TIRO. They're coming. We'd better hurry.

CICERO. I hear trumpets.

TIRO. From the Field of Mars. Caesar's leaving Rome.

CICERO. He's off to conquer the world. Let's hope he leaves us a place to hide – somewhere that's escaped his notice.

CICERO and TIRO steal away. Trumpets of CAESAR's army grow louder, CLODIUS, with young MARK ANTONY, leads in his MOB, drumming, with torches shouting slogans.

MARK ANTONY. Death to the tyrant!

CLODIUS. Burn out the Enemy of the People – vengeance, vengeance, vengeance!

CLODIA drags on TERENTIA – who is being flogged.

CLODIA. Kneel! Beg!

The MOB takes over Rome. CLODIUS burns down CICERO's house.

MOB. Power to the People! Freedom! Freedom! Freedom!

CLODIUS comes forward and speaks to the audience.

CLODIUS. Welcome to Rome!

The theatre fills with smoke and flames.

End of Play Three.

PLAY FOUR

CAESAR

Prologue

Trumpet calls. CICERO, TIRO, MARCUS *and* SERVANTS, *bedraggled, on the road, are returning to Italy. Sound of cavalry, and distant shouted orders.*

CICERO. Cavalry…?

TIRO. Praetorians. Red crests…

MARCUS. Kicking up a lot of dust… Four or five hundred – I'd say.

CICERO. Step off the road – let them pass.

TIRO. I don't like it. What if they're coming to arrest you? Or worse?

CICERO. If this is how my life is to end, so be it. The Saviour of the Republic – the Father of the Nation – hacked to death at the roadside by Julius Caesar's Praetorian Guard!

MARCUS. At least it will be quick.

TIRO. There are worse endings.

CICERO. Tiro – it was a joke! If Caesar wanted my head he'd have taken it years ago.

MARCUS. Can that be…? Yes! It's Caesar's personal standard –

TIRO. He's right – it's the man himself.

MARCUS. That's a good sign, isn't it, Father?

CICERO. Where there's life there's hope.

TIRO. Wouldn't count on it. Not with Caesar.

POPILLIUS. Clear a way – keep back!

Enter CAESAR, *with* ENTOURAGE *in riding cloaks, including* MARK ANTONY, HIRTIUS, PANSA, DOLABELLA *and* DECIMUS, *others.* POPILLIUS *carries* CAESAR*'s personal standard.* CAESAR – *unreadable* – *looks* CICERO *up and down.*

CAESAR. Just as I expected – not a scratch on him – entirely unscathed! I've fought a civil war – Death runs amok in every corner of Rome's Empire – yet Cicero gives fate the slip – again and again… How does he manage it?

Sycophantic laughter from his people.

I've always said he'd outlive us all? Was I not right, Tiro?

TIRO. Only time will tell, Caesar.

DECIMUS. You're right – you're always right, Caesar.

CICERO. I'm glad of your prediction, Dictator… As, these days, you're the only man with the authority to make it come true.

CAESAR. Good! I see we understand each other. (*Bursts out laughing.*) Oh, I've missed you, dear friend! Walk with me. See – I've come to meet you to show my respect… What do you want to do?

CICERO. I'd like to return to Rome. If you'll permit it.

CAESAR. Hmmmm. Promise you'll cause me no further trouble?

CICERO. I'm ready to swear it.

CAESAR. But what would you do in Rome? You'll want to celebrate my Triumphs – who wouldn't? But the law courts are closed – nothing to occupy you there. I'm not sure I want you making speeches in the Senate.

CICERO. I'll not go near the Senate. I shall retire from public life – I'm finished with politics.

CAESAR. How will you spend your time?

CICERO. I'll write.

CAESAR. What?

DECIMUS. Nothing against Caesar, I hope? –

CICERO. Philosophy. I thought I might usefully adapt the Greeks for our own times – Plato – Aristotle –

CAESAR. Excellent! We approve of statesmen who know when it's time to leave the stage, and transform themselves into harmless philosophers. You may return to Rome.

CICERO. Thank you, Caesar.

CAESAR. Might you lecture too? I could send you a couple of my more promising young men for instruction. (*Looking at* HIRTIUS.) Hirtius here will be Consul one day – and Pansa. You could teach them how to handle the Senate.

CICERO. Philosophy tends to give young men ideas. Freedom of thought is dangerous to dictators – wouldn't you worry I might corrupt them?

CAESAR. You've never worried me, Cicero! (*Laughs*.) There are lines you dare not cross. You've not been a military man, have you? Afraid of risking your skin... Everything on a throw of the dice? (*Studies him*.) Any other favours?

CICERO. I'd like to be relieved of my Governorship of Cilicia.

CAESAR. It's done.

CICERO. Doesn't it require a vote of the Senate?

CAESAR. I am the vote of the Senate.

Sycophantic laughter.

CICERO. Ah... Then you're not planning to restore the Republic?

CAESAR. Rotten timber. Can't rebuild with rotten timber. This your son?

CICERO. Marcus.

CAESAR. A soldier?

MARCUS. Yes, Caesar – I... fought at Pharsalus.

CAESAR. Against me?

MARCUS. Yes, Caesar.

CAESAR. Brave boy!

CICERO. Marcus is going to be a philosopher too – I'm sending him to study in Athens.

CAESAR. Wise father, wise son! (*Strokes* MARCUS.) But you'd be happier soldiering, wouldn't you, lad?

MARCUS. Oh yes, Caesar!

CAESAR. Thought so. Well then… (*Laughs.*) Oh, how I've missed you! Embrace me. Goodbye. Live a little longer – if you can manage it.

Goes suddenly – his ENTOURAGE, *wrong-footed, hurry after him. As he leaves,* CAESAR, DECIMUS, *and others roar with laughter – we presume at some joke* CAESAR *has cracked about* CICERO.

POPILLIUS. Keep up, lads! Follow the standard.

MARCUS. I just met Julius Caesar – he touched me – he saw right into my soldier's heart!

CICERO. I've fathered a fool – how could it have occurred?

TIRO. He seemed perfectly amiable – as tyrants go.

CICERO. You see only his calm and glittering surface, Tiro. You've never peered down into the murky depths –

TIRO. You have, I suppose?

CICERO. I've caught an occasional glimpse of the monsters that lurk and coil there…

He sets off back the way he came.

TIRO (*to* MARCUS). Lurk and coil. That's one for the book.

MARCUS. You'll be back in Rome for Caesar's Triumphs then. That will be something!

CICERO. Yes – something to avoid.

Exeunt. TIRO *hangs back.* CICERO *remains centre, worrying – not really in the action, nor out of it. He listens to* TIRO's *summary with a sinking heart. Revolted by all the slaughter.*

Scene One

TIRO. I've misplaced a volume of this book I'm writing about Cicero's life. In it I tell how many of the characters you got to know last time perished…

Military music.

Pompey fought Caesar for the mastery of the world and lost – his armies were defeated at Pharsalus and he was murdered in Egypt. Some eunuchs cut off his head.

EUNUCHS *bring in* POMPEY*'s head. It's placed near* CICERO *– as if he's guilty of failing to prevent civil war.*

Cato committed suicide – sliced open his stomach and dragged out his own intestines. Ughh…

The loathsome Crassus led seven legions – that's forty-five thousand soldiers – against the Parthians. They were massacred – Crassus had his head cut off too.

PARTHIANS *bring in* CRASSUS*'s head. And other* SOLDIERS*' hacked limbs.*

Who else? Clodius's reign of terror ended when he was beaten up and murdered in a roadside brawl.

GLADIATORS *drag in* CLODIUS*'s bloody corpse.* FULVIA *follows and beats her breast and weeps. The body parts and heads form a pile. The pile of corpses is too much for* CICERO *– he leaves in disgust, sickened and queasy.*

Clodius's wife – Fulvia – after shedding a few crocodile tears, married Mark Antony – now Caesar's right-hand man –

FULVIA *goes off with* MARK ANTONY.

And Caesar, having conquered Gaul, Spain, Egypt, Africa – and a few other places – including a poky little hole nobody's ever heard of called Britain – I believe it's somewhere just beyond Europe – boasted of the millions – yes millions – he'd slaughtered – marched his army into Rome, made himself Dictator for life, and established a kind of order…

Suddenly he's shedding tears.

At the cost of liberty, freedom of speech, good laws – and
the many other Republican values that – for men of integrity,
like Cicero – make life worth living. Forgive the tears…
I also tell how my master gave me my freedom. I am no
longer his slave. We live mostly in the villa in Tusculum now
– or the villa in Naples – or the one in Pompeii – and spend
our time growing roses, watering the plants, and writing
philosophy… I think we're well out of it.

A blast of trumpets – drums.

His wars being over, Caesar enters Rome in Triumph.

SOLDIERS (*singing*).
Alleluia! Godlike Caesar. Home to Rome we bring
the spoils
Bald as your knob end – lock your wives away,
Wars and whores are all he knows.

(*Shouted over trumpet blasts.*) Io triumphe! Io triumphe! Io
triumphe!

Braying trumpets, MOB *cheering wildly. A Triumphal
procession. Enter* CAESAR, *face painted red, robes of
Jupiter, red boots, in a gold chariot – a* SLAVE *holding a
laurel wreath above his head.* OCTAVIAN (*sixteen here*)
MARK ANTONY, DECIMUS, BRUTUS, CASSIUS,
DOLABELLA, HIRTIUS, PANSA, *etc., etc. The chariot
axel breaks.* CAESAR *pitched to the ground near the corpse
and the heads. A groan from the crowd.* MARK ANTONY
and BRUTUS *rush to help him to his feet.*

MARK ANTONY. A terrible omen. The mob won't like it –

OCTAVIAN (*laughing*). The gods are angry!

CAESAR. Antony? What do I do – what's the form? Brutus?
Quickly –

BRUTUS. There's no precedent, Caesar. We should call a
meeting of the College of Priests –

CAESAR. How? In the middle of my Triumph? Antony – what
d'you say? You're an augur –

MARK ANTONY. You're the Pontiff – make a ruling.

OCTAVIAN. Act quickly, Uncle – it'll be taken as a sign of
Jupiter's displeasure –

CAESAR. How? What's to be done? Advise me!

OCTAVIAN. Smile at the People – mount the steps of Jupiter's
Temple on your knees as an act of atonement – Anything! So
long as it looks as if you know what you're doing –

CAESAR. Wise above his years! That's my boy!

DECIMUS. Not on your knees – it would be humiliating –

OCTAVIAN. Not the way my uncle would stage it – he'll turn it
into the climax of the show.

CAESAR. I'll do it.

CAESAR *kisses* OCTAVIAN *and presents him to the crowd.*
Cheers.

On with the Triumph!

He opens his arms to the crowd. Wild cheering. The
procession moves on – the body parts have gone.

SOLDIERS (*singing*).
Bald as your knob end – better lock your wives away,
Wars and whores are all he knows.

CAESAR. I'm not bald…! Just thinning a little. (*Angry.*) I don't
like that song! Make them sing something else.

SOLDIERS (*singing*).
Alleluia! Godlike Caesar.
Conquered Gaul and shagged their girls,
When King Nicomedes shagged him
All the world could hear his squeals –

CAESAR. I like that one even less –

SOLDIERS (*shouted over trumpet blasts*). Io triumphe! Io
triumphe! Io triumphe!

Scene Two

Peace. Birdsong. The terrace of villa overlooking the Bay of Naples. SLAVES gardening. CICERO, HIRTIUS, PANSA, TIRO. CASSIUS – a little apart – brooding. HIRTIUS is declaiming:

HIRTIUS. 'Let us rather blame those weak-willed men who fail in their duty to the State, in the vain hopes of avoiding toil and pain.'

CICERO. That's enough, Hirtius – spit out the pebbles... Good!

HIRTIUS. Thank you. (*Spits out the pebbles.*)

CICERO. Demosthenes taught us that the voice is like a muscle. Daily exercise will give it strength to reach the back row of the Senate, or the theatre – you may even be heard above the noise of the mob in the Forum.

PANSA. You should write a book on oratory.

CICERO. I have. Tiro is making a fair copy. I shall dedicate it to Brutus.

HIRTIUS. Because you admire his integrity?

CICERO. Because, of all my younger friends, Brutus needs it most. He says I've had my day – considers my style too high-flown – vulgar – full of tricks, dramatic pauses – (*Pause.*) appeals to heaven – (*Gesture.*) funny voices –

PANSA. All the tricks you're teaching us.

CICERO. The greatest orators in the world were my tutors – in my old age I pass on their wisdom to you. Wisdom doesn't date. I believe it's accepted I'm the foremost speaker of our times –

TIRO (*touch of mockery*). The voice and conscience of the nation.

CICERO. But Brutus says I am orotund and actorly. He favours a flat emotionless delivery, weighed down with dull facts and figures –

Enter DOLABELLA.

When I was Consul, I used to call on him to speak when I needed to empty the House quickly. Actorly? What is oratory but a dramatic performance? Dolabella?

DOLABELLA. Caesar has sent for me, Father-in-law – I must return to Rome.

CICERO. Must you?

DOLABELLA. Then… Farewell. Caesar asks me to remind you of your agreement – not to speak in the Senate.

CICERO. I've spoken once only, and that was in praise of his clemency. I never heard your master was averse to a little shameless flattery? Or has Caesar changed – now that he's a god?

DOLABELLA. Why do you provoke him?

CICERO. Farewell, Dolabella.

DOLABELLA. Caesar loves you, Cicero. He's forever saying you and he are the last two standing. Nevertheless… Well then, farewell

Exit DOLABELLA.

CICERO. I cannot bring myself to hate that young man. I suppose he loves my daughter… in his way.

HIRTIUS. It has to be said – he's treating her abominably.

CICERO (*through tears*). He is.

PANSA. All Rome knows of the mistress he keeps. His endless adulteries are –

TIRO. I think perhaps this is not the time for…

CICERO. I live only for my Tullia's happiness… I wish I'd kept her with me… Let's not…

He turns away. HIRTIUS *and* PANSA *look at each other.* CICERO *controls himself.*

HIRTIUS. Caesar has sent for us too. There's a great deal of work to be done before the army leaves Rome –

CICERO (*a forced laugh*). Ah yes – our Dictator's off to conquer the revolting Parthians – I'd forgotten. I suppose it will mean another fat book – *Caesar's Conquest of Gaul* – the sequel – *Parthia*. Dreadful Latin – 'With swords and spears Caesar made war on the Dalmatians, and laid waste the territories of the Alsatians.' It has all the poetry and stylistic beauty of a shopping list...

HIRTIUS. Do you think so? (*Winces – clutches his neck.*)

CICERO. Are you unwell, Hirtius? Has my lecture on *The Good Life* wearied you? You realise I'm doing my best to corrupt you? By the time you're Consuls I'll have lured you away from Caesar and turned you both into good Republicans – I have great hopes of you both.

HIRTIUS. I seem to have lost all my energy since I stopped soldiering – that's all it is.

CICERO. We'll continue our studies in Rome.

TIRO. He can't keep away. He's like the faithful dog that lay by his master's grave – hoping the old Republic might yet twitch back into life.

PANSA. I've noticed a change in Caesar since his return. He's less tolerant – harsh even. Take Dolabella's advice. When you do come to Rome, stay away from the Senate.

CICERO. That is my intention.

HIRTIUS. Farewell.

CICERO. You're good pupils – quick studies.

PANSA. Farewell. Caesar has appointed us next year's Consuls.

CICERO. Ah! In my day – there were still such things as elections. Farewell.

Exeunt HIRTIUS *and* PANSA.

TIRO. That was rather tactless. Had you forgotten that Hirtius helped Caesar with *The Conquest of Gaul* – in fact, he wrote most of it.

CICERO. Of course I'd not forgotten. That's why I made a point of mentioning it. You're very quiet, Cassius. What has Caesar in mind for you?

CASSIUS. He's sending me to govern Syria.

CICERO. Syria? I suppose there are worse places.

TIRO. Are there? Name one.

CASSIUS. I'm no jack-in-office – I'm a soldier. I should be leading this campaign against Parthia. Nobody knows the enemy and the terrain as I do – I saved the day after the Crassus disaster – who is Caesar? He's made himself Dictator for life – but he'll not be satisfied until he has a crown?

CICERO. Did I tell you about the last time he came here?

CASSIUS. Caesar? He was in this house?

CICERO. Just where you're sitting. He was spending Saturnalia across the bay – sent round a note inviting himself to lunch –

CAESAR. Don't go to any trouble – oysters, quail – a little lightly grilled turbot would do.

Lighting change. CAESAR *and senior officers –* MARK ANTONY, FULVIA, HIRTIUS, DECIMUS, PANSA, DOLABELLA, LEPIDUS, PISO, CALPURNIA, *others – are suddenly in the room. They are given wine, and canapes.*

TIRO. Twenty for lunch in the dining room – two thousand of his bodyguard picnicking outside – ruining the lawns –

CICERO. Pissing in the lavender beds. And worse.

CAESAR. Dear friend, I've been reading your books – wonderful stuff, and what style! You should have given up politics years ago, and written more –

CICERO. Times are bad – our children no longer obey us, and every fool believes he has a book in him…

CAESAR. Though I take issue with an argument in your *disputations*… You say only the man who leads a good life can overcome his fear of death.

CICERO. It's what I believe. What is the whole purpose of philosophy? To prepare ourselves to look death in the face, and not be afraid. The good man –

CAESAR. But I can prove your argument false. Nobody could say *I've* lived a good life. Yet I have no fear of dying. What's your answer to that?

CICERO. For a man with no fear of death, Caesar – you certainly travel with a large bodyguard.

Laughter – CAESAR *remains unreadable.*

CAESAR. As Head of State I have a responsibility to the People – to the nation. Rome needs me more than I need Rome.

CICERO. And what of the soul? Do you believe the soul immortal? Or is it extinguished as the body dies?

CAESAR. How can we know? What does it matter? In my own case the question is irrelevant. The soul of Caesar shall live in eternity. Naturally. Because I'm a god.

Nervous laughter from a couple of his entourage. CAESAR *silences them with a black look. He's not joking.*

CICERO. Tell me, Caesar – was this your plan from the beginning?

Pause.

CAESAR. Plan?

CICERO. Your dictatorship?

CAESAR (*studies him for a moment*). There was no plan. All I ever asked was the respect due to my rank and achievements. I responded to circumstances. Dictatorship… followed on quite naturally. It's just… politics. Now you tell me something: there was a time during your Consulship when you could have had me executed – quite legally – on a vote of the Senate. Do you ever regret not having me strangled?

CICERO. I never think about it.

CAESAR. Aha! A politician's answer! You should write your memoirs, you know.

CICERO. Perhaps.

CAESAR. But you'll let me glance through them before you publish, won't you?

CICERO. I'd be honoured.

CAESAR *and his* ENTOURAGE *vanish.*

Would you change places with such a man? I wouldn't...

CASSIUS. I have two regrets – accepting a pardon when I was taken prisoner after Pharsalus – and not killing him when I had the chance.

CICERO. Careful! – Walls have ears...

CASSIUS. I'd made up my mind to stab him – on the Cydnus River – but his luck held. His boat moored on the far bank – I couldn't get across. If only –

CICERO. If only! We sit contemplating the 'if onlys' of history while Caesar and his gang dismantle our Republic. I wouldn't repeat that story. You've not mentioned it to Hirtius and Pansa, I hope? Or, gods forbid, Dolabella? My house is full of Caesar's men.

CASSIUS. I trust nobody. Except you, Cicero. Our nation's faithful watchdog.

Scene Three

Antechamber in POMPEY*'s theatre. Preparations for a Senate. A big bust of* POMPEY*, high in a niche.* SLAVES *trying to knock a laurel wreath off the bust's head.* SLAVES *bring in* CAESAR*'s gold and ivory throne and place it on a dais.* SENATORS *assemble.* DECIMUS *is talking to a pair of* GLADIATORS.

SLAVE 1. Can't reach it.

SLAVE 2. Get a longer pole.

SLAVE 3. There must be a ladder somewhere.

Enter MARK ANTONY, *a little drunk, and* HIRTIUS.

HIRTIUS. Antony – wait!

MARK ANTONY. I'm not serving alongside Dolabella –

HIRTIUS. There's nothing you can do – Caesar appointed him –

MARK ANTONY. Well, what was Caesar thinking? He knows
I caught Dolabella screwing my wife –

HIRTIUS. Whose wife were you screwing at the time? Accept it
– like the rest of us – we all have to –

MARK ANTONY. Dolabella! Let's see what the Senate has to
say about it – I'm an augur – I'll block his appointment –

HIRTIUS. What's the point! Caesar will overrule you –

MARK ANTONY. Let him try!

HIRTIUS. I thought you were his friend –

MARK ANTONY. So why does he treat me like his messenger
boy? Who does he think I am? –

    DECIMUS, TREBONIUS *and* DOLABELLA *enter.*

DECIMUS. Antony.

DOLABELLA (*under his breath*). He's like a petulant child –

    MARK ANTONY *turns his back.* DOLABELLA *and*
    TREBONIUS *walk on and join* BRUTUS *and* CASSIUS.

DECIMUS. What's the matter with you?

MARK ANTONY. Where's Caesar?

DECIMUS. His throne's arrived. The spirit of god has entered
his temple – the bodily form won't be far behind.

HIRTIUS. We can't start without him. What's on the agenda?

MARK ANTONY. Who serves with me as Consul when Caesar
leaves Rome –

DECIMUS. I thought that had been settled –

HIRTIUS. It has – it's Dolabella.

MARK ANTONY. Nothing's settled until I've settled it!

SLAVES *take* CAESAR*'s throne away.*

DECIMUS. What's happening now?

HIRTIUS. Caesar must have cancelled the meeting.

MARK ANTONY. He can't!

DECIMUS. Can't he? I'd better go fetch him.

DECIMUS *joins* CASSIUS, BRUTUS *and others. Huddle.*
DECIMUS *leaves. Enter* PANSA.

PANSA. Is Caesar not coming?

SLAVE 1. Got it!

Loud cheers from the three SLAVES *as they knock the laurel
wreath from* POMPEY*'s statue. Enter* CICERO *and* TIRO –
apart.

TIRO. You're not thinking of speaking?

CICERO. Haven't made up my mind.

TIRO. You've been warned. Twice. You shouldn't even be here.
Caesar –

CICERO. Caesar's off on campaign – with luck, it's the last
we'll see of him for years.

TIRO. He's leaving Antony in his place. Better the devil you
know –

CICERO. Oh, do stop nagging! Who do you think you are – my
wife? Why are they so late starting? (*Studying the audience.*)
Who are all these strangers? Immigrants from Gaul and
Spain? I'll bet some of them can't even speak Latin... let
alone Greek.

TIRO. They're our new Senators. Caesar's appointments.

CICERO. Bought their seats I suppose. The Senate I knew bled
to death on the battlefield of Pharsalus. What's the point of
us now? Caesar tells us what he's going to do – we shout our
approval... I shame myself by remaining here. I have my
garden – I have my library – what more does a man need?
Gauls on the Senate! I ask you! It'll be the Germans next.

Find out why the session's cancelled – there's Cassius – ask
him. I'll wait outside in the sunshine.

Exit CICERO. TIRO *goes over to the* CONSPIRATORS.

TIRO. Forgive me for disturbing you, Cassius – Cicero wants to
know what's happening.

CASSIUS. But...

BRUTUS. What does he mean?

CASSIUS. What does he think's happening?

TIRO. I –

DOLABELLA. Where is he?

TIRO. Outside. He sent me to ask if the meeting's cancelled –
that's all –

BRUTUS. Caesar won't leave his house – the omens are
unpropitious. We've sent Decimus to make him change
his mind.

CASSIUS. Tell Cicero to be patient –

BRUTUS. Make him stay, Tiro.

Cheering, off.

TIRO. Well... He's not supposed to attend Senate meetings –

BRUTUS. We may need him. Just... Make him stay.

TIRO. He's lost interest in politics. Or politics has lost interest
in him –

CASSIUS. Caesar's coming.

SLAVES *bring back the throne. Exit* TIRO. *Re-enter* MARK
ANTONY, *followed by* TREBONIUS.

TREBONIUS. Dolabella will only serve out what's left of this
year. Accept it.

MARK ANTONY. I refuse to accept it! I'm an augur – I'm
Consul!

TREBONIUS. He's Dictator!

MARK ANTONY. Caesar appointed me to govern Rome in his place – now he ties my hands – damn him!

MARK ANTONY *storms off*. TREBONIUS *follows him*.

TREBONIUS. Antony – wait!

MARK ANTONY. Damn him!

SENATORS *file in*.

CICERO (*studying the gallery*). What are those gladiators doing up there? Thugs...

TIRO. What an ugly bunch! It's Decimus's turn to stage the games – they belong to him.

CICERO. Let's hope Caesar doesn't notice them – he'll probably make them Senators.

TIRO. He'll be putting slaves on the Senate next.

CICERO. Slaves? We're already in a majority. I've had enough – I'm going home.

TIRO. Too late. He'd see you leaving.

CICERO *joins the others*. CAESAR *enters fast, with an entourage, rejecting petitions thrust at him*. DECIMUS *telling him a joke*. CAESAR *wears a purple-and-gold toga – he is twirling a stylus – looking about him. He stops suddenly*.

DECIMUS. And the cook said: 'But you told me to brown my meat...'

CAESAR (*laughs*). Cicero! Come to see me off? Let's get on with it then. Where's Antony?

DECIMUS. Over there – arguing with Trebonius.

CAESAR. Fetch him.

DECIMUS *propels* CAESAR *forward*. SENATORS *stand*. CAESAR *sits on his throne*.

CAESAR. Sit. Dolabella?

DOLABELLA. Here, Caesar.

TILLIUS CIMBER. A petition, Caesar –

CAESAR. Not now.

TILLIUS CIMBER. A pardon for my brother –

CAESAR. Go away! Our only business is to settle this dispute between Antony and Dolabella –

TILLIUS CIMBER. But, Caesar –

CAESAR. Fetch Antony. Let them face one another –

TILLIUS CIMBER. I beg you, Caesar –

CAESAR. No! No more pardons! I've been too mild with my enemies – too merciful. The men I pardoned after Pharsalus broke their oaths – sneaked off to join the rebels in Spain – and –

TILLIUS CIMBER. My brother was not among them! Caesar, I beg you –

TILLIUS CIMBER *grabs the folds of toga around* CAESAR's *neck and pulls him towards him.*

CAESAR. Take your hands off me! –

TILLIUS CIMBER. On my knees, I beg you –

CAESAR. This is violence!

CASCA *stabs* CAESAR *in the neck. A mere scratch. He pulls back – shocked at himself.*

Casca? What are you doing?

CASCA. Tyrant!

CAESAR (*laughs*). Are you mad?

CASCA *tries to stab him again.*

CASCA. Help me!

TILLIUS CIMBER *feebly knifes* CAESAR *in the ribs.* CAESAR *laughs and swats* TILLIUS CIMBER *away.* CASCA *tries again. Nobody helps.*

CAESAR. Casca – you useless…! That's not how you do it!

CAESAR grabs CASCA's dagger, but then is overwhelmed in a confused frenzy of stabbing. He fights back furiously – wounding several with his stylus. BRUTUS and CASSIUS join in. CASSIUS accidentally stabs BRUTUS in the hand.

BRUTUS. Aghh – Cassius! That's my hand!

CAESAR. Useless! The whole pack of you!

CAESAR appears to be enjoying himself. Finally, DECIMUS rushes up to CAESAR and stabs him in the back – deeply and expertly – just once. CAESAR turns and holds onto him – looks into his eyes.

Decimus… Oh, not you… Surely not you…

Confusion. The ASSASSINS stab, then run out shouting slogans: 'Liberty! Freedom! Peace! Long Live the Republic! No kings! No Dictator!', etc. Frightened SENATORS run away. As BRUTUS runs past CICERO, he briefly grasps his hands.

BRUTUS. Cicero! We need you, Cicero! The Republic needs you! Come with us! Come to the Capitol!

BRUTUS runs out. CICERO – frozen to the spot – horror on his face. CAESAR – feet pointing towards POMPEY's statue – looks at CICERO – smiles.

CAESAR. They can't kill me… I'm not dead, old friend… I'm just… God…

He dies. CICERO has blood on him – where BRUTUS has touched him – horrified, he tries to wipe it off – still staring at CAESAR. Enter TIRO.

TIRO. We must get you away. Do you hear me? Take my arm –

CICERO. A few breaths ago the heart of the Empire… Now no one dares go near him – look…

TIRO leads CICERO, in a daze, out into the sunlight.

Don't they trust me? Why wasn't I told – ?

Outside, confusion. TIRO and CICERO are joined by QUINTUS. CICERO is slowly coming back to life. DOLABELLA and DECIMUS arrive.

DOLABELLA. Follow us to the Capitol – we need your voice.
Do you hear me? Father?

CICERO. Even you knew about this? –

QUINTUS. Brother?

DOLABELLA (*to* TIRO). Bring him to the Capitol, Tiro. I'll be
acting Consul now – I need his advice – (*Exits.*)

QUINTUS. What's happening? You've blood on your hands –
are you hurt?

DECIMUS. Caesar's been killed –

QUINTUS. Not possible!

CICERO. This is his blood.

QUINTUS. Tiro? Is he dead?

TIRO. As mutton.

QUINTUS. You mean…? Then Rome is free – Praise Jupiter!

DECIMUS. Offer thanks to the gods – and us. Tyranny is dead.

CICERO (*to* DECIMUS). Did they think me leaky? I ought to
be offended –

QUINTUS. You wouldn't have had the nerve – to look him in
the eye – to plunge in the knife…

DECIMUS (*to* CICERO). Could you have done it?

QUINTUS. I could.

DECIMUS. I did. I struck the blow that finished him.

CICERO. You're soldiers… So much blood…

QUINTUS. It's wonderful!

Cheering and anger from the CROWDS.

TIRO. Don't you feel any pity? A few weeks ago, you were
laughing with him over dinner – proud to have him as your
guest –

CICERO. Tiro! I'm amazed you could ask such a question –

TIRO. Seems a little two-faced – he was always very kind to me –

CICERO. Kind? Kind! We were his slaves! Have you forgotten what that feels like – to be given your freedom? Let's have no talk of pity!

TIRO. I was just saying –

CICERO. I shall go and offer my support –

TIRO. You can't! Caesar's people will think you were part of it –

CICERO. Let them!

TIRO. Lepidus – Caesar's Master of Horse – has five thousand soldiers on Tiber Island – if he turns them loose in the City there'll be a bloodbath... And where's Antony?

QUINTUS. Lepidus might be part of the conspiracy –

CICERO. They came together as one – friend and foe – united to save the Republic –

TIRO. That's more than you know. Best go home and bolt the doors – wait until dark – and then... We might get as far as Tusculum –

QUINTUS. That would look like cowardice in my brother.

TIRO. Well! Ha!

CICERO. Go on – say it.

TIRO. I'm only trying to stop him getting his throat cut. They'll all be running for their lives. We'll go to Tusculum – then on to Athens, to young Marcus – we must get right away –

CICERO. I shall go up to the Capitol and thank the men who've given me back my liberty.

QUINTUS. I'll come with you.

TIRO (*to himself*). You'll live to regret it.

They climb up to the Capitol. Doorway of the Temple of Jupiter Optimus Maximus.

GLADIATOR 1. Hey – hey – hey – you're not going in there.

CICERO. I am a Roman citizen – a free man.

GLADIATOR 2. I don't care who you are –

CICERO. This is my City – I go wherever I choose. Don't you know who I am?

GLADIATOR 1. No.

CICERO. I am Cicero. Saviour of the Republic – Father of the Nation.

TIRO. He's come to speak to Brutus and the rest.

GLADIATOR 2. They look harmless. Let 'em through.

CICERO, TIRO *and* QUINTUS *go into the Temple.*

GALDIATOR 1. Who was he?

GLADIATOR 2. Just some old fart. I think he once served as Consul.

Scene Four

Temple of Jupiter. Gloom. Statue of Jupiter. CONSPIRATORS *and their* SUPPORTERS. *Including:* CINNA, BRUTUS, CASSIUS, CASCA, DOLABELLA – *his arm round* DECIMUS*'s shoulder – many others.* CICERO, QUINTUS, *and* TIRO *enter. Applause.* BRUTUS *and* CASSIUS *and the rest come to shake* CICERO*'s hand.*

BRUTUS. Are you with us, Cicero?

CICERO. Not since your ancestor expelled Rome's kings, has there been anything to equal it! It's the noblest deed of our times! But why are you cooped up here like criminals? Come down to the Forum – rally the People to your cause. What's the plan?

BRUTUS. There is no plan. We're patriots, not demagogues. We've removed the Dictator – freed Rome of his tyranny.

CICERO. But, Brutus… Who's running the country?

CASSIUS. Nobody.

BRUTUS. Things will sort themselves out. In due course a new government will establish itself.

CICERO. How? Go down to the Forum – declare *yourselves* the new government –

BRUTUS. Ha! I hardly think that would be constitutional –

CICERO. But… But –

BRUTUS. We didn't pull down the tyrant in order to set ourselves up as tyrants in his place. How would it be legal?

CICERO. Make it legal! Call the Senate – now – here to this temple. You're both Praetors – you have the authority – declare a state of emergency – anything – but act! Act now – you must take control –

CASSIUS. He's right –

CICERO. Explain yourselves to the Roman People –

BRUTUS. Well… I don't know… Isn't it up to the Consul to summon the Senate? Perhaps someone should ask Mark Antony –

CICERO. Antony's alive! By all the gods – you mustn't let him anywhere near this business!

CASSIUS. Didn't I say so?

DOLABELLA. We should have put him down – along with his master – I offered to do it –

BRUTUS. Murder a Consul? What crime has he committed? It wasn't Antony who was trying to make himself king over us –

CICERO. Oh, give him time! Where's Antony now?

Enter GLADIATOR 2 *who talks to* DECIMUS – *they hurry out.*

CASSIUS. He'll be working the City – weeping with the mob – testing opinion among the Senators – gathering support –

CICERO. Which is exactly what you should be doing –

BRUTUS. Oh, come! (*Slight pause.*) Support? Support for what?

DOLABELLA. Antony will be out for blood once he sobers up
– mine especially. I am Consul elect – don't I have the
authority to call a meeting of the Senate?

BRUTUS. No, I don't think so. Not until your appointment has
been ratified by the Senate. But if –

DOLABELLA. Unless a meeting is called, how can –

Distant trumpet calls. Drums.

CICERO. Trumpets? What's happening?

CASSIUS. They're signalling. A legion's on the move –

CICERO. I beg you – go down into the Forum – win over the
People before it's too late!

DECIMUS. It's Lepidus – he's moving Caesar's veterans off
Tiber Island.

BRUTUS. What! No! He can't – he has no authority to bring
armed men into the City.

DOLABELLA. Can't he?

BRUTUS. It would be unlawful – no!

CASSIUS. We'll able to see for ourselves from up here.

*They rush out of the Temple to look down from the heights of
the Capitol.*

BRUTUS. This is all wrong! I sent messages to Lepidus – why
hasn't he sent an answer?

CASSIUS. There's your answer.

DOLABELLA. He's marching his soldiers onto the Field of
Mars.

BRUTUS. Lepidus is my brother-in-law – he wouldn't break
the law –

CICERO. Brutus, I beg you – before it's too late – speak to the
People! Fire them with the spirit of the old Republic. If
Lepidus traps you up here – if Antony seizes control –

BRUTUS. I'm not sure… If –

CICERO. Give the People a lead! –

CASSIUS. We've given them their freedom – why are we behaving as if we've done something shameful?

BRUTUS. Shameful! My ancestor drove King Tarquin out of Rome – today I've rid Rome of a tyrant – I'm ashamed of nothing –

CICERO. Then tell that to the mob down there!

BRUTUS. But… Well… I suppose somebody should say something – I can see the sense in that – if –

CICERO. Address them from the Rostra – win their hearts –

DECIMUS. My gladiators will protect you –

BRUTUS. But…

TIRO (*aside*). When they start tearing you apart, you can always run back up here and barricade yourself inside the citadel.

CICERO. Really, Tiro –

Exeunt – equivocal crowd noises, off.

Scene Five

CAESAR's *house. Panic.* PISO *comforts a weeping* CALPURNIA. FULVIA *is ordering* SLAVES *about – they are hurrying away chests full of documents.* PISO *leads* CALPURNIA *away.*

FULVIA. Carry everything to my house – hurry. Everything must go – we'll sort through it later –

MARK ANTONY *stumbles on, drunk and dishevelled.*

MARK ANTONY. Fulvia! What am I going to do, Fulvia? Tell me what to do! What's in those chests?

FULVIA. Caesar's papers. I've persuaded the wife they'll be safer at our house. I'll keep what's useful and burn the rest. Leave everything to me –

MARK ANTONY. The game's up – I'm finished –

FULVIA. Finished! I've not started. You're going to pull yourself together and take control – stop behaving like a fool –

MARK ANTONY. We'll all be dead by tomorrow –

FULVIA. The treasury's in the Temple of Ops – it's vital we get our hands on the money. If we're to seize control we need… Give me that! (*Snatching his cup – smacks him about.*) For once in your life, sober up! Is that too much to ask? Come with me!

Exeunt.

Scene Six

Noise of the MOB. *Temple of Jupiter. The* ASSASSINS *return gloomily from the Forum. Last on are* TIRO *and* CICERO.

TIRO. Could have been worse.

CICERO. Could it? I don't see how. Oh, Brutus! Where was the performance – the rousing call to arms – the speech of fire!

TIRO. It was like a history lecture – I've already forgotten everything he said –

CICERO. Not one single ringing phrase – no grand gesture – no tempest, no tears…

TIRO. Cassius spoke well.

CICERO. Well, of course – he's my pupil.

DOLABELLA. You should have spoken too, Cicero – you might have saved the day. They were all waiting for you – they know you always have the last word. Talking's what you do – it's all you do!

CICERO. I had no part in it – I wasn't thought trustworthy! What right had I to speak for Brutus and the rest? They're dithering – and now they've left it too late – Lepidus's soldiers are streaming into the City…

TIRO. We can't even make it home. The streets are too dangerous.

CICERO. We'll be safe enough in the Temple.

TIRO. They'll come up here tonight and cut our throats.

CICERO. Decimus's gladiators will protect us.

TIRO. What? Hired thugs? What do they care for the Republic? If you'd listened to me we'd be halfway to Athens by now.

CICERO. I defended the Republic in my youth, I shall not desert her in my old age.

TIRO. And fine words butter no parsnips. Too late now – barricaded in up here on the Capitol – the mob prowling around down there – Caesar's veterans out for blood –

CICERO. For gods' sake, let me think! Liberators! What a spineless, gutless nest of ninnies –

TIRO. Careful.

BRUTUS, *and* CASSIUS, *join them.*

BRUTUS. I thought my speech went rather well. The People listened intently. Nodding their heads –

CICERO. Now listen to me, Brutus. All is not lost. Lepidus and Antony are both Caesar's men – Antony has power as Consul but no soldiers – Lepidus has soldiers but no legal authority to deploy them. They've always disliked each other – so our best course would be to drive a wedge between them.

BRUTUS. No. If Antony is willing to convene a meeting of the Senate. If –

CICERO. I say we deal directly with Lepidus – cut out Antony altogether –

BRUTUS. But Antony is Consul! –

CICERO. And if we don't stop him –

DOLABELLA. Couldn't I –

BRUTUS. How many times must I say it! The law – *the law* – is on Antony's side! We must keep on the right side of the law –

CICERO. Very well then, let's talk about law: Antony is Consul only by Caesar's decree –

DOLABELLA. As am I –

CICERO. Caesar is dead! – his dictatorship died with him – and as Caesar's dictatorship – obtained by force – was illegal, so Antony's Consulship must be illegal. We cannot allow Antony to continue in office. That's law for you – chapter and verse.

BRUTUS. Yes, I see... Well... I concede the point... But if the People think Antony is Consul then he's Consul, whatever a lawyer might say –

CICERO. Oh, 'the People'! Brutus! Try and understand! It was not enough to kill Caesar –

BRUTUS. Someone should call a meeting. If –

DOLABELLA. I'd be prepared to step in –

BRUTUS. Perhaps we should reconsider –

CICERO. OH, ALL YOU GODS!! (*Collapses.*) Do as you please – I've finished with you. Your lack of resolution will get us all killed!

BRUTUS. Very well. Then we're agreed?

CASSIUS. Are we?

BRUTUS. We'll send a delegation to Antony – men who have served as Consul – and who took no part in the assassination?

SERVIUS SULPICIUS. I'll go.

MARCELLUS. I'll volunteer.

BRUTUS. Cicero?

CICERO. Try to imagine what's going through Antony's head. He's positioning himself to take over Caesar's dictatorship – the repulsive Fulvia will be urging him on. Our one remaining hope is to lure Lepidus over to our side. We need an army!

CASSIUS. I agree with Cicero.

BRUTUS. But…

TIRO (*to* CICERO *aside*). Come outside – something's happening down in the Forum.

CICERO *and* TIRO *leave them arguing and come to look down onto the Forum.*

See – on the rostra – talking to the mob. The one in a General's red cloak –

CICERO. Lepidus.

TIRO. And behind him – waiting to speak?

CICERO. Antony… They've already joined forces. We're lost – finished…

TIRO. You did your best.

CICERO. It wasn't enough… In a way I'm glad, Tiro. A great burden has been lifted from my shoulders. The fate of the Republic – my own fate – everything's out of my hands now. What incompetence! Such manly resolution in striking Caesar down – such childlike folly in their lack of forethought! If only they'd taken me into their confidence!

TIRO. If only!

CICERO. At least I shall die on the side of right. I've always acted according to my conscience – always dealt justly, without fear or favour.

CASSIUS *joins them.*

TIRO. Well… most of the time. Although –

CICERO. I saw a flicker of hope for the Republic – I allowed myself to imagine it restored, renewed, surer, stronger… I've been deluding myself, haven't I?

CASSIUS. Antony – unprompted – has summoned a meeting of the Senate tomorrow, at first light. We've taken a vote. Will you go and speak for us, Cicero? For the Senate and the Republic?

The ASSASSINS *join them.*

BRUTUS. Cicero? What do you say? Will you once more be the voice of Rome?

CICERO. But this is Antony! Antony... Oh, very well! I'll do what I can. If they cut my throat, what does it matter? I am old.

CASSIUS. To die in defence of freedom – could there be a better death?

BRUTUS. None.

BRUTUS *embraces* CICERO.

TIRO (*aside to* DOLABELLA). If push came to shove I could think of a few.

BRUTUS. Father of the Nation!

Exeunt all but CICERO *and* TIRO.

CICERO. It may well be my final speech, Tiro – it must be my finest. You'll record it for posterity. I shall speak of liberty – of the nature of a republic, and the healing role of statesmen... And conclude with incontrovertible arguments for the moral justification of the slaughter of tyrants.

TIRO. You're infuriating! Why couldn't you have stayed away? Sometimes you can be such a... a... philosopher!

Scene Seven

Temple of the Goddess Tellus – the Earth. A crowd of menacing
VETERANS. MARK ANTONY *makes a sacrifice at the altar*
on the temple steps. He leads the Senate inside, followed by
LEPIDUS *(red cloak),* CICERO, TIRO *and* DOLABELLA.
An ivory curule chair is set on a dais. MARK ANTONY –
sober for once – stands, and takes out a written speech.

MARK ANTONY. Caesar was my dearest friend… but I place
love of my country above my love for Caesar… As your
Consul, guided by that patriotic love, I set aside all thoughts
of revenge, all personal sorrow – every private consideration.
Last night I was with Caesar's widow, and Piso, here – her
father. Calpurnia requests only two things – an end to
bloodshed.

Murmurs of approval.

And funeral rites for her husband appropriate to the honours
he won in life.

Silence.

Brutus, Cassius, Decimus and the rest are patriots – men
from Rome's most distinguished families… We deplore the
brutality of their act, but we salute the nobility of their aim.
Gentlemen, too much Roman blood has been spilt over these
past five years – now comes a god-given opportunity for a
lasting peace. Clemency was the mark of Caesar's statecraft
– let us show clemency to Brutus, Cassius, and the rest. In
the interests of peace and reconciliation we pardon them…
guarantee their safety. Let's ask them to come down from the
Capitol – to join us in our deliberations.

CICERO. Gentlemen, let us praise Antony for his wisdom. Let
reconciliation and moderation be our watchwords. I take
issue with only one small point: 'clemency' means pardon –
pardon implies a crime. The killing of the Dictator was many
things, *but it was no crime.* Do you remember the story of
Thrasybulus, who, three centuries ago, overthrew the Thirty
Despots of Athens?

TIRO (*aside to* DOLABELLA). Who could forget it?

CICERO. Thrasybulus instituted what was called an 'amnesty' for his opponents – amnesty from their Greek word 'amnesia' meaning 'forgetfulness'. That, I suggest, is what's needed here – not forgiveness but forgetfulness… A noble undertaking lies before us. I urge you all – let's join together to unite the Senate and People of Rome, and rebuild our wartorn Republic in a spirit of friendship and peace.

MARK ANTONY. I pray to all the gods –

DOLABELLA (*interrupting*). As your Consul-elect I propose that we offer amnesty to all who took part in the assassination of the tyrant –

PISO. No! –

LEPIDUS. No! Wait! It can't be right for us to pardon Caesar's murderers – grant an amnesty – call it what you will – until we've heard how they can excuse themselves –

PISO. Lepidus is right. And it's not only Brutus and Cassius who have done this – the guilty men are those who incited them to the murder –

DOLABELLA. There's a motion before the Senate – to grant amnesty to Caesar's assassins. Those in favour?

Approval.

Opposed?

LEPIDUS. I am opposed.

PISO. And I –

DOLABELLA. The motion is carried.

MARK ANTONY. Lepidus's objection is noted. And Piso's –

DOLABELLA. Send a messenger to the Capitol inviting Brutus and Cassius to join us. We'll adjourn until we have their reply –

MARK ANTONY, DOLABELLA *and* LEPIDUS *argue furiously in the background.*

CICERO. I am… speechless!

TIRO. Wrong-footed you, didn't he? Moderation was *your* theme – Antony got in before you.

CICERO. What's his game?

TIRO. Perhaps there isn't a game. Perhaps he's sincere.

CICERO. Sincere! Antony! No – he has a plan, but he's keeping it well hidden.

TIRO. Unless it's somebody else's plan... Tread carefully. The Temple's surrounded by Caesar's veterans – itching to cut your throat.

CICERO. Thank you for reminding me.

MARK ANTONY *returns to his chair.*

MARK ANTONY. Gentlemen, the Senate's first responsibility is the security of the State. When news of Caesar's death reaches Gaul – those tribes he recently pacified may imagine Rome weak and leaderless. They may rebel. So, in this time of emergency, we must show ourselves strong, and single-minded. I therefore propose that all laws promulgated by Caesar – his appointments of Consuls, Praetors, and Governors made before the Ides of March – be accepted and confirmed by this Senate.

Worried mumbling.

CICERO. Including your own appointment as Consul?

MARK ANTONY. Unless you've some objection?

CICERO. And Dolabella's as your fellow Consul? That was also Caesar's wish. I believe you are seeking to block Dolabella's appointment with your auguries?

MARK ANTONY (*flash of anger*). In the interests of unity, I am prepared to serve alongside Dolabella –

CICERO. And Brutus and Cassius will continue as Praetors for the rest of the year? And afterwards will serve as Governors of Macedonia and Syria?

MARK ANTONY. I –

CICERO. And Decimus – as appointed by Caesar – will be Governor of our northern territories, and take immediate command of the legions allotted to him?

MARK ANTONY. Yes – yes, and yes.

Surprise, applause, some protest.

Now will your side now agree to my motion? All acts and appointments issued before Caesar's death to be confirmed.

LEPIDUS. Yes – together with the grants promised by Caesar to his loyal soldiers – I want my men paid, or they'll riot.

TIRO (*aside*). Compromise – live to fight another day.

CICERO (*aside*). Cato would be ashamed of me.

TIRO (*aside*). Cato's dead.

CICERO (*stands*). I can't speak for Brutus, Cassius, Decimus and the rest. But if the Senate judges the laws imposed upon us by Caesar best serve the good of the State – I say with the others – let Caesar's acts and appointments stand.

Approval.

MARK ANTONY. These motions are carried.

Applause.

So that future strife may be avoided, let us here and now abolish forever the title and functions of Dictator. On pain of death, let no one man ever again seek to set himself above the laws and wishes of the Senate and People of Rome.

Approval. Enter BRUTUS, CASSIUS, DECIMUS *and others, who take their places.*

Welcome back to your places, gentlemen. I hope, Cassius, you've left your dagger at home today?

CASSIUS. And I hope, Antony, you've abandoned any thought of stepping into the tyrant's shoes? I could easily run home and fetch a big sword.

Laughter.

DECIMUS. With the Senate's permission, I shall go and take up the governorship of my northern province.

MARK ANTONY. That has been agreed.

DECIMUS. I shall have twelve thousand men under my command. If there are disturbances in the City, you have only to summon me. The People are confused – leaderless – angry… Anything could happen.

MARK ANTONY. Our only other business is to decide what to do with Caesar's body.

PISO. And his will. The Dictator – my son-in-law – made a new will six months ago – nobody knows its contents. I am named executor – I intend to read the will to the People –

CASSIUS. No! Our laws say that the body of a tyrant shall be dragged through the City and thrown in the Tiber – and that all his property is forfeit to the State –

PISO. Absurd! We have just ratified Caesar's laws. We can't dishonour the memory of the man who gave us these laws – the People would riot –

LEPIDUS. If they riot, I'll deal with them –

CASSIUS. I say no public funeral. At Clodius's cremation his supporters burned down the Senate House. We have made a fragile peace – it would be madness to put it at risk.

MARK ANTONY. I shall preside over Caesar's funeral. There will be no riots. I shall speak with moderation – words of reconciliation. I shall calm the City with mildness and reason. I know what's in the People's hearts. The dignity of my consular office will ensure good order.

BRUTUS. In the interests of concord, I will support the proposal. I share Cassius's unease. But I fear Caesar's veterans would revolt if we dishonour their much-loved commander – or deny him his burial rites.

PISO. What message would it send to the Gauls if we throw the body of their conqueror into the river?

MARK ANTONY. Anything to add, Cicero?

CICERO (*shakes his head. Faintly*). Nothing.

MARK ANTONY. We'll discuss Caesar's will tomorrow at my house. The Senate will decide who should be present as witnesses, and how we should proceed...

Scene Eight

Outside MARK ANTONY*'s* (POMPEY*'s*) *house,* CICERO, TIRO *and* DECIMUS *arrive.*

TIRO. We must get you away from Rome.

CICERO. Why? If I can make Antony respect the Senate – keep him on the path of moderation – after years of tyranny and chaos, I could be witnessing the birth of a revitalised Republic.

DECIMUS. I command the Senate's army – more than double the force Lepidus has. Leave me to deal with Antony. Stay away – go to Athens. The Republic is safe in my hands.

TIRO. Good advice. We wouldn't want to be anywhere near Rome when they cremate Caesar's body.

CICERO. I'm worried about this will... I wonder if Antony knows what's in it?

TIRO. How could he? It's been locked up in the Temple of Vesta.

CICERO. Caesar died the richest man in the world – he might have left Antony enough money to bribe his way to another dictatorship.

They go into MARK ANTONY*'s house. A group of* SENATORS *waiting.*

If Antony – forbid it, gods – ever gets his hands on Caesar's gold...

DECIMUS. I wish you'd stop worrying about Antony, he's a spent force.

DECIMUS *joins the other group.*

CICERO. I hope he's right.

He sees FULVIA, FULVIA *sees* CICERO, *scowls, and turns her back on him.*

The loathsome Fulvia? What business has that bloodsucker at the reading of Caesar's will? There's a rank smell in here – a distinctly fishy smell. Were poor Cato not dead, I could think he'd got here ahead of us.

TIRO. D'you think Fulvia makes it a point of principle to marry all your bitterest enemies – first Clodius, now Antony? How does she manage it? Master?

CICERO (*lost in thought*). I'm wondering –

TIRO. It's not Antony's game, is it? –

CICERO. It's Fulvia's. Of course it is!

TIRO. Puts things in very different light.

CICERO. More poisonous than Antony and twice as cunning, she won't sleep until her husband's the second man in the State.

TIRO. Second?

CICERO. She'll be first. And a worse tyrant than Caesar ever was.

Enter CHIEF VESTAL.

MARK ANTONY. Lucius Calpurnius Piso will read Caesar's will.

PISO. Examine the seal, gentlemen. Untampered with – unbroken. And now…

CHIEF VESTAL *hands* PISO *the will – he breaks the seal.*

Won't bore you with the usual preamble… Let's come to the substance – (*Reads.*) Caesar leaves his whole estate to… 'Any son born to him after the drawing up of this document…'

FULVIA. I think we can be certain no son has been born to Caesar in the past six months.

PISO. 'In the absence of a son, and failing of his heirs in the first degree, his estates…' As far as I can make out… would go to Mark Antony…

FULVIA. Oh, Caesar!

PISO. And to Decimus…

DECIMUS. To me!

FULVIA. It's an outrage! – He enriches the man that killed him! –

MARK ANTONY. But… Who are these heirs in the first degree?

PISO. Er… They are… 'The three male descendants of his late sister.'

FULVIA. Are they living? I'm confused –

PISO. All his wealth – money, properties, interest – is to be divided as follows: 'one eighth each to Lucius Pinarius, and Quintus Pedius' –

MARK ANTONY. Never heard of them –

FULVIA. That can't be right –

PISO. 'And three quarters to his great nephew Gaius Octavius.'

Silence.

FULVIA. Who?

CICERO (*aside*). Who?

PISO. Three quarters? But that must amount to nearly –

FULVIA. Gaius Octavius?

DECIMUS. So, I get nothing?

PISO. 'Further – Gaius Octavius is…' Surely not… can this be…? (*Reads.*)

FULVIA. What is it, man? What does it say?

PISO. 'Gaius Octavius – whom he here adopts *as his son* – is henceforth to be known as Gaius Julius Caesar.'

TIRO (*aside*). His niece Atia's boy – a bright lad of eighteen – he's with the army – overseas in Macedonia.

PISO. 'To every citizen of Rome, Caesar leaves three hundred sesterces to be paid in cash... And his estates beside the Tiber are to become "The People's Park".'

FULVIA. A son? An adopted son?

PISO. That's what it says.

MARK ANTONY. Give it to me.

FULVIA. Antony. Leave it!

She gives him a look and goes. MARK ANTONY *follows her. The meeting begins to break up, muttering, troubled.*

TIRO. Well! Brutus and Cassius aren't going to like this! All the trouble they gave themselves to rid Rome of one Julius Caesar, and a new one pops up before the old one's decently buried.

CICERO. The boy's an irrelevance – he'll not survive long enough to claim his inheritance... But the will! The will is Pandora's Box. Gifts of cash to the People? Why does Caesar need their love and support – even though he's dead and buried.

Enter QUINTUS.

TIRO. But he's not buried, is he? Not yet.

QUINTUS. You should never have allowed this public funeral, brother – it's madness! –

CICERO. How could I prevent it?

QUINTUS. If the mob riots – if you lose control of the streets –

CICERO. If *I* lose control? What can I do? Blame our liberators. All their energies and plotting went into toppling Caesar – they never gave a thought to what would happen once they'd pulled him down.

QUINTUS. It's you the People will look to for answers.

CICERO. Why me? Why is it always – *always* – left to me to –

DECIMUS *joins them*.

DECIMUS. There's a good deal of unease about this funeral, Cicero. Men of sense are packing up and leaving Rome –

CICERO. How will that help restore the rule of law, Decimus?

DECIMUS. There's no leadership here. Only Lepidus has soldiers – and it's by no means certain he can control them – I can see how this will end. I'll go north, put my legions in readiness – sit tight – and wait to be called.

CICERO. What good are they in the north? – They're needed here – now –

DECIMUS. Cassius and Brutus have gone. You should go too –

QUINTUS. Good advice.

DECIMUS. Mark my words, it will end in looting and burning – (*Exits*.)

TIRO. Catiline and Clodius all over again –

CICERO. Not necessarily. Nobody wants a City in flames. It's in Antony's interests to keep the peace. And I have high hopes of Hirtius and Pansa – if only we can survive the next few months – keep a semblance of order until they take up their Consulships, I might be able to save the day… I'm staying. I'll bolt my doors. Tiro here will attend the funeral – he'll keep me informed. Nobody will notice Tiro – nobody ever does. Besides, Caesar was his good friend – 'always very kind' to him.

TIRO. They say Athens is at its best in the springtime.

Scene Nine

The Forum. A wolf crosses the stage. Muffled drums. Braying trumpets. A theatrical procession, including the 'model' body of CAESAR, *naked except for a loincloth, showing his wounds, the real body, gilded, covered by a purple robe, and five actors playing* CAESAR, *in lifelike masks, each carrying a placard representing one of his conquests.* CALPURNIA, FULVIA, DOLABELLA *(who has changed sides)*, MARK ANTONY, LEPIDUS, PISO, HIRTIUS, PANSA, *others of* CAESAR's SUPPORTERS, *professional* MOURNERS, VETERANS *following.* MARK ANTONY *and* LEPIDUS *climb the Rostra and wait for the weeping and wailing to die down. The* ACTOR CAESARS *stand behind him.*

LEPIDUS. Citizens. This is your Consul – Antony. Give him a fair hearing –

MARK ANTONY. We come to bid farewell to a great Roman – struck down by men whose treasons he had forgiven – men he had promoted to the highest offices of the State.

Amazement.

The Senate has pardoned Caesar's murderers… Cicero defended their action – proclaimed 'an amnesty' for them… For those of you who have less Greek than Cicero – an amnesty is a veil drawn over the crimes of bloody assassins. I name Brutus, Cassius, Trebonius, Casca, Cinna, Decimus… Yes, friends – Decimus whom Caesar loved like a son. The Senate grants them amnesty… We must forgive the wrongs done to my friend…

Protest.

But oh, what a revenge should I take, were I not bound by oath to keep order here! They've sent me to reconcile you – the People Caesar loved – and the cowards who killed him – Rome's greatest benefactor. *Your* greatest benefactor. In his will, he freely gives you the wealth he brought home from his innumerable conquests.

ACTOR CAESARS *hold up a bloody garment to show the rips and holes.*

Look... Look here – Caesar's blood! Caesar – a god himself – who conversed with gods – who won from them the protection of your City... This deep cut for conqueror of the Gauls – a blow struck not by a Gaul, but by one of his own comrades... Here's another for the conqueror of Britain – of Germania, of Africa, of Spain... Stab after stab after stab... This one – in the back – from Decimus to whom the Senate has given command of our armies in the north...

Surprise.

Caesar extended Rome's boundaries to the limits of the known world – his sword and shield defended your homes and families... He defeated and destroyed millions upon millions of your enemies – yet he was unarmed and defenceless when men he loved slaughtered him – a judge in his Court of justice, a governor in his seat of government, a priest, sacrificed upon his own altar... A loyal friend to you all...

ACTOR CAESARS *drop the garment. Behind it is the actor playing* CAESAR's *corpse* (CAESAR), *painted white with the wounds outlined in livid red.*

CAESAR'S CORPSE.
    O that I – most unfortunate of men – should nurture
    Those wretches who have brought me to my grave!
    I that so often, crowned with oak and laurel,
    Led my adversaries captive – in Triumph – down the
        Sacred Way –
    I – of men most merciful to my many enemies –
    Mercilessly slain by those I thought my dear companions.

Avenge me! Avenge me! Avenge me!

Uproar. MOB *runs on with torches.* POPILLIUS *and his* THUGS *beat people up. A glow grows reminiscent of the end of the first play.* CINNA *is murdered. Drums,* MOB *chanting.*

End of Play Four.

PLAY FIVE

MARK ANTONY

Prologue

TULLIA, *pregnant and with a black eye.* DOLABELLA *angry.*
Enter CICERO.

DOLABELLA. I'll not give her up. She's my mistress – you're
my wife – I've given you a child – what more do you want,
woman?

CICERO. Tullia?

DOLABELLA. Stay out of this – it's no concern of yours,
Cicero –

CICERO. Yes it is – she's my daughter – I'll not have –

DOLABELLA. She's my wife! Don't –

TULLIA. Please, Papa –

DOLABELLA. I've nothing more to say on the subject. Obey
me, Tullia. (*Exits.*)

CICERO. What has he done to you?

TULLIA. It's my own fault… He was the husband I set my
heart on.

CICERO. But you knew what he was like. Leave him – come
back to me.

TULLIA. I'll not break my marriage vows.

CICERO. He has!

TULLIA. Papa… Forgive me… Forgive me…

They embrace, and part. CICERO *is broken.*

Scene One

Peaceful scene. Naples. CICERO*'s house.* HIRTIUS *and*
PANSA. *Gloom.*

HIRTIUS. This stillness... In the whole of Italy, I believe
there's no prospect more beautiful... Such an immense
blueness... I know nothing to compare with it – nowhere in
the world –

PANSA. A world with no Caesar in it... My mind can't take it
in... Everything's falling away. We'll be at war before
summer's over.

SERVANTS *bring wine.*

HIRTIUS. If a man of Caesar's genius could find no way out,
who will find one now?

PANSA. Not Antony.

HIRTIUS. Antony's nothing without Caesar. He's dismissed the
Senate until the first day of June. The world stands still –
holding its breath...

Enter TIRO.

TIRO. The master's in his library – he's had letters from his
friends in Rome –

HIRTIUS. Will he go back to Rome for the Senate meeting?

TIRO. I hope not.

PANSA. No point. Shouldn't think they'll get a quorum.
There's nobody left in the City to keep order. Decimus has
taken his legions north to his province – Cassius and Brutus
have abandoned us – half the Senate is down here on the bay
– barricaded in their villas – wondering when it'll be safe to
poke their heads out.

TIRO. Will it ever be?

PANSA. We have no leader. On days when Antony is sober,
he's either planning his next banquet or hiding from his
creditors. State business is completely neglected. Rome's full

of angry drunks trying to pick fights with themselves. How's your master spending his time?

TIRO. Gardening. Weeping over his daughter's unhappiness...

HIRTIUS. We hear Dolabella has abandoned her. Got Tullia pregnant and walked out on her –

TIRO. Say nothing to the master – he finds it too painful –

PANSA. He must try to put his griefs behind him – help us take back control. He's forever telling everybody how, as Consul, he saved the Republic. If half the Senate is down here, surely he could organise some sort of –

TIRO. No – he's given up politics. He sees nobody – refuses all invitations. I've instructions to turn away visitors – he's very firm. Up to you now – you're the next generation –

Enter CICERO.

CICERO. Gentlemen – you must think me very rude. Both of you Consuls-elect, and I keep you dancing attendance. All my hopes are pinned on you.

HIRTIUS. We were admiring the view. You can see as far as Misenum. And Capri.

PANSA. What's the latest news from Rome?

CICERO. All bad I'm afraid. On the night of the assassination, Fulvia tricked Calpurnia into handing over the Dictator's papers. So now our Consul writes his own edicts, says he found them among Caesar's documents, and pretends they have the force of law. If you bribe Antony or Fulvia heavily enough, dead Caesar will grant you any favour. It's a sort of financial necromancy.

HIRTIUS. He has the money too?

CICERO. Yes – a midnight raid on the Temple of Ops. Fulvia had all the Dictator's gold removed to Antony's own house. For safekeeping.

PANSA. Three quarters of it is supposed to go to the boy, what's his name?

TIRO. Octavian.

CICERO. Octavian, yes…

PANSA. I don't give much for his chances. He'd not be foolish enough to come and claim it, would he?

HIRTIUS. If he knows what's good for him he'll stay in Macedonia.

SLAVES *are unpacking books.*

CICERO. My books – at least I saved my books –

TIRO. I don't know why you're unpacking – we can't stay here. Sooner or later, Antony will send his thugs to burn us out.

HIRTIUS. Tiro's right. The People are blaming you –

PANSA. Antony's spreading rumours you planned the whole conspiracy –

CICERO. Planned! Nothing was planned – that's why the Republic is facing disaster.

TIRO. Athens, go to Athens!

CICERO. Tullia may need me here… I can't make up my mind. I'm getting as bad as Brutus… You know… Perhaps I should go back to Rome.

TIRO. There is no 'Rome'. Antony is Rome – Caesar's soldiers are Rome – the mob is Rome – rioting, looting, burning – hunting down the conspirators –

CICERO. But the Republic – my daughter –

TIRO. Fat lot of good you'd be to Tullia – or the Republic – without a tongue – without a head! You've never been in such danger – not even when Clodius and his gang came after you –

CICERO. I did not aban–

TIRO. Oh, you're not going to trot out the old 'I did not abandon the Republic in the days of my youth', speech! We know it by heart! The Republic is dead! Just – for once in your life – run away!

SERVANT. Sir, there are visitors –

CICERO. Send them away. Tiro, say I'm unwell – say I'm dying of grief –

TIRO. Or an upset stomach – that should get rid of them. (*Exits.*)

CICERO. Are you in pain, young man?

HIRTIUS. Not really – a tiredness – a lack of energy –

PANSA. Are you going to desert us? When we become Consuls, your advice –

CICERO. No, no – absolutely not – Tiro's right – I'm finished with politics. If – gods forbid! – we've another civil war coming, I want no part of it. War's a young man's game – I'm growing old… I shall retire to Greece with my son – persuade Tullia to come with me – we'll all study philosophy. There! The decision's made. No turning back.

TIRO (*returns*). You've a visitor.

CICERO. No, Tiro –

TIRO. I think you'd better see him.

CICERO. More bad news? Who is it?

TIRO. It's Gaius. Gaius Julius Caesar.

HIRTIUS. What!

PANSA. Caesar!

TIRO. The new one – the adopted son.

CICERO. He's here?

TIRO. With soldiers – a hundred or more –

CICERO (*suddenly scared*). They're going to kill me… But… I'm not prepared – I'm…

TIRO. I don't think it's your head they're after – he's a very polite young man. And I mean young – you'll see.

PANSA. I'm surprised he dare set foot in Italy –

HIRTIUS. He's either very brave – or incredibly foolhardy.

SLAVES *bring in* OCTAVIAN (*nineteen*) *with* AGRIPPA (*nineteen*).

OCTAVIAN. Marcus Tullius – this is one of the greatest moments of my life.

CICERO (*wary; still unconvinced he's in no danger*). You're very kind –

OCTAVIAN. I've read everything you've published – your philosophy – your speeches... Your prosecution of Verres – the trial that made your name – I have it by heart: 'It was not Gavius you nailed up on that cross, Verres... You crucified the universal principle that any Roman citizen is, and will always be, *a free man* – entitled to the protection of good government and the rule of law!' Marvellous stuff! I wish I'd half your powers oratory –

CICERO. Well –

OCTAVIAN. And some small part of your sagacity, and political skill.

CICERO (*relaxes*). You overwhelm me, young man... But... before we go any further, please tell me what I'm to call you –

OCTAVIAN. I insist on Julius Caesar – in public. To my friends I'm Octavian.

CICERO. Could it be Octavian for me too? At my time of life, I'd find another Julius Caesar hard to get used to.

OCTAVIAN. I'd be honoured to count you among my friends. This is Marcus Vipsanius Agrippa – he's advising me on military matters –

PANSA. He's very young –

OCTAVIAN. He's my age. And he's already distinguished himself in battle –

AGRIPPA. Sirs.

CICERO. Do you know Aulus Hirtius, and Gaius Vibius Pansa –

OCTAVIAN. Sirs, I hope I may count on your friendship too.

CICERO. They were trusted officers of your...

OCTAVIAN. Of my father. Yes – I know. Hirtius and I are old friends.

HIRTIUS. Yes... I... We...

OCTAVIAN. We served together – with my father in Spain – against the sons of Pompey... (*Takes in* HIRTIUS *for a moment*.) Marcus Tullius, I'll come straight to the point. I'm here to seek your advice. May I speak freely?

CICERO. Of course – all friends here! Though I'm sure you're aware I've aligned myself with those who removed your adoptive father?

OCTAVIAN. As have many honourable men. What's past is past – I can't allow myself to be distracted by old quarrels. My only concern is for the future of the Republic. At all costs, we must avoid another civil war... So what am I to say to my father's veterans? What do I do about Antony? Should I go to Rome? My family thinks my only safe course is to renounce my inheritance and go into hiding. What's your advice? What would Caesar have done – what shall Caesar do?

PANSA. Calling yourself Caesar doesn't make you Caesar. You'll be taking your life in your hands if you go to Rome.

HIRTIUS. Do you really believe Antony will simply hand over the millions he's stolen? It's probably spent by now –

PANSA. Why would Caesar's legions follow you rather than Antony?

HIRTIUS. Antony commanded the right wing at Pharsalus. No – Caesar's name's a target on your back. They'd kill you before you got within fifty miles of the City.

OCTAVIAN. You think so? My soldiers tell me I'd be welcomed there with open arms.

AGRIPPA. We can get him to Rome safely enough.

OCTAVIAN. Cicero? What's your opinion?

CICERO. There's no safety anywhere – all our lives hang by a thread. (*Considers*.) Not long ago Caesar – in this very place – assured me he'd risen above the fear of death. I never have. At your age I dreamed of glory. I'm too old to start again... But what I'd give to be in your place now!

OCTAVIAN. You'd go to Rome.

CICERO. I would. I'd stand for election.

HIRTIUS. But he's a boy! Election for what? He's not even old enough to vote.

CICERO. A Tribune was killed by the mob at Caesar's funeral – you should propose yourself for the vacant post.

PANSA. Antony would forbid it.

CICERO. Then he'd be playing into your hands. To stand for Tribune would show your determination to continue Caesar's policy of championing the People. The mob will love you for it.

PANSA. Antony will reject your candidature.

CICERO. If he does, he'll be opposing the People's will.

OCTAVIAN. You believe Antony is my enemy? I think so too. Come to Rome with me.

CICERO (*laughs*). No! I've just decided to retire to Greece. I'm going to study philosophy.

OCTAVIAN. But your counsel would be invaluable to me.

CICERO. Reconcile with those who removed your father. If you're willing to do that, in the interests of the Republic, I'll help you all I can.

OCTAVIAN. I'm not opposed to reconciliation. I don't bear grudges. It's my legacy I want, not vengeance.

CICERO. May I tell our friends that?

OCTAVIAN. Please do. Be my voice in the Senate. Assure Brutus, Cassius, Decimus and the rest, my only purpose is to bring a lasting peace to the Roman People. And I shall succeed. The only obstacle in my path is Antony. I see I must go and confront him. May I write to you?

CICERO. By all means.

They embrace.

OCTAVIAN. I wish you'd change your mind and come with me. Your fatherly guidance would mean a great deal to me.

HIRTIUS. We'll walk part of the way with you. You know your father has chosen us as next year's Consuls?

OCTAVIAN. Yes. I'd heard.

Exeunt OCTAVIAN *and* ENTOURAGE, *with* HIRTIUS *and* PANSA.

CICERO. Well, there's an old head on young shoulders!

TIRO. I wonder how long he'll keep it there.

CICERO. I didn't care for his companion. Agrippa, was it?

TIRO. Why did you encourage him? I should have thought the last thing you wanted was another Julius Caesar in Rome.

CICERO. The cub will tweak the old lion's tail – he'll cause problems for Antony – with any luck he'll split their faction – that'll be good for our side.

TIRO. What if he and Antony join forces?

CICERO (*considers it*). Then I'm a dead man – and the Republic dies with me. But I can't see it happening. Antony will tolerate no rival – he wants absolute power. Or Fulvia does. Anyway, Octavian's hardly a force to be reckoned with, is he? He's a nice boy but he's no Caesar – you only have to look at him. I wonder… Perhaps…

TIRO. What?

CICERO. Do you think I should postpone Athens? This Senate Antony has summoned for the first of June –

TIRO. There are hundreds of angry soldiers on the streets, too quick to draw their swords –

CICERO. You're right, as always… But if –

TIRO. No!

Scene Two

Rome – MARK ANTONY*'s house.* FULVIA *is studying a pile of correspondence – dealing with secretaries.* MARK ANTONY *(drinking) is watching.* OCTAVIAN *and* AGRIPPA *are shown in.*

MARK ANTONY. So... you've been kept waiting, boy. Drink? I wish I could say you're welcome –

OCTAVIAN. Don't apologise, Consul. We're both busy men. This house was Pompey's, I believe?

MARK ANTONY. Mine now.

OCTAVIAN. Well, it will be when you've raised the money to pay the auctioneer. *(Laughs.)* It has fine gardens. I was glad of the opportunity to spend an hour reflecting on the past – imagining the future – with Agrippa here.

MARK ANTONY. The future! Could anything be more uncertain? I worry for you, boy. And in this state of emergency more worry's the last thing I need. Look around – you've been on the streets, have you? Among the mob? Do you expect me to guarantee your safety?

AGRIPPA. No, he doesn't. That's what I'm here for.

MARK ANTONY. Ha! *(Sneers at* AGRIPPA.*)* Had I known you were intending to absent yourself from your legion and come to Rome, I'd have advised against it. Why *did* you come?

OCTAVIAN. Family business.

MARK ANTONY. But... you're not thinking of accepting this adoption – this legacy? I'm not even sure it's legal –

AGRIPPA. Oh, it's legal all right –

OCTAVIAN. I've been to the Urban Praetor – made the necessary declaration, sworn the oaths, signed the documents. I'm Caesar's heir – and yes, I've been among the People of Rome... Everywhere I've gone they've welcomed me.

FULVIA. We hear you've been to see the old man.

OCTAVIAN (*a withering look*). You are?

MARK ANTONY. This is Fulvia, my wife. Have you? Have you spoken to Cicero?

OCTAVIAN. A sound Republican and a great orator. Yes, I've been in the south. I had the honour of an audience – Cicero behaved like a father to me.

FULVIA. Is that what you're about? Acquiring fathers?

OCTAVIAN. I'm here to protect my interests.

FULVIA. Good luck to you!

OCTAVIAN. And to thank your husband for looking after my property in my absence. You may take from my father's house any trinket you wish as a keepsake, but I want the money immediately.

FULVIA. You're speaking to the Consul, boy.

OCTAVIAN. Whom I've known since he was my father's apprentice, legate and friend. There's always been plain speaking between us.

FULVIA. Times change –

OCTAVIAN. Enough of this! My father left to each of three hundred thousand citizens a substantial sum of money to be paid in cash. I intend to honour the terms of the will. I need his money. If it comes short, perhaps you'll authorise a loan from the public treasury to be repaid at a reasonable rate of interest?

FULVIA. I'm speechless!

OCTAVIAN. Then, while she is, Antony, you'll be interested to hear that it's my intention to stand for Tribune – the office is vacant I believe? I'm young, I know –

FULVIA. Far too young – and far too full of yourself! –

OCTAVIAN. An Assembly of the People will silence any procedural objections. I'm confident I could win the election with a large majority. I am Gaius Julius Caesar. I have the People's support – and I warn you, Antony – a great many of them blame you for not hunting down my father's murderers and bringing them to trial. You've been slow to restore order here. Without order there can be no good government – surely you learned that from my father?

MARK ANTONY. How – Who – What?! I'm not answerable to you, boy!

OCTAVIAN. We are all answerable to the People of Rome.

MARK ANTONY. Had I not defended your father against his murderers, he'd have been condemned as a tyrant! They'd have dragged his body on hooks through the streets and thrown it in the Tiber! Yes – and his money would have been confiscated by the State!

FULVIA. Where would your inheritance have been then, boy? Eh?

OCTAVIAN. I have already thanked your husband for protecting my father's interests and my own –

MARK ANTONY. I don't need your fucking thanks! And all his property would have been put up for auction and sold at knock-down prices to any thief, slave, or grave-robber that took a fancy to it –

OCTAVIAN. As was the case with Pompey's properties, I believe?

FULVIA. Get out of my house!

OCTAVIAN. I must also ask you to return my father's papers. The ones you removed from his home on the night of his murder –

MARK ANTONY. Those were State papers – I'm the fucking Consul.

OCTAVIAN. I'll send my lawyers to you. They can go through the documents with your people and decide what's mine, and what belongs to the State. I'm told you stand accused of inventing laws – claiming they were authorised by my father and discovered among his files. A careful scrutiny of everything would be in both our interests. It would reveal the truth – which, I'm sure is as precious to you as it is to me. But that's for later. For now – I want my money.

MARK ANTONY. What money?! What fucking money?! There is no fucking money!

OCTAVIAN. My father was the richest man in the world. If you're saying his estate is insufficient to pay the People of Rome the sums he left them in his will… Let's just say the People might find that lie difficult to swallow. Where are his chests of gold? It's well known you removed them from the Temple of Ops?

MARK ANTONY. That was the State's money – and there was precious little of it left!

OCTAVIAN. Then it's not true that you – a near bankrupt – have recently paid off your debts of forty million?

MARK ANTONY. Don't go there, boy! Or I'll – I'll – I'll –

AGRIPPA. We should leave now.

OCTAVIAN. Yes. I'm sorry, Consul. I won't prolong this interview – I have a pressing engagement with some of my late father's military advisers. I'll send you my lawyers.

AGRIPPA. It would be a mistake to think that because we're young, we're innocents and fools. We're all Caesar's men. It would be better, Consul, if you worked with us, rather than against us.

OCTAVIAN. Agrippa's right. We should work together. The People have swept away all the old certainties – Tribune, Consul, Dictator… In the current state of emergency, they're merely empty titles. What matters now is whom they'll follow – whom they believe – whom they'd fight and die for.

OCTAVIAN *and* AGRIPPA *leave*.

AGRIPPA (*aside*). Thought that went rather well.

OCTAVIAN (*aside*). I have his measure now.

MARK ANTONY. A boy! A sneering, fleering boy! I shall destroy the little – crush the little – the little! (*Roars and exits*.)

FULVIA. Antony. Antony – Antony! (*Follows him*.)

MARK ANTONY. A boy!

Scene Three

BRUTUS's *villa in Antium.*

TIRO. Brutus, Cassius, Decimus? Whatever happened to them? Would it surprise you to know that Brutus is still dithering? This is his villa – we're at Antium on the coast. He talks about returning to Rome – while making all the necessary preparations for a quick escape. His luggage is packed – there are boats waiting. Dither, dither...

Enter SERVILLIA *and* BRUTUS, *arguing.*

His mother – the redoubtable Servillia – has called a council of war. She was once Julius Caesar's mistress – though that's no great distinction – they say half the women in Rome – and not only the women –

Enter DECIMUS.

CICERO. Tiro? To whom are you talking?

TIRO. Nobody. Myself.

CICERO. I should never have agreed to this meeting.

DECIMUS. Cicero? She's summoned you too, has she?

CICERO. Decimus? Shouldn't you be with your legions in the north?

DECIMUS. Yes, I should. But –

SERVILLIA. A grain commissioner! In Asia! It's an insult!

CICERO. Servillia – Brutus –

SERVILLIA. He ignores the Senate – uses an Assembly of the Unwashed to deprive you of your province – and sends you to haggle with savages in the marketplace. Rome's liberator, a corn merchant! What are you doing here, Cicero?

CICERO. You asked me to come –

SERVILLIA. Antony rules by edict – and the mob sanctions everything he decrees –

DECIMUS. He's asking the Assembly to force me to hand over my province and my legions to him –

CICERO. You'll do no such thing!

BRUTUS. But if a legally constituted Assembly –

SERVILLIA. You should have crushed Antony – killed him! –

BRUTUS. But, Mother – the law –

SERVILLIA. The law! It's mob rule now! Whatever a lawyer says, it's mob rule!

BRUTUS. I can't remain in hiding forever, Mother – I lose respect with every day that passes. I ought to go to Rome. I'm still Praetor – I'll call an Assembly – I must speak to the People –

CICERO. Oh dear, no! I'd advise against that. The People are Caesar's heirs – they'd tear you in pieces. Listen to me, Brutus. You're the rallying point for all who love freedom. Accept this commission – lie low in some backwater until opinion shifts back in our favour. Fortune is changeable – the good times will return – in politics they always do.

SERVILLIA. My son Brutus – slayer of tyrants – humping sacks of wheat!

Enter CASSIUS.

CASSIUS. It's an insult! Antony is offering me *a grain commission*!

SERVILLIA. You too? Well, there's a surprise!

CASSIUS. Did Cassius save Syria from the Parthians to end his days among Sicilian market slaves? It's a studied insult! Decimus? Shouldn't you be with your legions in Mutina?

DECIMUS. Yes, I –

CICERO. What will you do?

CASSIUS. Leave Italy – go to Syria – the province Caesar awarded me.

CICERO. Sicily is safer.

BRUTUS. It would keep you on the right side of the law. If you comply with the ruling –

CASSIUS. Antony's ruling!

BRUTUS. Backed by the People –

CASSIUS. The People!

BRUTUS. You'd be doing your duty like a good constitutionalist – surely – that must still count for something – or why are we –

CICERO. Cassius. Listen to me. If Antony declares war on us, we'll need a military man – a commander-in-chief. You and Decimus here are the Republic's last hope. In Sicily, you'd be close – ready to strike when the opportunity arises –

CASSIUS. What opportunity?

CICERO. In half a year, we'll have new Consuls – Hirtius and Pansa, both honourable men. And I have high hopes of young Octavian – he's creating all sorts of trouble for Antony – the People love him for Caesar's sake –

CASSIUS. The tyrant's heir!

BRUTUS. What are you saying, Cicero? That the People still love their Caesar – that they'd willingly return to their slavery?

CICERO. The more Antony bullies Caesar's son –

SERVILLIA. He's no son of Caesar! He's just a boy – a snotty little boy!

CASSIUS. He's more likely to *join with* Antony and come after us –

CICERO. That could never happen. He doesn't bear grudges. He told me so himself.

CASSIUS. And you believed him! Anyway, he's no soldier – Antony will crush him.

CICERO. He'll try. But the boy is under the protection of his father's veterans.

DECIMUS. Antony would have to deal with me first. I have two loyal legions in the north – and I'm recruiting a third.

BRUTUS. But if an Assembly of the People orders you to hand over your legions to Antony –

CICERO. I'll make the Senate order him to stand firm.

SERVILLIA. So, we'll have the Senate and the People's Assembly sending contradictory orders to the military? Has everybody run mad!

CASSIUS. It's you I blame most, Decimus. If only you'd moved your army down to Rome in March!

DECIMUS. And where did you disappear to, back in March, Cassius?

CICERO. Oh, if only – if only…! Why blame Decimus? The seeds of disaster were sown when you failed to rally the People to our cause – failed to seize control of the Republic –

SERVILLIA. Well! I never heard anything like it – to be accused of a lack of resolution by Cicero of all people. A coward – who'd do anything to avoid a fight!

DECIMUS. I'm wasting my time here. I'm needed in Mutina.

CASSIUS. Only one course of action is open to me. I'll go to Syria – take up the governorship Caesar awarded me – and start drilling my legions there – if they want war, I'll give them a war!

CICERO. No – that's –

SERVILLIA. At last, someone's talking sense! And you'll go to Macedonia, Brutus. When the Senate ratified Caesar's decrees you were given Macedonia.

BRUTUS. I don't know. Would it not be unconstitutional? Cicero?

CICERO. Don't ask me. I give up. Tiro and I are off to Greece to study philosophy.

CICERO *and* TIRO *leave.*

I can't take any more of this. I should have followed your advice and left Italy months ago… I want to see my son. I need my daughter. I want peace and quiet – I want

grandchildren… I miss Tullia… She's everything to me…
Anyway, as everybody's accusing me of cowardice, my
running away will come as no surprise.

TIRO. You've made up your mind, have you? Well…

CICERO. What's the matter? Finally, we're off to Greece – it's
what you want, isn't it?

TIRO (*uncomfortable*). I've been meaning to speak to you for
some time… But I'm not sure I can bring myself…

CICERO. Are you ill?

TIRO. No – I've decided not to come with you to Greece.

CICERO. Ah… (*Studies him.*) Where will you go instead?

TIRO. To the farm you kindly gave me. Along with my
freedom… I need to rest. I'm growing old…

CICERO. I see. When do you wish to leave me?

TIRO. Whenever you'd find it convenient.

CICERO. Go whenever you wish. You're no longer my slave.

TIRO. I hope I'm your friend.

CICERO. Then the sooner the better. Tomorrow?

TIRO. If you wish it. I don't want to inconvenience –

CICERO. Tomorrow then.

TIRO. Well… I… Would it be all right if I borrowed some of the
slaves – and the little carriage to transport my belongings?

CICERO. Take whatever you need. (*Exits.*)

Scene Four

Pastoral music. TIRO *and* SLAVES *arrive at the farm, and unload bags and books (scrolls). Bucolic lighting change.* TIRO *puts on a straw sun hat – is brought wine olives, etc. A writing desk is set in front of him.*

TIRO. A month passes... I imagine the master sitting in Athens writing profound works of philosophy – here I am in this pleasant spot – worrying a little – wondering how he's managing without me – setting down his life for the future instruction of lawyers, politicians and schoolboys. Oh, the good life! I have unpacked my books – and now my little house has a soul. I sit in the shade in the cool of the evening... Look down there – I have a view of the entire bay – can you see... there's Capri floating in a blue mist – all those little white boats bobbing... And there's a girl at the baths in town who –

CICERO (*off*). Tiro?

TIRO. Oh no...

Enter CICERO *looking different – happy.*

CICERO. Tiro? What's happened to you? I leave you alone for a month and you turn into a scarecrow. What a glorious place to live out your declining years! Your own wine – (*Helping himself.*) not bad, not bad at all – a little young perhaps – your own olives... Surprised to see me?

TIRO. Nothing surprises me any more, Master. Not where you're concerned.

CICERO. What's this? (*Picks up a scroll.*) My life?

TIRO. Yes... I'm settled here now. I wouldn't want to... (*Waits.*) This isn't just a friendly visit, is it?

CICERO. Of course – that's all it is! I happened to be passing your gates. Aren't you pleased to see me?

TIRO. Why aren't you in Athens?

CICERO. Ah well, I decided against Athens – got as far as Sicily, but the wind was against us – kept blowing me back into harbour. I believe the gods may have been trying to tell me something. And then I heard about an extraordinary attack Piso made on Antony in the Senate –

TIRO. Piso!

CICERO. Piso of all people! Antony's definitely losing his grip. Decimus has three legions in Mutina now. And all the time more and more of Caesar's old soldiers are rallying to the boy.

TIRO. Octavian? But Brutus and Cassius –

CICERO. Gone to Syria and Macedonia – to strengthen and drill their legions.

TIRO. Surely, you're not hoping they'll go to war?

CICERO. They're preparing to defend the Republic. Oh, Tiro – a whole new spirit has infused us – a flame – pure, white, sublime!

TIRO. Us?

CICERO. All good Republicans.

TIRO. You're not thinking of going back to Rome?

CICERO. The Senate meets in nine days' time.

TIRO. Please don't. You've done more than anybody – I beg you –

CICERO. What's the worst that can happen? I'll die – so what? I'm past sixty – my race is run. It would be a good death – which, as you know, is the supreme object of a good life.

TIRO. It may sound good on paper – but when some thug of Antony's with a big sword –

CICERO. Tell me – do I seem happy? Do you know why, Tiro? I've conquered my fear of death.

TIRO. Ha!

CICERO. Oh, you don't believe me –

TIRO. Well, I mean!

CICERO. You think me still the timid creature of old! You couldn't be more wrong. Slowly and silently, philosophy has been working a profound change in me. I shall go and put

backbone into the Senate. We can't leave it to idiots like
Piso. The Republic needs its saviour – Rome is calling me!

TIRO. You're asking me to come with you?

CICERO. No – not at all! I wouldn't dream of allowing you to
share the dangers I shall face – to come with me on the
greatest adventure of my life. We parted badly. I came to
remedy that. And to bring you this. (*Gives a scroll.*)
Goodbye, dear old friend. When we have our Republic back,
I hope we'll meet again.

They embrace. CICERO *goes.* TIRO *reads the scroll.*

TIRO. '*On Friendship...*' He's marked a passage: 'If a man
ascended into heaven and gazed upon the whole workings of
the universe and the beauty of the stars, the wondrous sight
would give him no joy if he had to keep it to himself. If only
there had been someone with whom to share the spectacle it
would have filled him with delight. Nature abhors solitude...'

Oh... The cunning old bugger!

Master... Wait!

Scene Five

CICERO, *carrying armfuls of flowers, returns to his Rome
house. Cheering – mobbed by well-wishers.*

TIRO. Quite a welcome!

CICERO. It's not me they're cheering. I don't flatter myself.
They're welcoming home the spirit of the Republic –
remembering the good times long gone – the days of my
Consulship...

TIRO. Or it might just be their way of protesting against
Antony. Any stone to throw at a dog.

CICERO. I'd like to think I mean rather more to Rome than that.

TIRO. I'm sure.

Enter TERENTIA.

CICERO. Where's my daughter – where's Tullia?

TERENTIA. Husband… So you've found your way home at last –

TIRO. I'll leave you… you'll need to…

CICERO. No, Tiro – I want you to stay.

TERENTIA. I can't think why you came.

CICERO. I'm here to see my daughter – and my grandson.

TERENTIA. Tullia is very weak – it was a difficult birth. The child is healthy – it's with its father's people – she's too ill to feed it –

CICERO. I must go to her.

TERENTIA. You should never have come back to Rome.

CICERO. You forget, Terentia, I tried that once – running away. See where it's left us.

TERENTIA. Left *us*?

CICERO. The only hope of ending the chaos here was my return. As for this coldness between us – I hope –

TERENTIA. Do you honestly believe there's still hope? For us? I gave up all hopes of you long ago. What will you do?

CICERO. I still have influence – tomorrow I shall speak in the Senate –

TERENTIA. How? You can't even walk in safety down a busy street in broad daylight. And you were never the most courageous of –

CICERO. I shall find a way –

TERENTIA. Where does that leave me? What sort of life do you think we've been leading here?

CICERO. The fault's not mine. If we no longer have a future together –

TERENTIA. Whose fault –

CICERO. You've shut me out of –

TERENTIA. My life? My bed? You want to know why? Take a look.

She starts to undo the top part of her dress.

Help me. Undo the clasps.

CICERO *opens her gown revealing her back – criss-crossed with ugly old scars.*

CICERO (*gently*). Who did this to you? Who did it? Was it Clodius?

TERENTIA. Clodius? When they burnt us out – when they chased you out of the City – when you were too proud to accept help from Caesar... I went to reason with Clodius's sister – woman to woman – to plead – to beg – for you.

CICERO. I never thought –

TERENTIA. But Clodia's not a woman. She had me whipped off the premises. Her brother and her louche friends were with her – laughing at my shame.

CICERO. *Your* shame! The shame was theirs – you should have told me.

TERENTIA. Told *you*? A man who greets the whole of Rome before he greets his own wife. Stay and die in this City if you wish. Your follies – your vanity will ruin you but you'll not pull me down with you.

CICERO. You're divorcing me?

TERENTIA. Oh, my husband... (*On the point of tears, which she controls. Hard.*) You'll find a good deal of your property is missing. Don't blame the slaves – they're not thieves – I've sold it. I'm taking back my dowry. I have to live.

CICERO. Terentia –

Enter TULLIA – looking close to death – and a NURSE.

TULLIA. Father...

CICERO. My darling girl – what's happened to you –

TULLIA. I heard your voice –

TERENTIA (*to the* NURSE). You shouldn't have let her… Take her back to her bed – you fool!

CICERO. My love –

He embraces her.

TULLIA. Papa – you're hurting me –

CICERO. Oh… (*Weeps*.) Come back to Tusculum with me – I beg you, Tullia – let me care for you –

TULLIA. I shall – I shall…

NURSE. Lady…

The NURSE *takes* TULLIA *away.* CICERO *stares straight ahead.*

TIRO. Master –

CICERO. She's dying, isn't she?

TERENTIA. I'm afraid she is.

CICERO. Does she know it?

TERENTIA. The doctor's said nothing to her – but she was always a clever girl… I think she must know, don't you?

CICERO. Yes.

TERENTIA. She may have a week or two – a month perhaps. She waited for you. (*Starts to go*.)

CICERO. Terentia?

She turns, then exits.

I think I'll go and sit with my daughter now.

But the SENATORS *arrive.* PISO, VATIA, QUINTUS, HIRTIUS *and* PANSA, *others.*

VATIA. Oh, there you are, Cicero – welcome home.

CICERO. Gentlemen – brother…

CICERO *embraces* QUINTUS.

PISO. We were beginning to wonder if you'd ever dare to show your face –

PANSA. You really shouldn't have come – you're not safe here –

CICERO. When have I ever been safe?

VATIA. Our liberators have all fled abroad it seems.

PISO. Abandoned us in our hour of need –

CICERO. I'm here to provide some much-needed direction. Hirtius – you don't look well.

HIRTIUS. It's nothing. What will you do?

CICERO. I shall address the Senate – tomorrow –

PISO. No – that's the last thing you'll do!

PANSA. Nobody's going – nobody of importance. With any luck Antony won't get a quorum –

HIRTIUS. They've laid a trap for you.

CICERO. What sort of a trap?

PISO. Antony intends to propose a motion – granting the dead tyrant new honours –

CICERO. We've made Caesar a god – what further honours could he possible need? –

PISO. He'll surround the Senate with soldiers – and propose that every public festival should commence with a sacrifice to the deified Caesar.

CICERO. It'll be laughed out of Court.

HIRTIUS. He'll call on you to speak first –

VATIA. If you speak in favour –

CICERO. Of course, I won't! Nobody would take me seriously ever again!

HIRTIUS. And Antony's trap snaps shut.

QUINTUS. Because, if you speak *against*, you'll never reach home alive.

CICERO. But… if I refuse to attend I'll look like a coward still. What sort of leadership is that?

PANSA. Send word you're ill – exhausted from your journey. You're getting on in years. People will understand.

CICERO. Hardly the heroic return I was hoping for.

PISO. You must follow our lead. Stay away tomorrow – send Tiro to Antony with an apology.

Exeunt all but TIRO, QUINTUS *and* CICERO.

QUINTUS. What's the matter with you?

CICERO. Nothing – never better – tiredness – the long journey –

He bursts into tears.

QUINTUS. Brother…

CICERO. I must rest… Please… We'll speak tomorrow. I'll…

QUINTUS. Well, if you're sure… Do something, Tiro.

Exit QUINTUS.

CICERO. You were right, as usual, Tiro. I should never have come here.

TIRO. Then you'd have not been here with Tullia, when…

CICERO. I'm being tested. Am I strong enough yet to look death in the face?

Exit CICERO, *leaving* TIRO. TIRO *goes to* MARK ANTONY's *house and hands in a letter.*

Scene Six

MARK ANTONY*'s house*.

TIRO. Cicero sent his apologies. I took the letter. How did Antony react?

MARK ANTONY, *drunk in a rage, kicking* SLAVES, *waving* CICERO*'s letter*, DOLABELLA, FULVIA.

MARK ANTONY. He's tired! He's sick! I'll make him sick – the old –

FULVIA. Antony –

MARK ANTONY. Get my lictors! Get round to his house – break his doors down – I'll rip his tongue out – knock his head off – he needn't think he can get the better of me – I'm the fucking Consul now, not him –

FULVIA. *Antony.*

MARK ANTONY. I want him dragged to the meeting – I want to hear him heap praises on the man he hated – I want him on his knees – begging – the way I begged on the day he executed Roman citizens!

FULVIA. Don't be a fool – all our enemies are staying away – all of them who matter –

DOLABELLA. Piso – Vatia – many others have sent apologies –

MARK ANTONY. Then they'll all be dragged there – they'll not make a fool of me! (*Exits.*)

FULVIA. Antony – Antony!

Exeunt FULVIA *and* DOLABELLA.

TIRO. Badly. Antony reacted badly. The Senate meeting went ahead – though it was barely quorate. The god Caesar got new honours – under duress.

CICERO. Come on. I haven't returned to Rome to cower underneath my blankets! Go call the others, Tiro – we'll go together. Antony can hardly massacre us all. Where's the meeting to be held?

TIRO. In the Temple of Concord.

CICERO. Oh, the wonderful irony of it!

Scene Seven

QUINTUS, PISO, VATIA, PANSA, *and* HIRTIUS, *sick, join them and they all head for the Temple of Concord.*
DOLABELLA*'s chair is set up.* DOLABELLA *meets them at the door.*

DOLABELLA. Antony is sick – I'm presiding in his place.

PISO. Sick? Do you mean drunk?

CICERO. You're very close to Mark Antony these days, Dolabella – what can have turned you from bitter enemies into fast friends I wonder?

VATIA. Syria. Antony's given him Syria to govern.

DOLABELLA. Antony and I working together now – for peace and reconciliation.

CICERO. Ah yes – I remember – 'Let reconciliation and moderation be ever our watchwords!'

DOLABELLA. Be careful, old man – the game is getting rougher.

CICERO. I'm going to make it rougher than you could possibly imagine, son-in-law – I'll make you curse the day you were born – though men like you are not born – they're excreted.

PISO. He's worse than Antony –

CICERO. Their term as Consuls is almost over. I've high hopes of Hirtius and Pansa here. The good times will return.

DOLABELLA *exits to the Senate. They go into the meeting.*
CICERO *is applauded.*

SENATORS. Cicero! Let him speak! (*Etc.*)

CICERO. Gentlemen… Yesterday I was sick. I could not attend the session. Antony – in a rage – threatened to send soldiers to drag me here. Why? Were the barbarians at our gates? Had our legions suffered a crushing defeat in Gaul or Africa? Was Rome facing earthquake, plague, flood, or fire? No, gentlemen – Antony wished to discuss a public thanksgiving – prayers and flowers for a dead tyrant. Hardly a national emergency! But do you think – had I been here – I would have supported Antony's proposal? New honours for dead Caesar? I say rather we should heap honours upon Brutus – the man who struck him down – and rescued us all from lives of abject slavery.

DOLABELLA (*standing*). Senator! –

CICERO. Sit down, *Consul*! I am outraged that when Lucius Piso there stood up in this House to condemn the gross abuses rampant in this City – not one of you – not a single man raised his voice in support of him. (*Addressing the audience*.) What is the meaning of your servility? Are you Senators of Rome – are you men? Shame on you all! I say you have all fallen short of what the Roman People expect of you. You shift uncomfortably in your seats – have you lost your voices?

DOLABELLA. Cicero – sit down!

CICERO. No.

Protests at DOLABELLA.

SENATORS. Let him speak! Let's hear Cicero! Throw Dolabella out! You're useless, Dolabella! (*Etc.*)

CICERO. Back in March I agreed – against my will – that Caesar's acts should stand. Today, any law of Caesar's Antony dislikes is ignored. Other laws – supposedly discovered on scraps, and jottings – or in the holes and corners of Antony's febrile and wine-soaked imagination – are finding their way onto our statute books. Criminals are pardoned by the dead Caesar. Favours are granted to Antony's friends by the dead Caesar. New taxes are imposed by the dead Caesar. But why do we need more taxes? What's become of the State Treasury? What happened to the vast fortune Caesar left for safe keeping in the Temple of Ops?

DOLABELLA *leaves with his* LICTORS.

Why won't Mark Antony come to this House and explain himself? Dolabella – oh, there he goes! – says Antony's sick – a privilege only yesterday he denied to me. I'm told he's angry with me. Well, I imagine he's going to be a lot angrier now! If, in future, I can speak in safety to you I shall. I've lived a long life – I have achieved an unprecedented degree of respect. What time remains to me shall not be my own – it shall be devoted to the service of the Senate and People of Rome.

Stunned silence. CICERO *exits. Followed by* TIRO. *A roar of applause begins as* POPILLIUS *and* THUGS *arrive.*

Got it all down? Send copies to Octavian, Brutus, Cassius, Decimus – anybody you can think of.

TIRO. We'll need bigger bodyguards – iron bars on the doors – a whole pack of savage watchdogs.

Exeunt TIRO *and* CICERO. *Re-enter* DOLABELLA *with* MARK ANTONY, *who is drunk and in a rage. Joined by* POPILLIUS *and* THUGS. *The* SENATORS *protest – confusion.*

MARK ANTONY. Shut the doors – nobody leaves! (*Throws up.*)

SENATORS *laugh, point and jeer at him.*

Where is he? Where is this Enemy of the People – this executioner of Roman citizens – this hypocritical, arrogant, trembling coward who incites men to kill but leaves others to wield the knife?

DOLABELLA. Antony –

MARK ANTONY. What right has Cicero to condemn me – he was the sole cause of the civil war! Now he wants to start a war with me! I'll give him a fucking war!

DOLABELLA. Consul!

MARK ANTONY. Catiline's rebellion – Clodius's murder – Caesar's assassination – he masterminded all these crimes!

PISO. The meeting's over – we are no longer quorate?

MARK ANTONY. I'm your Consul! Obey me! The session's not over until I say it's over. Come back! Do you hear me – I'm your fucking Consul!

PISO. But only for a few more weeks.

The SENATORS *leave jeering.*

Scene Eight

Birdsong. Tusculum. AGRIPPA*, muddy with hard riding.* TIRO *is reading him extracts from* Philippic II.

TIRO. Listen to this bit. 'When, at the end of your boyhood, Antony, you first put on your manly toga, you immediately took it off again and began to ply your trade as a rent boy – chalked up your bill of fare and your price list – you didn't come cheap – and for the first and only time in your life you found a profession you were suited to.'

AGRIPPA (*laughs*). He wouldn't dare!

TIRO. 'But soon the besotted Curio, at that time in search of the stability of married life, rescued you from prostitution and, as it were, made an honest woman of you – '

AGRIPPA (*laughs*). Cicero can't stand up in the Senate and say that – Antony would cut his tongue out!

Enter CICERO.

TIRO. He can't say it – but he can publish it. The power of the pen –

CICERO. Agrippa. This is a surprise.

AGRIPPA. It was meant to be. Letters from Caesar. (*Handing them over.*) He likes your speech.

CICERO. Wait until he sees the one I'm working on now. Am I to gather Tiro has been reading you edited highlights?

AGRIPPA. You're taking a great risk.

CICERO. Antony vilified me in the Senate. The bile he spewed out must be answered in the kind of language he understands –

AGRIPPA. Leave Antony to us – we'll soon have him on the run. Caesar has raised an army from his father's veterans in Casilinum and Calatia.

CICERO. So I hear. There are some in the Senate who question the wisdom – and I may say legality – of it –

AGRIPPA. But not you, I hope?

CICERO. Octavian agreed we'd do everything in our power to avoid any fighting.

AGRIPPA. Yes – that is the agreement. But if Antony picks a fight we'll finish it.

CICERO. Well… Antony would be a fool to start a war. He's lost most of his support in the Senate.

AGRIPPA. Caesar is confident his legions will desert, and come over to us.

CICERO. How will you persuade them?

AGRIPPA. The usual way – money. We've plenty – much more than Antony, despite all his thefts. And we have the name – Julius Caesar's name counts for everything. He's sent me to ask your advice.

CICERO. I'm not a military man.

AGRIPPA. You know how Antony thinks –

CICERO. It's Fulvia you're dealing with. She's the better tactician.

AGRIPPA. Look – we've three thousand battle-hardened veterans – more joining every day. Do we bring them into Rome? Or do we dig in at Capua and block Antony's route north?

CICERO. Tell Octavian he'd be welcomed in Rome. If he can persuade the People he wishes only to restore the Republic he'll have the backing of the honest men too.

AGRIPPA. And yours? (*Studies him.*) Will he have your backing? He's expecting it.

CICERO. I hope he numbers me among the honest men. I shall always be a father to him – assure him of that.

AGRIPPA. A politician's answer? We're relying on you to keep a tight rein on the Senate. Look – once Antony's dead, you'll get your Republic back. But if it comes to a war, Caesar will have to be commander-in-chief. He wants the Senate's blessing – and he needs you to deliver it. (*Pause*.) What's your answer?

CICERO. I… I shall write to him.

AGRIPPA (*studies him*). I've ridden hard. I'll go have my feed – and sleep until you've finished your letters. (*Exits*.)

TIRO. This is a melancholy season. It's so cold… The skies are growing dark – countless thousands of starlings – are sweeping down from the north – listen to their shrieks…

CICERO. Like great black flags unfurling over the house.

TIRO. A superstitious man might think they're warning us of coming disasters.

CICERO. Who can we trust? Hirtius – Pansa? Brutus and Cassius over the seas – Decimus in the north… Octavian at the gates of Rome?

TIRO. Octavian has youth on his side – the name of Caesar is a powerful recruiting sergeant.

CICERO. I was once First Man in Rome. I'll not take orders from a mere boy leading an armed insurrection… He's precious little chance of coming out of this alive. I don't know what to do… I wonder if I should go and talk to him? Face to face?

TIRO. To Octavian? No, you shouldn't.

CICERO. I've a friend who has a house on Lake Volsinii – not far from the boy's camp –

TIRO. Too far for an old man in the middle of winter… Don't get involved. And who knows! When Antony sees the forces ranged against him, discretion, being the better part of valour, might turn him into a good Republican.

Enter TERENTIA *and the* NURSE. *Red-eyed.*

CICERO. Terentia?

TERENTIA. If you wish to say farewell to your daughter, you must come with me now...

The sky is darkened by shrieking starlings. Exeunt TERENTIA, CICERO, TIRO *and the* NURSE. MARK ANTONY *and his huge army occupy the stage.* FULVIA *and* POPILLIUS *with him at the head. Eagles, drums, trumpets.*

End of Play Five.

PLAY SIX

OCTAVIAN

Prologue

Drumroll. The walls of Mutina – manned by DECIMUS*'s*
SOLDIERS. DECIMUS *dictating a letter to a* SECRETARY.

DECIMUS. A letter to Cicero in Rome, from Decimus, in
Mutina.

I have strongly fortified the town and am preparing for a long
siege. I have recruited an extra legion – encircled the town
with ditches and palisades – stockpiled weapons – my
granaries are full – we have a good supply of water. We can
hold out for several weeks – possibly into February of the new
year. Antony has sent messengers to me with a ruling of the
People's Assembly ordering me to vacate my province and
hand over my legions to him. You have sent me the Senate's
order commanding me to hold fast and defend Mutina to the
last man. As my orders are contradictory, I shall remain loyal
to you and the Senate and ignore the People. Antony is
advancing on us with an army of twenty thousand men.
Persuade the Senate to muster a strong force and send it to
relieve us. If Antony is attacked from the south, I shall bring
my legions out of Mutina and join the fight. We are in good
heart – but hope to hear soon of decisive action from Rome.
You are no military man, Cicero – take advice from men of
experience and proven valour. Don't delay – act!

May all the gods, et cetera, et cetera, et cetera.

Got that? Give it to a man with a good horse.

Scene One

Darkness. OCTAVIAN *emerges from the gloom – lights a couple of candles.* AGRIPPA *appears – dripping – covered in snow, disguised in hooded riding cloaks, they're both in armour.*

OCTAVIAN. What is this place?

AGRIPPA. Belongs to a friend of Cicero. What if he's lured us into a trap?

OCTAVIAN. Why would he? He needs me to save his Republic. Anyway… you'll protect me.

Enter CICERO *and* TIRO, BODYGUARDS *and* ATTENDANTS *with torches.* AGRIPPA *half-draws his sword. It should seem like a possible ambush.*

CICERO. My dear boy! Is that you – what are you doing in the dark? Tiro was beginning to think the house was deserted –

A warm embrace.

OCTAVIAN. Dear, loyal friend – how good of you to ride – what is it – a hundred miles from Rome and safety –

TIRO. It felt like more –

OCTAVIAN. And in the middle of winter!

CICERO. I have turned away old age. In the cause of peace, how could I refuse? But we saw no sign of your people – where are your men?

OCTAVIAN. We came alone.

AGRIPPA. I judged it safer.

CICERO. Well, then… I thought Tiro here could make a note of everything –

AGRIPPA. You're empowered by the Senate to negotiate on their behalf?

CICERO. Not exactly. But it would be useful to have something to show them.

AGRIPPA. Then –

OCTAVIAN. I'd prefer it if nothing were written down – that way we can speak more freely.

AGRIPPA. How much support in the Senate do you have? What about Hirtius and Pansa – the Consuls-elect? Until they take office, who's giving the orders? Because, without their support –

OCTAVIAN. Agrippa –

CICERO. Some might say it's reckless of me – to involve myself with a couple of boys at the head of an army of doubtful legality –

AGRIPPA. An army that's growing by the day –

CICERO. An army that will, I trust, never see action. My hope is that even at this late stage Antony won't risk opening hostilities – once he understands the strength of the opposition he'd be facing.

OCTAVIAN. Two legions Antony shipped home from Macedonia have deserted him, and come over to me –

CICERO. That's good news indeed –

OCTAVIAN. Dear friend, we cannot allow this to end in bloodshed – Roman killing Roman –

CICERO. It wouldn't be the first time I've pulled the Republic back from the brink. When I foiled the conspiracy of Catiline, I alone –

AGRIPPA. It worries me you don't have the Senate's authority to deliver what we need –

OCTAVIAN. Agrippa –

CICERO. Young man, there is no authority in Rome. Power lies in the dust – for any man of courage to pick up. If anyone can put backbone into what's left of the Senate, I can.

AGRIPPA. If you're saying –

OCTAVIAN. Agrippa… The sacrifices Cicero has made – and will make – on my behalf are sufficient proof of his loyalty

to me. What help can we offer you? In what capacity would
Caesar be most useful to the Republic?

CICERO. Let's examine the facts. Decimus commands three
legions. He has fortified Mutina, and dug in for a long siege.
Antony is marching north to challenge him –

OCTAVIAN. He refuses to obey the direct order of the Senate?

AGRIPPA. We can't let Antony take Mutina –

CICERO. No – it would give him the power base he needs.
He'd control the whole of Northern Italy. Rome would be at
his mercy.

OCTAVIAN. It would be a setback –

CICERO. What it boils down to is this. You, young man, have
raised an army to defend your country – all seasoned fighting
men – but it has no legitimacy. We of the Senate have law on
our side, but few soldiers. We do have a common enemy –

OCTAVIAN. Antony –

CICERO. Somewhere in the mix – surely there's the basis of an
agreement between us?

AGRIPPA. An agreement you have no authority to make.

CICERO. Oh, for the love of god, Octavian, call off your dog!

OCTAVIAN. Agrippa – enough –

CICERO. Take it from me, young man – if you want a deal, I'm
your best bet! There are plenty on our side who'll say, 'We
didn't rid Rome of one Caesar to welcome in another – '

AGRIPPA (*real anger – we get a hint of what he's capable of*).
And take it from me, old man – there are plenty on our side
who'll say, 'Why should we fight to defend men who
betrayed and murdered our leader!'

OCTAVIAN. Agrippa –

AGRIPPA. It needed saying! –

CICERO (*slams his arms on the chair – rises in a huff*). If that's
really how you feel, there's no point in continuing –

OCTAVIAN. There's no need to take offence… Dear friend, be in no doubt, I shall destroy Antony… I'd prefer to do it with the blessing of the Senate. Can you deliver that blessing?

CICERO. I can. But let's be clear about what the Senate will demand of you. If – when – Decimus comes under attack, I'll have Antony declared an Enemy of the People –

AGRIPPA. Can you do that? –

CICERO. You'll march your legions north to rescue Decimus. You'll work with him – you'll fight alongside him – together you'll destroy the enemy. And let's be clear about this too – we're talking about *Decimus* – that's the Decimus who lured Caesar – whom you call father – to his death and struck the fatal blow.

OCTAVIAN (*fixing* CICERO *with a stare*). What's past is past. I can work with Decimus.

CICERO. Then I'm willing to propose a motion that, despite your age, the Senate gives you an Imperium – the legal authority to wage war on Antony.

OCTAVIAN. I shall be the Senate's faithful officer.

CICERO. But only while this state of emergency lasts.

OCTAVIAN. Agreed.

CICERO. You'll place yourself – and your army – under the supreme command of the new Consuls – Hirtius and Pansa. You'll obey their orders at all times.

OCTAVIAN. You have no reason to doubt me…

CICERO. Well then…

The three shake hands – AGRIPPA *reluctantly.*

OCTAVIAN. I was sorry to hear of your daughter's illness. I hope she'll make a speedy recovery.

CICERO. Tullia is dead.

OCTAVIAN. I… Oh, my dear father…

OCTAVIAN *embraces* CICERO.

Enter SERVANTS *with wine.*

TIRO. We've found some rather good wine.

CICERO. Youth and experience, arms and the toga, come together in solemn alliance to rescue the Republic.

AGRIPPA. We must be off –

CICERO. Let us go – each man to his post – resolved to do his duty to the Senate and People of Rome.

OCTAVIAN. To the Republic! (*Raises his cup to his lips.*)

OMNES. The Republic!

AGRIPPA. I'll fetch the horses –

CICERO. Won't you stay the night? We've still much to discuss –

OCTAVIAN. Saturnalia tomorrow – my soldiers will want their gifts. Gold is important to them… First and dearest of all my friends – your voice and my army will prove an unbeatable alliance. (*Embraces* CICERO.) Farewell! Good fortune prosper our enterprise.

CICERO. May all the gods protect you, my dearest boy!

Exeunt OCTAVIAN *and* AGRIPPA.

TIRO. You realise you may be delivering Rome from one tyrant – only to give it into the clutches of another?

CICERO. He's no tyrant – he's just a boy. A boy in need of a father. His natural father's dead – his adoptive father has left him the most dangerous legacy in history. He looks up to me now – and that's a blessing for him, for us, and for the Republic. Don't worry – I'll keep him on the side of virtue – at least until he rids us of Antony… I need to rest and think. You'll write up an account of what's passed between us, won't you?

TIRO. Of course. I'm not in the least bit tired – a hundred-mile gallop is nothing to me.

CICERO. Sometimes… I wonder why you put up with me.

TIRO. I wonder that too… All you have to do now is to persuade the Senate to agree to the deal… Look. Octavian's cup. He didn't touch a drop.

Scene Two

Near Mutina, drums, and trumpets. MARK ANTONY*'s army on the march led by* FULVIA *and* MARK ANTONY – POPILLIUS *carries the Eagle. Noise grows. Panic back in Rome. The Senate assembles –* HIRTIUS (*sick and wasted – a scar on his neck*) *and* PANSA *in animated conversation. Last of all,* CICERO *arrives – greeted by a buzz of expectation.*

PANSA. Gentlemen. Antony – in direct contravention of the orders of this House – has set down his army at the gates of Mutina. He's demanding the surrender of Decimus, our commander, and our legions. Decimus has taken an oath that he will fight to the last man to keep the north loyal to the Senate – he requests immediate rescue.

SENATORS (*muttering, troubled*). How? We have no army. Rescue? (*Etc.*)

PANSA. Cicero?

CICERO. What action shall we take against this rank traitor Antony? He opens hostilities by laying siege to the excellent Decimus in Mutina. Why? Because he needs a base from which to mount an attack on Rome. He plans to sweep down upon us – as once the elder Caesar did – to seize dictatorial power… Make no mistake – he would already be battering at our gates were it not for the intervention of a young man – I should say rather a boy – a boy of almost godlike intelligence and courage, who – on his own initiative – has raised an army to defend us.

Protest and approval mixed. CICERO *lets the noise die down.*

Oh? You can't believe what you heard me say? I'll say it again. Had not this boy single-handedly resisted the aggressor, Rome would today lie in ruins... Gentlemen, we cannot sit idly by, and allow the blackest chapter in Rome's history to repeat itself.

Therefore, I propose that this valiant youth – Gaius Julius Caesar Octavianus – be given full authority to wage war on Antony – no longer as a private individual, but as Rome's General. Let us give young Caesar his Imperium – and place in his hands the whole defence of her Republic. There's not a moment to be lost.

Stunned silence. Then:

SENATORS. No! He's bought you! You old fool! (*Etc.*)

Though there are louder shouts of approval.

CICERO. You are right to applaud this glorious young man. Together we shall find the strength to purge our government of corruption – and set it on new and firmer foundations! Antony offers us a stark choice: lives of shame and ignominy – or no life at all. With such a traitor, no terms are possible. Yet in the darkness, silence of these troubled times I intend to rekindle a spark of resistance which – with your support – will blaze forth in flames of liberty!

SENATORS (*cheering*). Cicero! Cicero! (*Etc.*)

CICERO (*aside*). If only Brutus had come to me for lessons in oratory.

TIRO. 'If only – if only...'

Scene Three

A tent. OCTAVIAN, AGRIPPA, YOUNG SOLDIER SCRIBES.

AGRIPPA (*reading*). 'Antony would already be at the gates of Rome were it not for the intervention of a young man – I should say rather a boy – a boy of almost godlike intelligence and courage.' Lays it on thick, doesn't he?

OCTAVIAN. He's giving me a lot to live up to. Come on – get to the important bit.

AGRIPPA. 'Gaius Julius Caesar has stepped forward to protect the State, and your liberty – '

OCTAVIAN. What does he say about sanctioning our war? –

AGRIPPA. Here… 'This valiant youth must be given full authority to wage war on Antony – no longer as a private individual acting alone – but as Rome's General entrusted by this Senate with the defence of her Republic.'

OCTAVIAN. Excellent! Have they given it?

AGRIPPA (*scanning the letter*). Er…

OCTAVIAN. Have they voted me my Imperium?

AGRIPPA (*searching the letter*). No. No, they haven't… the Senate has awarded you… 'A vote of thanks.'

OCTAVIAN. Let me see – (*Takes the letter and reads.*) The old man claims he has the Senate and the People eating out of his hand… But… 'Nothing can be done… Until the new Consuls take office on the first of January' –

AGRIPPA. What did I tell you!

OCTAVIAN. Now that's a *pity*!

AGRIPPA. A pity! Does he know nothing of soldiering! Dear gods – Antony's not standing around, is he? – waiting for a bunch of old farts to blow the whistle – he's dug in outside Mutina – his war machines are lobbing fucking great rocks at the walls!

OCTAVIAN. Mutina's walls are strong – the gates heavy –

AGRIPPA. This is what happens when you let politicians conduct a war!

OCTAVIAN. It's a setback – not a disaster. Decimus should be able to hold the town until the first of January.

AGRIPPA. So what do we do now?

OCTAVIAN. We wait. You drill your soldiers – recruit more – put everything in readiness... I'll draft Cicero a flattering reply to his disappointing letter.

AGRIPPA. Plenty of oil and little vinegar – keep up the pressure... You know...There's nothing to stop us moving north without the Senate's sanction...

OCTAVIAN. Stick to soldiering, Agrippa. Leave the politics to me.

AGRIPPA. And your 'almost godlike intelligence and courage'?

OCTAVIAN *throws a cushion at* AGRIPPA – *laughter – a mock fight* – SCRIBES *join in. Suddenly they're just children fooling around.*

Scene Four

New Year. We're at the end of the familiar swearing-in ceremony for the new Consuls. CICERO *networking.* HIRTIUS *and* PANSA. HIRTIUS *is very ill – cancer.* CICERO *is shocked by his appearance.*

CICERO. Hirtius? Are you able to carry on?

HIRTIUS. The surgeon removed the growth from my neck. I should make a full recovery.

CICERO. You must – Rome needs her Consuls. Caesar is eager to march against Antony – there's not a moment to be lost. The three of us should be able to settle everything quickly. Call me first – as senior ex-Consul I'll open the debate –

HIRTIUS. Pansa will preside. I'm not... yet...

CICERO. Octavian must have his Imperium.

The CONSULS *take their places.* PANSA *stands.*

PANSA. Each new day brings new reports of a worsening
situation. The circumstances of the threat we face are well
known to every man here… Before I open the debate –
I speak both for myself and for my fellow Consul who has
risen from his sickbed to attend – we believe we should seek
a reconciliation with Mark Antony.

Surprise.

Grave as things are, I trust we have not yet abandoned all
hope of a peaceful solution.

HIRTIUS. I concur.

CICERO (*aside to* TIRO). What are they doing?! What a pair of
spineless mediocrities!

CICERO *gets up – expecting to be called.*

PANSA. I call upon Calenus to open the debate.

CICERO (*aside to* TIRO). Calenus – why Calenus?

TIRO (*aside*). Antony's man.

CICERO (*aside*). He's a clown.

CALENUS. This difficulty has been made out by Cicero to be
a struggle between all of them Senators what are on the
Republic's side, and Mark Antony on the other one. But it's
not like that, is it? Cicero's not correct. It's just a row between
three different parties what are all in it for themselves. Look –
I know I'm no great speaker – I'm not an intellectual – but I'm
good with people. It was Caesar what put me in this place
because I keep me ears open – I get to know what people
think. And what people think is that Decimus could save us all
a lot of bother by handing over his soldiers to Antony. But he's
not going to, is he? Even though the People's Assembly tell
him he's got to. And then there's this lad what's dropped in on
us out of nowhere – going around raising armies. Well, he's
just out for what he can, get isn't he? And if you ask me, I say
Antony's in the right. And if Decimus won't budge out of his

northern what-do-you-call-it – *province*... Well, we should think about offering Antony some other place instead. Like Macedonia for instance.

CICERO (*as if in pain*). Oh!

CALENUS. If you won't go for that then I say we should stay neutral – just do nothing – it'll be sure to sort itself out sooner or later.

CICERO (*aside to* TIRO). *This* – a Senator! (*Stands.*)

PANSA. Lucius Calpurnius Piso.

PISO. Gentlemen, I'm no friend to Mark Antony. I was the first to speak against him in this House when his depredations against the State grew too blatant for an honest man to bear. I've always regarded him as unpredictable, and dangerous – I do still. But, gentlemen, most of us here have lived through a long civil war – and I for one have no desire to live through another. Let the Senate try one last time to make peace with Antony. I propose we send envoys to offer terms.

CICERO. No! That will buy him the time he needs to strengthen his hold on –

PISO. Cicero – I'm speaking! Sit down!

PANSA. Cicero –

PISO. If Antony submits himself to the will of the Senate – if he abandons his siege of Mutina, and withdraws with his army over the border to the Italian side of the Rubicon – many Roman lives will be saved. If he agrees terms, even at this late stage, war may be averted. If he rejects them – if he plunges the nation into another bloody conflict... Then at least the whole world will know whom to blame.

PANSA. Vatia.

VATIA. Let me be brief. Mark Antony has lost the confidence of this House, of most of his former friends, of the People, and almost all the legions he once commanded. His term as Consul is over – yet he seeks to cling onto power. He would seize by force the province we awarded to Decimus. So much for Antony!

Approval – especially from CICERO.

But what of this boy – this strutting cub of Julius Caesar – upon whom some pin their hopes of salvation? Octavian has incited the People to violence – raised a private and illegal army – and declared his intention to bring Caesar's killers to justice. If we appoint this laddish would-be warlord – make him 'the sword and shield of the Senate' – as Cicero urges – what guarantees can Cicero give us that his boy won't come and use his sword on us?

CICERO. He has my absolute trust!

VATIA. I'd sooner trust Antony. I'm with Piso, we should send envoys – let's make peace.

CALENUS. I'm telling you – peace is all what Mark Antony wants.

CICERO. Antony wants peace, does he? (*On his feet.*) Then let him lay down his arms, come here, and beg for peace! We wait – we debate – listening to faint hearts and appeasers. Antony doesn't wait – he invades our territories, attacks our officers, batters at the walls of our towns – and you say *we should send envoys to this monster*! Antony appointed *himself – at an Assembly ruled illegal by the augurs*! –

Jeers from MARK ANTONY*'s* SUPPORTERS.

You jeer – but we ignore the gods at our peril! Antony is forging decrees – he's a thief and he's a traitor. To give him a province – any province – would be to provide him with power base – the money, arms, and soldiers he needs to destroy us! He grows stronger by the day – he grows in confidence – because he sees we sit talking, talking, talking – and *doing* nothing. Envoys? Send him envoys? Send him defiance!

Agreement.

Proclaim a state of emergency – put on your armour – declare Antony an Enemy of the People!

Roars of applause.

It is on Rome and Romans Antony makes war. Let him feel Rome's anger – let him face the full force of a Roman Senate and the Roman People acting together with strength and purpose!

Louder applause.

Had not young Caesar – upon whom Vatia heaps such scorn – come to our rescue, which of us here today would have had the courage to speak freely in this House? How many of us would still be alive? Give Caesar his Imperium! On this god-given boy all hope of liberty rests. Nothing is dearer to him that the opinion of good men, the importance of just law, and the health and strength of our Republic. I give my word to the Senate and to the Roman People – I promise – I solemnly pledge that Caesar will always be the humble and obedient citizen he is today. He has no thought of vengeance, no desire for personal advancement, no guile... His only ambition is for his county's good!

Massive applause.

TIRO. I hope you know what you're doing.

CICERO (*stands*). I propose that Gaius Julius Caesar be given command of Rome's armies.

PANSA. The proposal is that young Caesar leads our legions in the field – under the supreme command of myself, and Hirtius, your Consuls.

Acclaim.

That motion is carried.

CICERO. I propose that Mark Antony be declared an Enemy of the People.

SENATE. Aye! Agreed! (*Etc.*)

CALENUS. I veto the motion.

Outrage, protest, confusion, calls for order – CALENUS jostled. Then enter FULVIA, MARK ANTONY's mother JULIA, and MARK ANTONY's baby son (carried), all in black. Silence descends. They kneel.

FULVIA. Reverend fathers – I humble myself before you – will you hear a woman speak? On my knees, I beg – do not make an enemy of my husband, Antony – spare his family that

humiliation! He's a good man – Rome's brave soldier – a
loyal servant of the People – he's only trying to find a way to
satisfy the many demands made on him by yourselves – by
our good citizens – and by his soldiers. He has his faults –
it's true! But he's not vicious – he has no ambition. There
may have been times when he's acted rashly – but only to
defend himself against attacks on his honour and his honesty.
There have been attempts on his life! My husband is a
simple soldier. He's no match for the smooth and cunning
politicians who speak against him. Why is there is so much
hatred – so much violence here? Antony tried his hardest to
keep order... and I... I... (*Weeps*.) His mother kneels to you
– his child kneels – we implore you – send to him – speak to
him! I'm willing to travel north with your envoys and plead
with him – he'll listen and obey... But do not brand him a
public enemy! We shall be destitute – a noble family ruined
and begging in the street. Send your envoys – come to terms
– I beg you – find ways to prevent this war. Can anything be
more precious to Romans than peace?

CICERO (*aside to* TIRO). Dear gods – that harpy ought to be
on the stage! Surely they won't fall for it?

TIRO. I'm not so sure... Look at them.

Scene Five

Mutina. MARK ANTONY*'s tent – HQ staff at work*.
POPILLIUS *and* THUGS. *The scene is punctuated by huge*
thumps as rocks pound the city walls. PISO *and two others of*
the delegation enter – CALENUS *and* VATIA. MARK
ANTONY *reads the Senate's letter*.

MARK ANTONY. Welcome to Mutina. Drink?

DELEGATES *shake their heads*.

I suppose Cicero drafted this? Yes – of course he did. Most
insulting... very peremptory... I'm ordered to grant you safe

passage into the town so you can discuss the Senate's requirement with Decimus. Well, I can't allow it – obviously. Hear that? We're pounding the walls – I should think they'll fall in the next day or so – far too dangerous. If I buried a Senatorial delegation under a pile of rubble they'd say I did it deliberately – certainly Cicero would. (*Reads.*) I'm to give up my claim to this province – well, I'm not going to do that either. The People gave it to me – it's mine by right. If Decimus plays dog-in-the-manger, the law's on my side if I choose to burn him out.

PISO. Then there's no more I can say.

MARK ANTONY. If you were to offer me Gaul instead – I mean the whole of Gaul – I might consider it. It would be for a term of five years – minimum – and Decimus would have to hand over his legions to me. I'd need at least another six to keep order beyond the Alps.

PISO. Is there nothing we can offer to prevent this war?

MARK ANTONY. Yes – what I've just said – Gaul and the legions. And the Senate must ratify all the decrees I've made in Caesar's name since the day of his murder – I want everything legal. And the investigations into the disappearance of the State Treasury from the Temple of Ops must cease immediately. Oh, and my followers – anyone I nominate – must be given immunity from prosecution. What was Cicero's fine forgetful word for it? Given an amnesty? And finally, the Senate must pay my soldiers – I'm short of ready money. It's Rome's army – Rome must pay.

PISO. It's clear now what your intentions are, Antony. You never wanted peace.

MARK ANTONY. Piso, I've no idea what my intentions are. All I've ever asked is a little respect. I respond to circumstances as they arise. This unfortunate war just followed on quite naturally.

Exeunt DELEGATES. *Enter* FULVIA.

FULVIA. Fools!

MARK ANTONY. Trudging all this way through snow and ice –

FULVIA. I've bought you the time you needed. Act quickly now – finish off Decimus before they bring up their reinforcements. Drink?

MARK ANTONY. No – not now. I've a town to take and other battles to fight.

Thumps of rocks on Mutina's walls.

Scene Six

PISO, CALENUS, VATIA, HIRTIUS *and* PANSA *on the rostra* – CICERO *addresses the* PEOPLE. *Starlings darken the sky.*

CICERO. Citizens – friends. Mark Antony has rejected our offers of peace. Our envoys did their best – their best was not good enough. As I forewarned them. Therefore, the Senate has declared a state of war exists between the Republic and Mark Antony. Tomorrow, Hirtius, our Consul will lead two legions north to join young Caesar, relieve Mutina, and rescue General Decimus. The Consul Pansa will follow on with an army of twenty thousand new recruits as soon as they are armed and battle-ready. May the gods prosper our enterprise!

SENATORS. May the gods prosper our enterprise!

Half-hearted CROWDS *concur and disperse.*

TIRO. You have your war.

CICERO. Write to Octavian. Tell him the good news.

TIRO. Is it good news?

CICERO. Antony is the last obstacle on our road to freedom – I shall destroy him as I destroyed Catiline. For a second time I've saved the Republic. Single-handed. Let the boy know nothing happens in Rome these days without my approval – nobody knows where my power begins and ends. It's better than being Dictator –

TIRO. I could have been home on my farm.

CICERO. Real power has nothing to do with the baubles of office – a curule chair, the fasces – power lies in an ability to sway a mob with a rousing speech – or to demolish all opposition in the Senate with a relentless assault on their argument – blow after blow – like missiles thrown against a town wall by some mighty ballista. The voice! That's real source of power...

TIRO. What has happened to my old friend and master who hated soldiering and loved his books? I rather miss him.

Enter QUINTUS.

CICERO. Brother?

QUINTUS. They've murdered Trebonius – in Syria.

CICERO. Trebonius!

TIRO. So the first of Caesar's assassins pays the price.

QUINTUS. He'll not be the last... Well, brother – you've started a war. I wonder how many of us will live to see the end of it.

CICERO. How did Trebonius die?

QUINTUS. Tortured with whips and red-hot irons – and his neck broken –

CICERO. Who did this!

QUINTUS. Dolabella – your son-in-law. He's shouting to the world he won't rest until he's avenged himself on all Caesar's assassins –

CICERO. But he was one of them! On the Capitol with them – he spoke up for Brutus and Cassius in that first Senate meeting –

QUINTUS. He's a weathercock. Perhaps he senses the wind is shifting back in Antony's favour.

CICERO. Antony is finished. I have united the Senate and the People against him.

QUINTUS. A snake's not dead till you cut off its head.

Drums, trumpets, rival armies marching towards each other – PANSA's and MARK ANTONY's.

Scene Seven

Night. Banging on CICERO*'s door – dogs barking.* TIRO
appears with lamps and SERVANTS. *Enter an exhausted
'bloody sergeant'* MESSENGER.

TIRO. It's the middle of the night – what's happening –

MESSENGER. You'd better wake up your master.

Enter CICERO.

A message from the Consul Pansa – he regrets to report a
catastrophic defeat –

CICERO. No – no – no! –

MESSENGER. At Forum Gallorum, Mark Antony ambushed
Pansa's army. The line broke and there was a terrible
slaughter – they were only farmers, bakers, laundrymen, and
stableboys – they were never going to stand up to the fury of
Antony's hardened veterans –

CICERO. Hirtius – and Octavian – where are they?

MESSENGER. Nobody knows.

Enter CALENUS.

CALENUS. You're in real trouble now, Cicero. There's an
angry crowd gathering in the Forum. You'd better get down
there, and tek your medicine – Father of the Nation! Grovel
– beg! I'd like to see you talk your way out of this one. All
them people what was cheering you on will curse you for
this – there's a lot of 'em as says you was aiming at the
dictatorship –

CICERO. It pains me, Calenus, that the People could believe
such a thing of me. It pains me almost as much as your
appalling Latin.

SERVANT. Master – there's another message –

CICERO. If it's more bad news – I don't want to read it –

CICERO *takes the letter and reads it, as he heads for the Forum. A gloomy Assembly of the People gathers.* CICERO *enters through the audience with* SENATORS *and a* BODYGUARD. *He mounts the rostra.*

Friends... I have dispatches from the front line... Here is a letter from the Consul – Hirtius. Let me read it to you: 'We have this day reversed an earlier disaster and won a great victory over the enemy! What was lost at noon was regained at sunset. I fell upon Antony's men as they were celebrating – prematurely – their earlier success. We have captured two Eagles and sixty standards. Antony is trapped in his camp with the poor remnants of his cavalry. Mutina is saved, Decimus rescued. Pansa is wounded but should recover. Tomorrow, with Octavian and Agrippa, I shall assault Antony in his camp and finish him. Thanks be to the gods! Long live the Senate and People of Rome!' This, friends, is your victory!

CALENUS. Oh, fuckin' 'ell!

CROWD (*wild cheering*). No – it is your victory! Long live Cicero! Father of the Nation! Saviour of the Republic! (*Etc.*)

They carry CICERO *off shoulder-high. Drums and trumpets. The victory celebration blends into the assault on* MARK ANTONY'*s camp. Fierce fighting. A bit like a bear-baiting.* OCTAVIAN *attacks* MARK ANTONY. OCTAVIAN'*s standard-bearer is killed.* OCTAVIAN *seizes the Eagle and holds it high.* HIRTIUS *joins in and is killed.* DECIMUS *joins in against* MARK ANTONY. AGRIPPA *drives* MARK ANTONY *off – gives him a severe thrashing.* MARK ANTONY, *badly wounded, is routed by the overwhelming force of* AGRIPPA'*s attack. He's dragged to safety, but clearly finished.*

Scene Eight

CICERO*'s house*. TIRO *reading*.

TIRO. Dispatches. More good news – nothing but good news!

CICERO. Is Antony dead? Have they found the body? Is he taken prisoner?

TIRO. Threw down his weapons and fled. Last seen heading for the Alpine passes, with a few of his cavalry.

CICERO. He'll never make it. The winter snows won't have melted. Still – I won't sleep soundly until I know he's no longer a threat.

TIRO. They'll hunt him down and kill him... Pity about poor Hirtius...

CICERO. Better a glorious death in battle than lingering on in agony. The cancer would have got him – he didn't have long... This war needs a dead hero – I shall put Hirtius on the vacant plinth – I look forward to delivering a eulogy to end all eulogies.

TIRO. What about Octavian?

CICERO. Oh, a pat on the head – a gilded statue if he's lucky.

Enter VATIA *and a* SLAVE.

VATIA. You've heard the good news – Antony's legions are utterly destroyed?

CICERO. Yes – letters come almost by the hour –

VATIA. They've not got him yet, but he can't cross the Alps – the passes are frozen. And even if he works a miracle we have our occupying army of sixty thousand men in Gaul waiting to arrest him. They'll bring him home to Rome in a cage.

CICERO. Shame we've lost our Consul though.

VATIA. Yes – he disgraced us. Such an ignominious end – to let himself be ambushed!

CICERO. What? Hirtius died gloriously – in the last battle.

VATIA. I'm talking about Pansa.

CICERO. Pansa isn't dead!

VATIA. He is – I've had a letter from Decimus – there's one for you too –

SLAVE *hands* CICERO *a letter. Who hands it to* TIRO, *who reads it.*

CICERO. And I've had a letter from the boy – it's Hirtius who died.

TIRO. They're sending home his body for a State funeral –

VATIA. But… can it be…? Do you mean to tell me we've lost *both* our Consuls?

CICERO. Dear gods! In the entire history of the Republic only eight Consuls have died in office. Eight – in nearly five hundred years! Now we lose two in the same week.

TIRO. To lose one Consul is unfortunate. To lose –

VATIA. So who'll command the Senate's legions now?

CICERO. Decimus, obviously. I've ordered Octavian to hand over the legions he raised illegally to him. It's Decimus's province. Now the battle's won we can't have boys tramping all over Italy with private armies at their back.

TIRO. Caesar might take a different view.

CICERO. I shall smother him in honours – baubles, laurels – things soldiers like.

TIRO. I doubt it would fool Agrippa.

VATIA. I suppose the Senate could vote the boy an ovation.

CICERO. You've changed your tune, Vatia. What happened to 'this strutting cub of Julius Caesar'?

ISAURICUS. Tall trees must bend, or break in a storm.

CICERO. Leave Octavian to me. I'll raise him to the heights – then drop him. Praised, raised and erased.

VATIA. Very good – I'll remember that – praised, raised and erased.

CICERO. He'll fall in with whatever I decide – a dutiful son always obeys a wise father…

Exeunt VATIA.

I shan't sleep easily until I have word Antony's taken, or dead. A true Roman would have fallen on his sword, but oh no – not Antony! –

Scene Nine

Night in OCTAVIAN*'s camp. Torches. Incense. The bodies of* HIRTIUS *and* PANSA *are carried in procession. Eagles. Funeral music.* OCTAVIAN *and* AGRIPPA *are last.* OCTAVIAN *is reading a letter.*

AGRIPPA. From Cicero?

OCTAVIAN. From Vatia … (*Reads.*) 'Praised, Raised, and Erased…'

OCTAVIAN *hands the letter to* AGRIPPA. *Exeunt following the bodies.*

Scene Ten

Night. CICERO*'s house.*

PORTER. There are soldiers at the door, Tiro. The one the master doesn't like.

TIRO. Agrippa?

CICERO (*looking up*). Impossible – Agrippa's in the north with the boy – a pair of buggers if ever I – My dear Agrippa – welcome to Rome!

AGRIPPA *has entered, with four* CENTURIANS – CAESAR*'s veterans – in muddy riding cloaks.*

How good to see you! And what a surprise. We've been starved of news here. I hope Octavian is well?

AGRIPPA. He is.

CICERO. The Senate owes him a debt of gratitude.

AGRIPPA. It does.

CICERO. Is Antony dead? Taken prisoner?

AGRIPPA *stares at* CICERO.

Is something wrong?

AGRIPPA. 'Raised to a great height and dropped? Praised, raised and erased'?

CICERO. Oh that! Tiro is forever telling me my foolish tongue will land me in trouble one day. If I've given offence…

AGRIPPA (*studying him*). If you feel the need to write him an apology, I'll see he receives it.

CICERO. I only wish you boys had been with me in the Senate the other day – I made the rafters ring with Octavian's praises – for his daring – his loyalty… He'll be the youngest commander in the history of the Republic to be granted the distinction of an Ovation. An Ovation, eh? What about that! Nor did I neglect to mention the heroic part you –

AGRIPPA. Caesar bears you no ill will. The same can't be said for his friends and soldiers… The veterans in our legions have not forgotten nor forgiven the discreditable part you played in the elder Caesar's murder –

CICERO. I played no –

AGRIPPA. 'The killing of the Dictator was many things, but it was no crime'? Caesar will do everything in his power to protect you – but you're not making it easy for him.

CICERO. I have zealously guarded that young man's interests at all times – I've no need to remind you of that. I'm determined that – in years to come – he'll play a leading part in Rome's affairs. Now what news of Antony?

AGRIPPA. The question is – old man – what part are *you* going to play in Rome's affairs… in years to come? (*Lets it sink in.*)

You've set yourself up as leader of the Senate – it's unclear on whose authority – but it seems to us that either you cannot control your people, or you're misjudging Caesar as badly as you once misjudged his father. That Senate edict – ordering him to hand over command of his legions to Decimus – *Decimus*! Was that your idea?

CICERO. But we agreed –

AGRIPPA. It was an insult! Even had he been willing to obey, do you imagine soldiers who served Julius Caesar faithfully in campaign after campaign would take orders from the coward who stabbed him in the back? You've never been a military man – you don't comprehend generalship – you've no understanding of that inward determination and strength that gives one man power to command the loyalty of thousands, and lead them to victory or death.

CICERO. Are you telling me Octavian refuses to accept the authority of the Senate?

AGRIPPA. It's a matter of whose authority *his legions* will accept.

CICERO. I –

AGRIPPA. Who speaks for the Senate? You? They'd never accept *your* authority. (*Studies* CICERO.) There's only one circumstance in which Caesar's army would place itself at the disposal of the Senate as far as I can see... If you made Caesar Consul –

CICERO. Consul! It's out of the question!

AGRIPPA. Why? Both Consulships are vacant. I've brought the bodies of Hirtius and Pansa home to Rome –

CICERO. The boy's nineteen!

AGRIPPA. I'm nineteen myself – feels good to me... You made Caesar Propraetor at nineteen – he led your army into battle at nineteen – defended your Republic at nineteen – gave Antony a thrashing at nineteen –

CICERO. But –

AGRIPPA. You yourself suggested he stood for Tribune at nineteen – so why not Consul at nineteen?

CICERO. I –

AGRIPPA. If his youth is the only issue, couldn't he take someone who is old as his Consular colleague?

CICERO. Well –

AGRIPPA. Someone whose wisdom and political experience would make up for his lack of it? (*Studies him.*) I'll leave you to think about it… (*Starts to go.*) Oh, and there's no news of Antony. Our best guess is he's dead – or trapped somewhere between our front line and our legions occupying Gaul. I'll wait outside while our horses and men have their feed. Any letters you'll want to write to Caesar, I'll see he gets… Along with your apology if you believe it necessary. Praised, raised, and erased…

Exeunt AGRIPPA *and* CENTURIANS. CICERO *deflates.*

TIRO. Is the boy suggesting what I think he's suggesting?

CICERO. That I serve alongside him as Consul?

TIRO. Naturally you'd never consider it.

CICERO. It would be a glorious culmination of my political career… Very few men have held two Consulships –

TIRO. It's just a title – you're doing the job anyway –

CICERO. A second Consulship – think of the honour –

TIRO. Think of your lost reputation. When Julius Caesar came with an army at his back demanding a Consulship – we fought a civil war to try and stop him –

CICERO. I don't see it quite like that –

TIRO. Brutus will see it like that – Cassius will see it like that. How could you explain yourself to the Senate? A nineteen-year-old as First Man in the State – you as his junior colleague? He'd demand your unquestioning support for anything and everything he proposed – and do you honestly see yourself working with the likes of Agrippa –

CICERO. I can control them! The important thing is to keep the boy on our side – it's maddening! Who's putting these ideas into his head I wonder?

TIRO. What if they're his own ideas? What if he's a cunning, scheming, ruthless little monster – what if lusting after absolute power runs in the family – what if that's what his uncle saw in him – and that's why he adopted him.

CICERO. You're wrong! He's nineteen… Oh you gods!

SERVANT. Master – The Urban Praetor has called a meeting of the Senate. There's news – from Gaul.

CICERO. Antony is dead. I'm certain of it. They've sent me his pickled head in a bucket…

Scene Eleven

The Senate assembles – CICERO, *stony-faced, is last in.*
As they troop in, TIRO *addresses the audience.*

TIRO. There was no pickled head – no bucket. Against all the odds Antony had escaped over the mountain passes into Gaul and incited our legions there to rebel. They were Caesar's men – Antony had led them in battle – he now had an army of sixty thousand battle-hardened soldiers.

Murmurs of alarm.

CICERO. All is not lost! Gentlemen, this is a setback – it is not a defeat. In Syria, in Macedonia, and in Greece, the Senate has many legions, commanded by the noble Brutus and the gallant Cassius. We shall summon them home. Decimus has kept his army intact. It's my confident belief liberty will triumph in the end.

Lukewarm response.

VATIA. As I speak, young Caesar is marching his victorious army down the Via Flaminia – he's less than a day's march away. I believe he is the man in whom we must place our trust. Therefore, I propose this House sends a delegation to welcome him into Rome. And that we hang laurels on the door of his mother's house on the Quirinal. It's there he'll be setting up his headquarters.

CICERO. May the Senate know how is it our friend Vatia is so well informed?

VATIA. I have been in constant correspondence with Caesar. In fact, I'm proud to inform you all that he has accepted the hand of my daughter in marriage. Therefore, to bind this excellent warrior still further to our cause, I propose the constitution be amended – so that Gaius Julius Caesar the younger may be permitted to stand for the office of Consul.

CICERO (*aside to* TIRO, *grim*). I should have seen this coming...

TIRO. You turned him down – he bought Vatia.

CICERO (*stands*). I congratulate the noble Vatia. My dear friend, young Octavian, is honourable, patriotic – everything a son-in-law should be. He has had no stronger advocate in this Senate than I. One day he will, no doubt, be Consul. Whether he should be Consul when he's not yet twenty, simply because he has an army at his back is a different matter...

We are all servants of the Republic – no one man among us can ever again be its master. I am opposed to Vatia's motion. I cannot permit the boy to sit in the Consular chair. I would sooner lie choking in my own blood than betray the principle on which the Republic stands – first and last – and always – *the rule of law*.

Lukewarm applause.

I feel it all slipping away from me, Tiro. When the young man arrives at our gates with his army they'll agree to anything he demands –

TIRO. They'll make him Consul, won't they?

CICERO. They're spineless – gutless –

TIRO. What pleases me... is that I've got my old master back. Everybody knows you're capable of behaving like a pompous fool – but when the Republic is under threat you

can always be relied upon to do the right thing – the
honourable thing – the noble thing…

CICERO. I should have listened to you – let you persuade me to
keep out of it and go to Athens – I was happy in my garden –
with my books. Do you have any advice for me, old friend?

TIRO. You'd better go and see Octavian – find out what he
means to do with you. Get it over with…

Scene Twelve

OCTAVIAN *is in the middle of dictating letters to a couple of*
SECRETARIES. VATIA *is standing in front of him.* AGRIPPA
watching.

OCTAVIAN. Was there something else?

VATIA. Do you mean to humiliate me, boy?!

VATIA *leaves, angry.* OCTAVIAN *continues to dictate.*

OCTAVIAN. Where was I? 'The African legions are intact. Not
a single ship was lost – so I have gained a further eight
thousand battle-hardened soldiers and a thousand cavalry.'

CICERO *and* TIRO *appear –* OCTAVIAN *hands a*
SECRETARY *a pile of papers* (*this is the* SECRETARY *who
will carry the last message*). AGRIPPA *smiles at* CICERO.
OCTAVIAN *continues to dictate.*

'I judge we shall soon be strong enough to move against
Brutus and Cassius, but nothing can be done until I have
destroyed Antony. Let me have numbers, and an estimate of
your costs, et cetera, et cetera. Gaius Julius Caesar. That'll
do.' (*Handing another large pile of letters to the*
SECRETARY.) And deal with those, would you?

Exit SECRETARY. OCTAVIAN *smiles at* CICERO.

Cicero! – the last of all my friends to welcome me to Rome!

CICERO. I imagined you'd be too busy with State affairs to
bother with meaningless gestures of friendship.

OCTAVIAN. 'For friendship is nothing less than an accord in
all things, human and divine, coupled with mutual goodwill
and affection. No greater gift was ever bestowed on man by
the immortal gods.' You see – I have your books by heart.
I couldn't think what had happened to you. I was beginning
to suspect you were avoiding me because you disapproved of
my actions.

CICERO (*shrugs*). I've given up approving or disapproving.
The world is as it is. Men do as they please, whatever I think
or say.

OCTAVIAN. What can I do to make you happy? Would you
consider serving alongside me as Consul?

CICERO (*relief*). Well, I… (*Wrong-footed.*) Ah! You're toying
with me. Raising my hopes –

OCTAVIAN. And dashing them. Cruel of me – this is no time
for jokes. Forgive me. My Consular colleague will be
Quintus Pedius – an obscure relative. I doubt you'll have
heard of him – I doubt anybody has. Which is the whole
point of him.

CICERO. So not Vatia?

OCTAVIAN (*laughs*). No – not Vatia!

AGRIPPA *and others join in the laughter*.

There seems to have been some misunderstanding there.
I shan't be marrying his daughter either.

CICERO. What will you do?

OCTAVIAN. Settle matters here – destroy Antony, as I promised
you – then I'll hunt down and kill the men who betrayed and
murdered my father. All of them. Well, there it is… Now you
may go too, old friend.

CICERO. Go… where?

OCTAVIAN. Anywhere you like. But you can't stay here in
Rome. And I don't want you creeping back while I'm

marching north – under no circumstances can I allow you to attend the Senate. Confine yourself to writing philosophy – nothing political. I forbid you to write your memoirs.

TIRO. Athens?

AGRIPPA. No.

OCTAVIAN. No. I forbid you to leave the country. We can't have you running off to join Brutus and Cassius, can we?

AGRIPPA. Decimus tried that. He was caught and executed.

TIRO. What's happened to his three legions?

AGRIPPA. They've all come over to our side – sworn allegiance to Caesar.

OCTAVIAN. Are my terms acceptable? Will you give me your word? My soldiers would not be so generous to you.

CICERO. I give you my word. Thank you.

OCTAVIAN. In return, in recognition of our past friendship –

CICERO. '*Past* friendship' – is it?

OCTAVIAN. In recognition of our friendship I guarantee your safety. No man will harm you while you're under my protection...

OCTAVIAN *hands* CICERO *a document*. CICERO *and* TIRO *start to leave*.

Tell me – was it a joke? Or did you mean it?

CICERO. A joke, Caesar?

OCTAVIAN. Would you really have tried to erase me?

CICERO. I would have done exactly the same to you, as you're doing to me. The difference between us is I'd have done it for Rome – for the Republic.

OCTAVIAN. It could never have happened. Everything I do is sanctioned by heaven. I had no mortal father – I was begotten by the god Apollo. I know this to be true because my father Julius Caesar told me it was true. And he himself is a god. The gods cannot lie.

Exit CICERO. TIRO *gives* OCTAVIAN *a black look and follows his master.* OCTAVIAN *is a little surprised. How serious is* OCTAVIAN *about his godhead? He smiles at* AGRIPPA *and the others, who laugh – he returns to dictating letters.*

A letter from Gaius Julius Caesar in Rome to Mark Antony in Gaul...

Scene Thirteen

Tusculum. Peace – birdsong. Sunshine. A bed in the garden. CICERO *asleep and dreaming – the ghost of* TULLIA *standing over him. She watches him for a long time. She senses* TIRO *and* QUINTUS *coming and disappears.*

TIRO. His eyesight is failing – he won't work – he can't write. Most days I read to him – we're going through his old letters. It's all there – his whole life – his early struggles to gain election to the Senate, the legal battles that made him famous – the prosecution of Verres – his Consulship – names from the past – Catiline and Clodius – Caesar, Cato – Tullia and Terentia – I'm putting everything in order. Secretly, of course.

QUINTUS. Octavian has been sworn in as Consul.

TIRO. His first step on the political ladder – and he's starting on the top rung.

QUINTUS. The Courts are busy passing death sentence on Caesar's assassins.

TIRO. Shhh... Keep that from your brother.

QUINTUS. He's getting ready to go after Antony. The boy has eleven legions now.

TIRO. If there are gods in heaven they'll destroy one another.

CICERO. Quintus...

QUINTUS. Brother... are you awake?

CICERO. I wasn't asleep... I've been helping Tiro write a history of our times. What an adventure it's been! History as it happened! Tiro has all my papers – drafts, copies, his own memories...

TIRO. My book might be read a hundred years from now.

CICERO. Longer – much longer – a thousand... It's the case for my defence. I lost the past – I shall lose the present – but the future will be mine. Put it all in, Tiro – the good and the bad.

TIRO. What – all of it? You wouldn't want to appear greedy, vain, duplicitous –

CICERO. Everything! Everything. Let me stand before history naked as a Greek statue. Let future generations laugh at my follies – just so long as they read me. I fought a good fight. I did my best... And I failed. What does it matter – set it all down, Tiro – tell future generations how magnificently I failed. Those who come after me will learn more from my faults than from all Caesar's Triumphs...

TIRO. I'll tell them the truth.

CICERO. The truth is all that matters. When all the Caesars lie in darkness, silence – dust and ashes my living voice will still be ringing out... Caesar prophesied I'd outlive Caesar. Unfortunately, he didn't specify which Caesar.

QUINTUS. You should leave Italy?

CICERO. I can't – I gave my word to the boy.

QUINTUS. The ports aren't watched – the weather's still clement. You could slip away – go to Marcus in Athens.

CICERO. I'm tired. I haven't the strength.

QUINTUS. Brutus and Cassius would welcome you with open arms.

CICERO. I love this house – Tullia loved it too – I buried her here. I'm no longer afraid of death, brother – I'm ready for it – I long for it... I must have lived a good life. I'm in no danger. The young man has guaranteed my safety. And now... I need to sleep. Where's my stick? Help me.

QUINTUS. Give me your arm.

> *Exeunt* CICERO *and* QUINTUS. *Drums and trumpets.*
> *Down the steps come* POPILLIUS, *Eagles, images, etc., etc.*
> *Then enter* MARK ANTONY *and* OCTAVIAN *in full*
> *armour. They embrace and acknowledge the audience.*
> SOLDIERS *cheer.* MARK ANTONY*'s team leave.*
> OCTAVIAN, AGRIPPA *and a* SECRETARY *remain.*

OCTAVIAN. Antony's offering a hundred thousand in gold for Cicero's head… It's a pity.

AGRIPPA. He still has a voice – a pen. He must be silenced.

OCTAVIAN. His death would be a stain on my honour.

AGRIPPA. For a month or two. After a couple of years, who will remember him?

OCTAVIAN. Still…

> OCTAVIAN'S SECRETARY *takes a letter to* TIRO.

OCTAVIAN'S SECRETARY. Are you Tiro?

TIRO. I am.

OCTAVIAN'S SECRETARY. I have a letter for you from my master, Caesar – (*Hands it over.*) He has joined forces with Antony. They will work together to hunt down and exterminate his father's assassins. You're to get Cicero to safety – you have Caesar's permission to go wherever you wish – there's not a moment to be lost. There are men on the road coming to kill him – they're not far behind me.

Scene Fourteen

Like the opening scene. On the road. CICERO *on a litter, and his* SLAVES. *Panic.*

CICERO. He gave me his word – his solemn promise –

TIRO. That was before he joined with Antony. The young man has betrayed us. We need to get you to the boat – they can't be far behind –

CICERO. Carry me to Rome – I'll cut my throat on Octavian's doorstep – let him die of shame –

TIRO. He has no shame. If they catch you –

CICERO. Let them –

TIRO. They'll torture you to death. I beg you – get back in the litter –

CICERO. I'm not afraid.

TIRO. For my sake, then – for the sake of your friends, and for your son – please – we must hurry.

SOLDIERS *appear from all entrances.*

POPILLIUS. Marcus Tullius Cicero.

CICERO (*to his* SERVANTS). Throw down your weapons. Nobody is to fight.

POPILLIUS. I have a warrant for your execution.

CICERO. I am a Roman citizen.

POPILLIUS. My orders are from Mark Antony himself.

CICERO. I am a Roman citizen.

POPILLIUS. I know who you are.

CICERO. I am a Roman citizen...

POPILLIUS. *So what?!*

CICERO. Come closer – my eyesight's not what it used to be. I know you, don't I? What's your name?

POPILLIUS (*taken aback*). My name is Gaius Popillius
Laenas...

TIRO. Gaius – it would be, wouldn't it!

CICERO. Remember him, Tiro? A spotty fifteen-year-old who
murdered his father – right at the beginning of my career?

TIRO. He was guilty. He'd have been put to death – but you got
him off.

CICERO. On condition he joined the army... It's a kind of
justice, I suppose.

POPILLIUS. The verdict of the Constitutional Commission is
that the death sentence should be carried out immediately.
Get him out of the litter.

CICERO. Oh, leave me where I am. It'll be simpler like this.

He lies back and offers his throat.

POPILLIUS. Why not? If that's what you want.

TIRO. At least it will be quick.

CICERO. I can think of worse endings. Try and make a decent
job of it. No fumbling.

POPILLIUS. Let's be having you then.

Epilogue

TIRO. They cut off my master's head and hands.

Enter FULVIA *with* CICERO*'s head.*

Fulvia pierced Cicero's tongue with the pin of her brooch –
the tongue that had hurled defiance at Antony, and so often
spoken of her with contempt. His head and hands were
nailed up on the rostra as a warning to any who might think
of opposing the new Government in thought, word, or deed –
or who might speak or think of freedom...

Brutus and Cassius were defeated at Philippi, they fell on
their swords, and the last hopes of the Republic died with
them. Antony committed suicide with his mistress Cleopatra
after the boy defeated him in battle. 'Which oft our stage
hath shown...'

The boy is now the Emperor Augustus. He rules the whole
world. And up in heaven Julius Caesar, his adoptive father, is
well pleased with his belovèd son...

OCTAVIAN *and* AGRIPPA, *dressed for a Triumph, lead the
full cast – a procession of characters alive and dead – ghosts
– cross the stage. Last on is the murdered* SLAVE *– the first
image of the play.*

I've finished my book – my *Life of Cicero.* My own life will
soon be over. In the summer evenings, I sit on the terrace and
look up at the stars... I think of what my master wrote in *The
Republic* – Scipio's dream of that place where statesmen –
well... the better sort of statesmen – go after their deaths:

Starlight.

CICERO. I gazed in every direction and everything appeared
wonderfully beautiful. There were stars we never see from
Earth – all larger than we could imagine – bright spheres much
greater than our own world... Indeed, the Earth itself seemed
to me so small that I grew scornful of Rome's great Empire –
so tiny it was scarcely visible. If only you will look up on
high, and contemplate this eternal home and resting place, you

will no longer concern yourselves with the gossip of the common herd – nor put your trust in great and powerful men – nor look to them for any reward for your labours. All that men do or say dies with them and is blotted out – lost and forgotten in the slow embrace of time. All that remains of a good man – a good life – is what is written down.

TIRO *rolls up his book.*

End of Play Six.

THE JUNGLE BOOK
Stuart Paterson
Adapted from Rudyard Kipling

KENSUKE'S KINGDOM
Stuart Paterson
Adapted from Michael Morpurgo

KES
Lawrence Till
Adapted from Barry Hines

MIDDLEMARCH
Geoffrey Beevers
Adapted from George Eliot

NOUGHTS & CROSSES
Dominic Cooke
Adapted from Malorie Blackman

THE RAILWAY CHILDREN
Mike Kenny
Adapted from E. Nesbit

SWALLOWS AND AMAZONS
Helen Edmundson and Neil Hannon
Adapted from Arthur Ransome

A TALE OF TWO CITIES
Mike Poulton
Adapted from Charles Dickens

TREASURE ISLAND
Stuart Paterson
Adapted from Robert Louis Stevenson

WAR AND PEACE
Helen Edmundson
Adapted from Leo Tolstoy

WENDY & PETER PAN
Ella Hickson
Adapted from J.M. Barrie

WOLF HALL *and* BRING UP THE BODIES
Mike Poulton
Adapted from Hilary Mantel

A Nick Hern Book

This stage adaptation of *Imperium* first published in Great Britain as a paperback original in 2017 by Nick Hern Books Limited, The Glasshouse, 49a Goldhawk Road, London W12 8QP, in association with the Royal Shakespeare Company

Imperium, Lustrum and *Dictator* (novels) copyright © 2006, 2009, 2015 Robert Harris
Imperium (play) copyright © 2017 Mike Poulton
Introduction copyright © 2017 Mike Poulton

Robert Harris and Mike Poulton have asserted their rights to be identified respectively as the author and adapter of this work

Cover image: RSC Visual Communications

Designed and typeset by Nick Hern Books, London
Printed in Great Britain by Ashford Colour Press, Gosport, Hampshire

A CIP catalogue record for this book is available from the British Library

ISBN 978 1 84842 698 6

www.nickhernbooks.co.uk

facebook.com/nickhernbooks

twitter.com/nickhernbooks